BLOODY BUT UNBOWED

A Memoir by John Seaman

Для Элена, моя подруга dlod шестьдесят лет

Иван Симан
12/13/15

McNally Jackson
New York
2012

Copyright © 2012 by John Seaman

ISBN 978-1-938-02228-9

Notes for Cover

The Memoir title, "Bloody But Unbowed," comes from the poem "Invictus,": by William Ernest Henley (1849-1903), an English, Victorian, poet. Henley, in "Invictus," is also responsible for the lines, "I am the master of my fate; I am the captain of my soul.", lines which I also like, and which might also make excellent book titles.

Below is the text of Henley's "Invictus":

Out of the night that covers me,
Black as the Pit from pole to pole,
I thank whatever gods may be
For my unconquerable soul.

In the fell clutch of circumstance
I have not winced nor cried aloud.
Under the bludgeonings of chance
My head is bloody, but unbowed.

Beyond this place of wrath and tears
Looms but the Horror of the shade,
And yet the menace of the years
Finds, and shall find, me unafraid.

It matters not how straight the gate,
How charged with punishments the scroll,
I am the master of my fate;
I am the captain of my soul.

The cover picture is an art photograph I created a few years ago. It has little to do with the book title, "Bloody But Unbowed," which only refers to my adventurous life. The photograph is an example of my life's work.

The photograph represents "Psyche," a figure from Greek mythology. Psyche was a Greek mortal woman who was beloved of the Greek God, Eros. Psyche and Eros had a good relationship, but Psyche was strictly forbidden from ever looking at Eros. One day, however, Psyche transgressed, and looked upon Eros. Zeus was furious, and banished Psyche to Hades. That would have been the end of it, except that Eros, after much pleading, was able to persuade Zeus to make Psyche immortal, to live forever among the Gods.

BLOODY BUT UNBOWED
A Memoir by John Seaman

Table of Contents

Section 1	1	To Begin a Tale
Section 2	24	Deep Waters
Section 3	40	Art and the Mind
Section 4	53	From Birth to Puberty, 1936-1949
Section 5	85	From Puberty to First Encounter, 1949-1956
Section 6	131	From First Encounter to Crisis, 1956-1960
Section 7	161	Interregnum, 1963-1967
Section 8	176	(Very Slow) Recovery and Renewal, 1967-1989
Section 9	236	From Renewal to (Some) Self-Realization, 1989-2010
Section 10	254	Some Friends
Section 11	283	More Friends
Section 12	295	Eleutheria, 1989-2010
Section 13	312	Holding to Tradition, 1968-2009
Section 14	316	Psychiatric Explorations, 1957-2010
Section 15	342	My Friend Diane
Section 16	357	More Diane

Section 17 369 Letters to Janet
Section 18 387 My Life in Photography and Art
Section 19 422 From the Model Stand
Section 20 426 Making Movies with Jane
Section 21 430 Notes on Family
Section 22 440 My Departed Sister Barbara
Section 23 448 Picknicking at Lighthouse Beach
Section 24 456 The Nude Gastronome
Section 25 485 More on Nude Beaches and Bodypainting
Section 26 491 Skydiving for Seniors…
Section 27 501 Legal Overseas and Nevada Brothels

To Begin a Tale

The biggest thing in my life from 1974 to 1987 was Patricia's brothel (not its real name) in New York City, where I was a regular patron, once or twice a week, throughout those 14 years, for a total of about 1,000 visits. You can check my multiplication. I have many delightful reminiscences of the place. I particularly remember many evenings in the 1970s when, at about 6:00 p.m., the original version of "Star Trek," starring William Shattner and Leonard Nimoy, would come on the house TV. All action in the two house bedrooms would stop and everybody would emerge to watch the episode, drinking free beer all the time. I guess Star Trek gave us all, all the clients and the hard-working women, something to dream about. But I'm sure those women accumulated a lot of karma doing what they were doing, and they gave many people like me something to rejoice about in our otherwise bleak lives, and if there is another life, reincarnation or whatever, as I fear, like a good Buddhist, I hope these girls come up with something at least as congenial as the "Enterprise." When the "Trek" episode ended, it was back to the beds for another hour's pleasure before closing time at 8:00 p.m.

The brothel was located in a well kept brownstone on a pleasant tree-lined New York City street. There were flowers, maybe tulips in season, around the bases of the street trees. The brothel itself was first floor rear, with a spacious yard in the back. The building and suite were well maintained, with nice rugs on the floor. I don't recall any wall decorations. There were the two large bedrooms, and a large dining room/cum kitchen where we waited our turn, drinking free beer. Waiting room entertainment was provided by conversation and also the aforementioned live TV. I wager that, before TV, there was a live piano player. Thus, it goes without saying, everything was handled very efficiently, but also pleasantly. The place was redolent with an odor of air freshener, but it was not too strong or offensive. In fact, I developed a pleasant association of the pungent smell of the air freshener with my image of the beautiful women in the place. I believe this particular NYC brothel has been at this location since the 1920s.

Anyway, more detail: the women were on a regular, well-organized circuit of many brothels in the Northeast. The circuit was probably organized and run by the Mafia or some other such group. More power to them! They met a great need.

But what was I doing in the brothel? I can only tell you that I was an ex-mental patient, recently released from spending the better part of a year on the violent ward of a state mental hospital. I was still very weak psychically. I could not relate to women socially in the normal way. The brothel provided a welcome refuge and escape from my otherwise very limited circumstances. It was nearby and convenient. And it provided an excellent solution to the constant overweening problem of finding sexual gratification. It helped immensely in my rehabilitation.

My time in the brothel ended in 1987, when AIDS became rampant. I couldn't risk my health any more. Counsel advises me that I can't be prosecuted for my activities there, because of the Statute of Limitations.

As a regular at Patricia's, I was sometimes invited to the backyard barbecue behind the brownstone where this house of pleasures was located. The house sported a spacious, fenced in backyard, with a bit of greenery. There was a picnic table with a beach umbrella and a couple of chairs. The franks and hamburgers here tasted better than the same fare anywhere else, because I was so happy to be there, and we had a good time. Two doors down, in another backyard, the nuns of a particular sacred congregation took their ease, as we did, on nice days. There was a lot of chatting over the back fence between the two groups of women. Everybody knew what everybody else was doing, over that fence, of course. The Pope would have been very happy to see the scene. As I understand it, in the Roman Catholic scheme of things, venial sins are almost a necessity, or there'd be no reason for the Church's existence (except for mortal sin) and nothing for the good nuns over the fence to pray about. I wonder if Father Carney of my neighborhood R.C. Church would accept my bastard Thomism.

I once saw a B&W movie, perhaps made before WWII, *The Whores' Picnic*, purportedly based on a short story by Guy de Maupassant. The movie was delightful, there were many contretemps. Particularly touching was the old fellow, now dysfunctional, who hung around the whorehouse because he still got something out of watching the action, at least the comings and goings. And of course, in the movie, everybody did have a very merry picnic in the country.

From this story, I was inspired to take the Madam of my favorite place, Nicky, a very gracious

Italian-American woman, and the lead woman prostitute, whose name I have forgotten, to the New York Philharmonic at Avery Fisher Hall, which was perhaps known as Philharmonic Hall at that time.

My friend and backer Ralph Bentley came along to make it a foursome. For the evening out, the ladies were dressed to the nines (better than Ralph and I were, although I was in a good blazer and slax) and we all looked nicer than a lot of the regular Philharmonic attendees. Anyway, the ladies had never been to Lincoln Center in their lives. It was a whole new world to them. They were very attentive to the music and we all had a very good time. I do not want to appear in the least condescending in writing this because both Nicky and her lead worker were very experienced ladies in the ways of the world, running an especially congenial house (I've been in many others of which I could not say this), keeping many people in good spirits, and keeping both the Police and the Mafia at bay. Can't recall if we went out for drinks and supper afterwards but I hope we did. The whole thing was a high moment for me, having planned and executed the whole thing. And we were rewarded. For weeks afterward, Ralph and I were given freebies (free girls) at the brothel.

I will mention here that I am setting out to write this memoir, a large project, on July 5, 1998, one week after my 62nd birthday. I retired from full-time wage-earning employment on June 22nd (I still work for wages one day a week), but I am very much occupied with my photography, art and writing. The Memoir is loosely inspired by the *Confessions* of Jean-Jacques Rousseau, which were in turn based on the *Confessions* of St. Augustine. Why these two? Because they represent the beginning of Western memoir writing in the modern age, and because both were concerned, implicitly or explicitly, with sex. St. Augustine wrote about his early life in the brothels of Carthage ("Lord, give me chastity and continence, but not just now") and Rousseau wrote about the courtesans of Venice in the 18th century. Thus, my memoir is an ambitious project, I realize.

I also learned a lot about Sex that I didn't already know at this marvelous brothel, and I want to tell about some of the revelations. Consequently, the next couple of paragraphs will not be for the squeamish. I will preface it with one of the juicy items I read in Rousseau's *Confessions*. He said the only women with clean linen in moribund Venice in the 1740s were the courtesans. And there's much racier stuff in Rousseau, some of which I will allude to later.

My first discovery at the brothel was something called "Around the World." In this practice, the woman inserts her index finger in your rectum while simultaneously performing fellatio on you. It's called "Around the World" because the woman's finger is only a fraction of an inch from her mouth, separated only by a thin barrier of soft tissue, if the action is done right. The pleasure, from the pressure on the prostate and the fellatio, is immense. The arousal is extreme. The whole idea of the thing is extraordinary. My friends and I learned of the practice from Pearl, a Venezuelan import. We all had a few misgivings about the rectal aspect of the art, but, nonetheless, when we heard Pearl was in town, we all dropped everything and rushed downtown to the brothel.

About the rectal practice, we all had slight misgivings because we thought rectal meant gay. I do know that my beloved therapist for 19 years, Diane Gregory, told me (some) married couples do rectal things to each other all the time. But, as young American males, we did have the fear of engaging in what we thought might be a "homosexual" practice. All I know is that when Pearl was in town, all our misgivings vanished, and my pals and I rushed to our Nirvana.

I was also very impressed that the working women at the brothel would "swallow it" after performing fellatio on me. This can be very empowering to a guy. This gives a sense of mastery to the man. None of the limited number of women I'd known socially would ever blow me to orgasm and then swallow it. Always, I had to warn them when I was cuming so they could "get out of the way." It's too bad. It's harmless protein, and it means a lot to a man if the girl will swallow it. It can be a very moving thing.

"Swallowing" should be part of every girl's education at her mother's knee. All this brings up something I heard about the education of girls (by their mothers, usually) in Latin countries. Young women are taught to be cognizant of a man's "necessity," and perhaps in some way to be accommodating to it.

The women at Patricia's definitely changed my opinions about what a woman can do in her sexual role. I never married and probably never will, so maybe I don't know what I'm talking about. But if I did have a wife, I would want her to become at least as sexually proficient as the women in Patricia's brothel. My social acquaintances have so far disappointed me in this regard. Is this asking too much? I do everything sexually that I am able to do for my partner. A woman should do the same. A woman who is squeamish or too genteel is no good in bed. I think the Latin mothers have the right idea.

I wondered whether the women in the brothels feel, or feign, pleasure? I can only say that most seemed to get something out of it, especially, a pride in giving pleasure. About 1974, a young woman Ph.D. candidate, a patient in a group therapy session I was attending, took me to a lecture by a medical expert on prostitution. I have since forgotten his name, but he said, "Most prostitutes are either nymphomaniacs or masochists, or both." Well, O.K. to that, at least the nymphomania. What's wrong with a woman being a nymphomaniac?

Anyway, all of this confirmed to me how wonderful a woman can be to a man, even these working girls. My social experiences outside had led me to a somewhat lower opinion of women. My social acquaintances were inexperienced, shallow, inhibited and reluctant to try anything in the least adventurous. Many of them just gave limited sex in order to be liked by the man, so he would dance attendance on her, and so they would have an escort. My experiences outside had been disappointing.

A close friend, a Ph.D. and M.D., was asked by me to read and comment on my manuscript. About this opening chapter, he asked for more detail on the procedures in brothels, saying that, "Not many of my readers would have experience of such things." That last comment surprised me. Many, or most, men have tried it at some time or other. I believe my respectable father did.

Apropos of the authorities, three or four times (only) in my more than 1,000 visits to Patricia's, I heard a disgruntled client shouting that he would go to the police and expose the place. But nothing ever came of it. I'm convinced the place enjoys some kind of immunity.

About Patricia's, the women came from all over, and are mostly but not all white or Latino. Occasional African-Americans. To my taste, the best women were from Appalachia. Intelligent WASPs, savvy but not highly educated. Impoverished backgrounds. The brothel was the Appalachian women's best opportunity to escape the limitations of their upbringing. On the other hand, the Latinos came from all of Central and South America and the Caribbean. The travel schemes must have been very elaborate. The women stayed a week at a time at each place, and you would sometimes see them again, eight or ten weeks later, in the same place. I didn't patronize many other brothels in the metropolitan New York area, but I've been to a few others. Very occasionally, I would see the same woman again in another brothel. Oh yes, a few of the women were very well educated. One or two particularly well-spoken young women claimed to have Ph.D.s.

Anyway, what was the routine? You would be admitted, if you were known, after a look through a peephole. New patrons had to be introduced by an old patron. The cover for the place was that it was a "leather goods" establishment. I found that to be a very exciting idea. On coming in, the Madam would greet you and offer a free beer, which was handed to you. Later on, when you were better known, you could take yourself from the refrigerator. You would wait for the women to come out, when they had finished their current trick. You would then pick the one you wanted. All were at least moderately attractive, young and with good figures, and some were rare beauties.

On going into the bedroom, the first thing was to take off your clothes and to hold in your hands a basin filled with soap and hot water, while the young woman washed your genitals. Hygiene was very important. I remember a story about the Chinese Communist revolution in 1949-1950, when the prostitutes were rounded up. The Communists made them all into public health nurses, because they were so good about hygiene. The Chinese Communists were very idealistic revolutionaries in those days. And no backsliding was permitted. If the woman reverted to her old ways, she would be warned once, then a second time, and on the third mistake, she would be shot. Of course, those days are long gone. Now, the laissez-faire Chinese Communists tolerate prostitution for the hard currency it brings in. Formerly, I would have favored the idealistic approach, but now I believe organized, well-run, hygienic prostitution is a social necessity. In most places around the world it is legal and supervised by the Government. In London, for example, prostitution is technically illegal, but it is tolerated by the authorities as long as it is conducted on a discreet basis. Perhaps that's also the situation in New York City.

After the washing, and an inspection for disease, sex would follow. The girls would perform all the sex practices I was familiar with, and a few I didn't know, such as "Around the World." Nothing violent or dangerous of course. But plenty of vaginal and even rectal intercourse, fellatio, coming in the girl's mouth with swallowing, and hand work. Many positions. All very pleasing. And you were never rushed. You had at least 45 minutes, if you needed it.

When you were finished, we would both come out into the living room, and I would have another beer. I would pay the Madam, and the Madam would give a regular playing card to the young woman, a marker for her trick, for which she would be paid, later. Half the fee went to the worker, half to the house. The flat rate for one woman (yes, I tried two once or twice, not very successfully) was $12 in 1974 and $30 in 1987 (for whatever you wanted done), when I quit. By now, it must be $150. $150 was the rate for a budget morning "job" in a legal Nevada brothel, when I was last there, a couple of years ago.

When I was living on the street, in flop houses, abandoned buildings, and sleeping in cold alleys, I vowed that I would never make capital of any kind out of what had happened to me because that would give some justification to it and to the faulty process of psychoanalysis that had brought me to that plight. Now, however, I have embarked on this memoir, which will necessarily include something of my experiences in the analysis and on the street, to give one last blow against the cult of Freudian psychoanalysis, which I am told by knowledgeable people is almost dead anyway, but I intend to give it one more kick.

I do not think suffering is necessary before you can learn anything. In fact, I think it warps you and to some extent, makes you unfit for normal human relationships or pursuits. And also, I have come to the belief or at least suspicion, foolish and unscientific as it sounds, that we may exist again in other lives after this one (Leopold Bloom's "metempsychosis" in James Joyce's *Ulysses*) as the Buddhists believe. The prospect of myriad lives of suffering, some of it much worse than I have experienced in my life (but I can imagine it getting very bad now, much worse than the very bad things I myself have experienced in this life) daunts me. In a way, I sympathize closely with the women working at Patricia's. These women got by, by remembering the childhood lesson that I spoke of earlier, that they should try to be accommodating to men's needs. Like me, some might say that these women have had very bad lives. This comparison might be true, but I'm not sure. But we do have some things in common.

#

Also, like the Buddhists, I seek oblivion, not eternal life. Of course, complete oblivion would be an *augenblick*, the "blink of an eye." My good and constant friend Ralph Bentley mentions with approbation the comment of one of his early professors that he "looks forward to oblivion, to being dead, with just enough awareness so that he can 'enjoy being dead.'" Incidentally, the Buddhist priest Dr. T.K. Nakagaki told me at one of my colloquia that a person can be a Buddhist and an Atheist at the same time. At least, I recall his saying this. Interesting, but I doubt it. Nakagaki added that the Atheist who was a Buddhist would need to at least admit Spirituality, which I will not do. That's not my kind of true atheist.

I foolishly thought Freudian psychoanalysis was a form of science, because it was endorsed by the American Medical Association and because Freud was purported to be an atheist. Now, however, I know better. To give one example: libido theory and the theories of bound energies are all entirely transcendental. Quasi-religious, in fact. I have come to believe that nothing in physical reality (including energy) exists if you can't measure it with a scientific instrument.

In my scientific studies at school and later at work, I had trouble with the problem of faulty perception, reading the scientific instruments. I would get one reading, glance away and back, and, when nothing had changed, get a completely different reading. I attribute this to my weak psyche's propensity, magnified later, to hallucinate. But, not too long ago, Professor David Sidorsky of Columbia University, in a course I was auditing, personally told me that scientific instruments can now be equipped with huge digital LED readouts, that even someone half-mad could read. No more struggling to match verniers as in that aeronautical laboratory where I worked at The National Bureau of Standards when I was just 16, or, a little later, the shades of coloration on the agar plates in the Cornell University Department of Plant Breeding, where I studied and worked (unsuccessfully) for a doctorate when I was just 20.

These experiences convinced me I could never be a lab scientist, because the results looked one way at one moment and the same specimen looked completely different to me ten seconds later. And this was before I had any psychological trouble. It was also before the advent of the big digital LED readouts. At that time, I decided I would write for a living, like my father. Faulty perception wouldn't matter. I could see enough to see the keys of a typewriter, or, later, a computer.

To consider further my psychological experiences, I am convinced that the overused paradigm of the Oedipus complex derives, not from Greek mythology, but from the symbol of the patriarchal Jewish God, overcoming everything before it. My Freudian psychoanalyst did not try to win me over by persuasion, or by personal example, but by trying to crush and dominate me. I, of course, resisted, partly because I sprang from a different culture. I was not crushed or dominated but I was reduced to such a state that survival became difficult.

I read somewhere that, within the framework of the Oedipus complex, 9 out of 10 men with unresolved Oedipal complexes are total failures but the one in 10 who has the total love of his mother, or of all women, goes on to great things. Napoleon was mentioned as an example. There were others but I have forgotten them.

#

I wanted to discuss Barry Silvers, my Swarthmore College roommate for two good years and a steadfast friend, at least most of the time, over these past 58 years. After I was often tormented, bullied and hazed in the Wasp Jock Wharton dormitory, at the suggestion of proctor Frank Sieverts, I took refuge with all the Jewish intellectuals, misfits and others who didn't fit in with fraternity, jock life, in the Mary Lyons dormitories, a mile south of the main campus, located in the buildings of an old girls' school the College had taken over. Barry Silvers was one of my first friends there.

Mary Lyons 1, the first building I lived in at that location, was as far off in the woods as it was possible to get in suburban Swarthmore. Several hundred feet below there was a small waterfall on Crum Creek. An army Nike missile group operating antiaircraft rockets occupied Mary Lyons 2. Some faculty lived in Mary Lyons 1 with us, including psychology professor Arthur Greenberg and his wife, Faith Lewis Greenberg (more about her later). In my sophomore year, I roomed with Barry Silvers on the third floor of aforesaid Mary Lyons 1. My academic work was mediocre, I was dissatisfied with the engineering curriculum I had started with, and I found refuge with the Outing Club. Barry Silvers was also active in the OC. Incidentally, later on, I read some Vassar literature at Swarthmore about how the "dim bulbs" at Vassar found solace in their Outing Club. Well, so be it, I thought at the time.

In either my junior or senior year, I was elected President of the Outing Club, nominated by Barry Silvers. I organized canoe trips and difficult spelunking expeditions (to the raw caves near Kutztown). But, best of all, during vacation breaks, I organized gigantic mountain trekking expeditions to places as remote as the Nantahala Mountains in North Carolina, the White Mountains in New Hampshire (yes, we climbed Mount Washington), the Mahoosuc Mountains in Maine and the Virginia Blue Ridge. Sometimes we went in the dead of winter, keeping warm with the girls in double sleeping bags, in temperatures as low as zero degrees Fahrenheit, while the army mountain troops in these mountains at the same time as us called it quits because it was too cold. We stuck it out and had a great time, however. Slab bacon and the girls kept us warm.

Of course, I was afraid to ask Virginia Rice, one of the pretty young women I shared my double sleeping bag with, to have sex with me. I was afraid to ask, afraid I wouldn't be able to perform, afraid she would get pregnant, afraid of the unknown female maw, just afraid. At that time, I still had only a rough idea of the intimate female anatomy. I was just afraid and wouldn't wing it for fear of a debacle. And Virginia, pretty little thing, was eager. She said to me, "You don't do anything!" I'm ashamed of this episode. Still, in my life, I have never wanted to try anything unless I had it all planned out from beginning to end beforehand. I still think that's the right idea. My psychotic episode would never have been precipitated if I'd stuck to my watchword.

But, even with the failure with Virginia and others, those weeks in the mountains with my little groups were unqualifiedly the happiest days of my life. We were away from our terrible parents, our schoolwork responsibilities, and we were facing and mastering a lot of new challenges. The mountains and the woods were very beautiful. There was a great camaraderie, and also everybody looked up to me as the leader. I foolishly thought at the time that these trips were the beginning of a happy, adventurous, productive life. I was wrong. It wasn't the Commencement of a good life, it was the End. Shortly thereafter, at age 24, I began psychoanalysis with Dr. Irving Sternschein. His non-directive technique drove me completely insane in nine months. Very briefly, he brought my unconscious mind to the surface, full of terrible things, and, when this happened, he offered me no support at all. When I suddenly cracked, he didn't offer me moral support or tranquilizers, but could only suggest a mental hospital. I stormed out of his office, struggled on, on the streets, for a couple of years, and then the police put me in an asylum.

When I made a minimal recovery, I was unable to work, for the most part of seven years, and half-mad, barely able to control myself and living a marginal life in furnished rooms, for another twenty. I've never had the same optimism and confidence as at 24, before this. I carry around with me now a lot of emotional, religious, transcendental, so-called "spiritual" and sexual baggage I'd like to get rid of. I'm trying now to get back to thinking abstractly, to thinking "like a machine," as decent Dr. Nathan Stockhamer said I did before the nondirective analysis. That kind of thinking was what brought me success in the early days—perhaps it will again. The only decent thing in all of my later life was the brothel.

#

I had a most interesting dream one Thursday night, the night after Rivka Kfia called me to tell me she getting divorced and would like to see me and possibly pose for me. In the dream, I found myself riding a horse, keeping my seat fairly well but not altogether comfortably, on a nice day. First, I rode through some pleasant wooded countryside, then, with difficulty, on a superhighway with a metal grill roadbed with fast cars whizzing by, and finally, through sand and scrub to an area which was a "silica waste."

What is the point of being convulsed by violent emotion? What is the point of strong emotion at all? Why do some people strive for it? I suppose it's pleasant, in the sense that it makes you feel more alive. Even if it's unpleasant, the previous may be true. But what is the purpose of it? What can it lead to? More often than not, when in the grip of violent emotion, you're incapacitated for anything else. Of course, you can write or tell about it (later), but that's just compounding the error. What kind of human endeavor is really helped by strong emotion? I fail to see any purpose to it.

My violent emotion when struggling with my many and varied hallucinations is an example of this. Yes, it was deep and passionate, but it was all totally useless. Maybe a well trained therapist (are there any?) could have channeled my emotion into something productive, but it would have taken a very long time and, from my present vantage point, I doubt the value of the outcome.

Deep Waters

How did my madness arise? What were the causes? Now that madness has passed, at least for now, I can tell you how it came about and give you, by way of introduction to this saga of desperation and survival, a few examples of what my mental state was like at the height of it. I give a more detailed etiology in Chapter 14, "Psychiatric Explorations," but I will start the story of my madness here.

In 1959, a couple of years out of college, and frustrated with my life and my (lack of) relationships with women, I entered into an intensive nondirective Freudian psychoanalysis. This was a mistake. After nine months of this, the analyst went on vacation, and, without him, I lost my mind. On his return, the analyst could only suggest that I enter a mental hospital, but I was determined to avoid that. So, in my miserable condition, I struggled on, sometimes on the street, until 1963.

On the night in November, 1963, that President John Kennedy was assassinated, I was transferred from the Bellevue psychiatric ward, where I had been taken by the police three weeks earlier after they found me trying to slash my wrists in the middle of Fifth Avenue, to what was then called Manhattan State Hospital, on Ward's Island in the East River. I then felt the date was significant. Perhaps, a little Jungian Synchronicity?

I was admitted to Manhattan State after dark, quickly processed and sent to a large ward to sleep. It was already dark in the ward, people were asleep. The big windows showed the patterns of the lights still lit in some of the other wards in the same building and the lights of the other buildings in the complex. But I could not interpret the pattern of the lights; I could not Gestalt the pattern and definitely recognize what I was seeing. I had some idea, of course, but it was still scary, or more correctly, awesome. All I could see was a mysterious light display, like an enormous city or spaceship.

Then, the staff, thinking the poor patients were upset by Kennedy's death (some were; it's amazing the hold that man had on so many people's imaginations), got the idea of playing the Death March (Largo), the dirge, from Handel's *Saul,* to comfort everybody. The loudspeaker played it over and over again, all night long. Actually, I think it was a radio broadcast piped in. Anyway, it was a moving introduction to what turned out to be a satisfactory refuge for almost a year.

Incidentally, from the picture window of my present 13th floor studio cooperative apartment in Morningside Gardens, where I have lived for nearly 28 years, I have a full view of the renamed Manhattan Psychiatric Center on the other side of Manhattan Island (perhaps more synchronicity?). No matter; I rather like the prospect and the view.

Later on, after release from State Hospital, I thought I was cured. I quickly ran through a succession of jobs, and in 1966, I ended up in a very good one. But between my two major psychotic breaks, when I was working in a fine job as a science writer at The American Institute of Physics (AIP), one of the deeper and more terrifying psychological experiences of my life occurred. I know now that these were hallucinatory or so-called "religious" experiences, but at the time, it was frightening.

I was already in a psychologically weakened state after my first trip to Europe, in the company of my then-fiancée, Rachel Chouxfleur, who had just gotten over being pregnant with my child. I had arranged an abortion for Rachel, well and safely executed, in 1967, when it was illegal to do so, in a little clinic in the mountains of Puerto Rico, .Rachel said the setting,

Spanish tiles on the wall, was very "pleasant," alleviating her distress. I was overstimulated by this event, and by everything else that was going on in my life, to say the least, and this manifested itself in the following episode:

In Europe with Rachel a few months later, I had relapsed and lost my way around London. It seemed the street map was changing around. Things looked completely different, like another reality. Different buildings, different streets. I finally found my way back to Rachel and she successfully brought me back from England. But things didn't work out well on my first day back at work. At AIP, I worked in a small office, with only three or four colleagues, in a small building totally occupied by the Institute I had as company a Director of Public Relations, an Assistant Director, and one Secretary. On my first day back, I quickly realized that I was out of control.

In my disturbed thinking, I had the notion that I knew what people in this AIP office were going to say and do before they did it, in the daily office activities. Then, the whole thing went a little further, and the people in the office seemed to shimmer and become phantasms, in that they ceased to have any independent reality. The staff seemed like personages in an El Greco painting. They seemed to be only creatures of my mind and will. Was this some kind of inversion of the ego which makes what is happening look like a product of the ego? My mind could not have actually been controlling these people, but it seemed as if this were so. There seemed to be NO objective reality at all—everything seemed to be a product of my mind. In the next stage, everything vanished (or was still present only as a meaningless kaleidoscopic phantasm) and there was nobody there but Me and God. In the final stage, there was nobody there but God. All this was so terrifying (especially to a professed Atheist like me) that I snapped out of it and fell exhausted on my desk.

All this experience was probably a gigantic hallucination, but I have been unable to entirely get the idea out of my head that it might have reflected a distorted view of some other reality of some kind. I have read of somewhat similar experiences in religious and philosophical literature, including in Evelyn Underhill's wonderful book, *Mysticism*, written in 1910 and telling of many similar experiences.

Later in 1967, after I'd left AIP, and my roommate had left me, I was in a total funk, knowing I couldn't pay the rent and would soon be on the streets again soon. In my distraction, I was destroying all the furniture and throwing the refuse out into the service hall for the porter.

In the middle of this, I tried to listen to classical music on WQXR to calm myself. But then the strangest, most unearthly, terrifying organ music came over the radio that spoke to the energies boiling up within me. It was the eeriest thing. I turned the radio off, but the music continued. Out of desperation, I smashed the radio, but the strange music still continued. I was very scared and fled out into the street.

The next thing I did was go into a $1.19 steak house across the street and, with a couple of my few remaining dollars, order a steak. I started to eat it, and realized that this was the most preternaturally delicious steak I had ever tasted. Nothing has tasted that good before or since. It was unnatural. I bolted up from the table and left the steak unfinished. Again, it was too eerie. On the way out, I had the terrifying fear that the other meat, the other steaks cooking on the grill, were going to "bellow on the spits," like the cooking meat from the witch Circe's cattle that Odysseus' men had killed. It didn't, but this observation shows the state of my mind. Of course, perhaps the meat only tasted so good because I was starving. But no, the impressions were too strong even for that.

Back in the apartment, now with most of the furniture gone, I tried to shave with an electric shaver. For some reason, the device flew apart in my hands. IT SEEMED that I was so charged up with energies of some kind that these had caused the device to fly apart. I did seem to be all charged in a way that I am sure no one could measure with a scientific instrument. Perhaps Freud's bound energies, now unbound, that I don't believe in because they are transcendental? What I mean here is that Freud seemed to believe that a large part of our psychic energy is tied up within us because of our various neuroses and other limitations. But I found out that these energies can be very dangerous if released at an inopportune time.

Over the next day or two, I had the same experience with electric clocks, transistor radios and other small electrical devices. They all seemed to fly apart in my hands when I touched them. I seemed to be all charged up and quaking with some kind of force or energy. Surely my "character armor" had been penetrated, as Dr. Wilhelm Reich used to say, and the so-called inner "energies" had been released. I never want to experience anything like that again. In the rest of my life, I have carefully avoided all such "surprises."

It's a low trick to reduce anybody to a state of mind where he or she will experience things like this. Though in some perverted way it might be interesting (and frightening), it serves no useful purpose, in that it does not reflect physical reality and leads to nothing, except perhaps RELIGION or the OCCULT. I must say that some people do not go psychotic when their psychic defenses are down. But it did happen to me (and others). Of course, maybe the unbound energies could be turned to sexual purposes, but I don't like that. Too "occult." I really prefer what is called "clinical" sex, to preserve my emotional balance. As I understand it, "clinical" sexual pleasure is focused in the genital organs, and does not take over the whole body and personality, as Reichian orgasms may do. Maybe I'm missing something, restricting myself to clinical sex, but I just don't give a damn. I value my sanity.

I sleep with four lights burning. I am a professed atheist and intellectually do not believe in anything transcendental, including disembodied spirits of any kind. However, unless I sleep with many lights on, I wake up completely disoriented with no idea where I am. Worse, I sense the presence of all kinds of entities, including departed friends, especially Otto Koch and George Michanowsky (more about them elsewhere), and lots of others.

There are my forebears, including both my died-young parents. Also my deceased heroes, such as Bertrand Russell. Of course, there's a full complement of guardian archangels, including Michael and Gabriel (I wish I had been spared the early sketchy religious indoctrination). Finally, I sense the space-opera creatures, including people from the future, coming back to give me much-needed advice.

I know this last derives from my course work at Columbia University, where my professor, Dr. David Albert, one of the two or three best minds in quantum mechanics in the country, and also teaching philosophy of science, maintains definitively now that time travel will be possible in five or ten thousand years. My idea is, what's to stop these future people from coming back and visiting us NOW, perhaps to save us from our mortality?

More so-called "transcendental" or "mystical" and/or "hallucinatory" experiences. At the height of my madness, I could no longer read anything. There were two problems. The first was that when I looked at a printed page, the words seemed to transpose and shift lines, in a manner very similar to that on a desktop screen when you scroll or add, move or delete bodies of copy. The page also seemed to glow in an unearthly fashion. Very strange.

The interesting thing about the similarity to a desktop screen was that, in 1967, when I had these experiences, the prototypes of desktops barely existed. Yes, I had seen one at the IBM headquarters in Armonk, where I was visiting as a representative of The American Institute of Physics (still sane) earlier in that same year. I had even been allowed to ask questions of this prototype interactive device. I remember thinking at the time, very impressed, that the computers (the "cosmic computer," as one mad friend put it) were coming back through time to rescue me from my mortality and the pack of fools around me.

The second part of this set of hallucinations was that I thought, when you put a book back on the shelf, its contents could change. I thought this because, in my schizophrenia (I was so diagnosed at one point, I believe), when I took a familiar book down from the shelf, I would open it and find a page I was totally unfamiliar with, even if the lines of text were not "visibly" transforming at the time. This notion that the contents of books were mutable persisted for a long while. It discouraged me, even when I was somewhat better, from trying to pursue any intellectual disciplines, because of the futility of it all, in the face of the ever-changing and multiplying realities (in the books and elsewhere) I was faced with.

One of the reasons for describing all these experiences, which I hope were purely subjective phenomena, is to bring up the matter that upset me the most. I must say that I thought then, and I think now, that if "miracles" can happen, if the entire natural order can be suspended, indeed, if God exists, then there's no point to anything, no point to any human endeavor. And, when I was quite mad, a "miracle" seemed to be happening every five minutes. But yet, when the fit of madness passed, ordinary reality returned, completely unchanged. But, in the presence of these "miracles," there would be nothing to do but wallow in the emotional opiate that is Religion. And, by extension, I suppose my negative attitude would extend to a lot of art, beauty and love. I thought when I was growing up that the only meaningful goal was to increase mankind's control over the natural order. By this, I mean natural science and mathematics. If this has no meaning, then nothing has any meaning for me.

I've noticed that many analysands lapse into "loving" relationships, do their specialized jobs, raise their families, and give up any hope of really amounting to anything or making any fundamental changes or improvements in the life of mankind. "Love" is not enough for me. I never accepted this. I still want to amount to something. Love is a trap. I refuse to recognize limitations and settle for love. I think anybody who does is misguided. And I think this business of marrying and making a home and a family is a dumb reflex. There are too many babies, anyway. This sort of thing has been going on for ages and we're still in terrible trouble. Better to make some changes or do nothing at all. And, of course, as an ex-mental patient, my chances of really affecting the fate of the race are nil. I knew I was ruined the day of the psychotic break in 1960 and I still know it. The best one can do in such a case is try to do something in the so-called "arts."

I know some of the standard explanations for these hallucinatory phenomena now. When your defenses are down, when your "character armor" has been penetrated, you take note of things you would otherwise ignore. In the more or less "normal" individual, the sensory data is "screened," and only those data which fit in with what the particular psyche needs and habitually uses are admitted and "used." The rest is cast away. But when your defenses are down, you get a lot more stuff, some of it painful. The psychiatrists do this to you deliberately to strip away your defenses, to effect fundamental "change." I don't know if they should. It didn't work (wasn't manageable) in my case.

My new, dear friend Rivka Kfia offers still another, but related explanation. First, a word about Rivka. She successfully defended her thesis and was awarded a double doctorate in physics and philosophy by Columbia University on August 31, 1998. I called her the same day from Cap d'Agde naturist resort on the French Mediterranean coast to congratulate her. Besides winning the double degree, she is an accomplished classical pianist (has performed professionally), is trained in classical ballet, and can do a creditable oil painting. I'm afraid Rivka has contempt for the intellectual capabilities of most people (she won't talk to them - ignores them) but she seems to have a lot of respect for me and my abilities, which helps me a lot, since I don't have her attainments.

Rivka also has a clever 3-year old son and is separated. She has spoken at one of my colloquia and at one of my Eleutheria Salons. Anyway, upon getting the doctorate in physics and philosophy, Rivka did a marvelous thing. She took a job in the schizophrenia project at Columbia-Presbyterian Hospital. Because she had a lover who was schizophrenic and later killed himself, she had first-hand knowledge of the problem. Because she was trained in logic, she tested her schizophrenic friend's ability to do different kinds of logic (while he was still alive), and, knowing (from texts) what parts of the brain carried out different kinds of logic, she was able to localize the seat of her friend's schizophrenia, or so she thinks.

Rivka now thinks there is a small physical anomaly in the brains of schizophrenics, one that could be corrected by only slightly invasive procedures. She wrote up her proposal to the National Institutes of Health and they awarded her a sizable grant to investigate. That's why she's now working at Columbia-Presbyterian. She wears a white coat, is called doctor, and puts schizophrenics from the psychiatric wards there into MRI scanners to search for the physical anomaly. She thinks she has found it.

I can relate all this to my aforementioned mystical, hallucinatory experiences mentioned in this section. Rivka points out, as we know, that the center of the brain is relatively empty of synapses, the switching points in the mental "circuits" where information is routed around the brain during its activity. Most of the synaptic activity takes place near the outer surface of the brain, where the furrows are, and where synapses are abundant.

However, says Rivka, in schizophrenics, a dense collection of synapses develops in the center of the brain, and because these synapses aren't "pruned" regularly, as happens in the normal brain, a lot more data, sensory and otherwise, is transmitted. (The purpose of the pruning is to prevent this and only supply the individual with the data he habitually needs and uses.)

Now, to pull all this together, what if this extraneous data is not all "garbage," but what if some of it shows aspects of some realities we ordinarily ignore? What is the relationship between schizophrenia and art and creativity?

It's all very interesting. What if one day, Rivka can fix me up with her laser, and I can "think like a machine" again? That's the only kind of thinking that has brought me any recognition in this Society.

Incidentally, Rivka is not so sure she can suggest a way to treat the anomaly, once it has developed, but she's very interested in its etiology. She suspects the etiology is genetic or traumatic, or both. She thinks the predisposition to this can be picked up in childhood and treated then. She is interviewing mothers of schizophrenics to see if there were any trauma during certain stages of pregnancy, for example.

My experiences were all very wacky, my mind rejects it all, but I still feel the effects of all of it (the experiences).

Art and the Mind

I have great trouble trying to conceive of myself as an artist, even though I enjoy such work and have demonstrated at least some talent in this direction, in my sketching, photography and writing. As my 1959 Rorschach put it, and as is still true, my psychological problems are philosophical. This is also true of my relationship to the artistic process.

Put simply, to a lot of thinkers, artists are second-rate citizens. Plato and Nietzsche and a lot of other philosophers said so (only a few did not) and Freud is known to have said that the artist is "inadequate," and only succeeds with women indirectly, by pandering his fantasies to them. Long ago, I clipped Ernest Jones' (Freud's gentile biographer) comments on this and I photocopied the excerpts. I still have these copies around the studio somewhere. In the past, I carried them around with me, so as not to waver from my then total dedication to science, computers and technology.

Also, now that I have something of an artistic career, I know many other artists, and universally, they seem to me to be flaky in one way or another, both in their artistic creativity and in the rest of their lives.

After I'd been fired from yet-another science writing job in 1977, I remember sitting in the Footlights Café, then located under Lincoln Center, with my friends Ralph Bentley and Otto Koch (the latter killed by a hit & run in 1990) trying to decide what to do with the rest of my life. I had started attending and enjoying classes at The Art Students League in 1974 (I started the same week that I began going to the local brothel—I hadn't wanted to confuse meeting my sexual needs with meeting my artistic needs, if you can understand that. Then and now, I still had some shreds of pride and dignity, even after being humbled by the psychiatrists and the institutional commitments.).

Anyway, after some soul searching, I decided to continue to commit myself, almost full time, to writing about computers, technology and the management of same. And I kept on with this until 1986, when I finally was forced out of the science writing career and took up art and photography.

A little more about my attitude and relationship to art. When I was hauled into Manhattan State Hospital in November, 1963, it took me a week or two to recover my orientation. Then I began to take note of the facilities that were offered us to help in our recovery. There wasn't a lot. Of course, there were the tranquilizers, including thorazine (generically, chlorpromazine) which were the best thing they offered. With these, I gradually recovered my senses and a limited ability to function.

There were a few other services, including art therapy. At the time, I knew little about art, except an average college graduate's acquaintance with famous artists and childhood and high school instruction in art. But I'd had such visions, hallucinations and transcendental experiences after, and only after, my psychotic break! My reaction to them was, I don't want to expand my awareness of distorted perception any further—I just wanted to batten down the hatches and get on with a normal life—so I always declined the offer to go to art therapy, when it was offered to us. Who knows, I might have become a great action painter at the time. Ha, ha! Instead, I went on to write about physics and computers for another 23 years. It seemed to be the right thing to do at the time. I wanted no part of this "new world" I'd been thrown into.

Instead, I went to the woodworking shop, which I then thought was a rational thing to do. I'd done a little woodworking when young, building many hamster cages, etc. But it turned out, I was afraid to operate any of the machinery, I was trembling so badly, in my new "liberated" emotional state. I just couldn't wait until I got my defenses and my "character armor" back. I felt like a complete fool, trembling like a newborn babe.

Incidentally, I was told they had magazines with photographs of nude women in the art therapy group, to draw from. But I didn't see the sense of getting aroused for nothing, or having some art therapist watch me work out my sexual fantasies and frustrations. Or would it have been for nothing? We did have social hours where we were allowed to meet with the girls, and one young couple that I met in the mental hospital told me they were making love in the broom closet. In retrospect, now, it seems like it might have been an invitation to share the girl, or that, with a little initiative, I might have made it into that. We did have a certain sense that we were all in this together and there was a certain camaraderie. But I was so backward in those matters, and so debilitated as well, that nothing came of it. Another missed opportunity, perhaps?

Still more on art, and the psychology of art. It seems to me that most art as we now have it panders to the conceits of the rich and established, and is used to help them maintain their position. The public is impressed with the sophistication of critics and collectors who understand, or purport to understand, this stuff. Maybe folk art is an exception. I know that all the museums and art schools I attend are heavily endowed by the Rockefellers, the Whitneys, etc. One leftist I once knew said the art schools were heavily endowed to get the riff-raff off the streets and to keep them from being politicized and turning into Communists and Anarchists. I know for myself that Beauty is a trap that keeps me from spending more time thinking about things that are really important.

It seems to me that if art and esthetics are undertaken seriously, they will partake of the transcendental. Proceeding to analyze this, the transcendental will partake of the spiritual and the spiritual will partake of the Religious. Now the Religious has almost always seemed to me to be a Drug and a Poison (following Marx, Albert Ellis and Bertrand Russell and a lot of other people). Consequently, most forms of art are to be eschewed. My work, photographing and drawing the nude, is reasonably objective and I hope O.K. for me. I do take the pictures and draw the sketches in an artful, esthetic way, and this makes me a little uncomfortable. Likewise, Otto Koch described my whole life style as that of a *lebenkunstler* or "life artist" (one whose whole life is a work of art) and I guess this is O.K.

As to my trying to be objective, I follow Goethe, who said, in a letter to the writer Eckermann, that "Societies in decline are subjective, while progressive societies are objective." I would fear my esthetic capacity if it would lead me into making any deep works of art that would tend to confirm the Subjective or Religious attitude. I know I once loved Abstract Expressionism until I read somewhere that it was a "spiritual movement" and I then became very wary of it. Yes, I still go to the Pollock and Rothko shows, with interest, but I have the feeling when I do so that I am venturing into the camp of the Enemy.

I had an interesting comment from a brilliant 23-year-old friend, Kacey Stamats, who was also a wonderful young stage director, that, "Why was Art a Last Resort for you?" But then she went on to say, "John, don't get me wrong. You're a damn fine artist! Your sketches are wonderful!" I believe Kacey was on to something. I don't believe I would have ventured into Art until I'd exhausted some other possibilities.

#

I'm well aware that there are art forms other than the visual arts. I want to say a little here about music and Manhattan State. Since my Swarthmore days, I had always loved classical music, to the virtual exclusion of all other kinds of music, except maybe a little jazz and salsa. But, briefly, when I was in the depths, classical music lost its appeal, and I began to dislike Mozart. One day I had the asylum barber cut my hair in a Bob Dylan style and I began to listen to and applaud rock music. This phase was very brief. I soon decided I was being foolish and irrational, and I began to deliberately cultivate my taste for Mozart, etc., again. This second change (the return to Mozart) happened when I began to feel a little better. I also went back to a crew cut. I will mention that, later on in life, I began to shave my head and I do so to this day.

For the rest of this chapter, I will leave the subject of art and its relation to madness and I will discuss other aspects of life in Manhattan State (Psychiatric) Hospital. Some of the things happening there were not too pleasant. When I arrived at that place in 1963, they were still performing occasional lobotomies there, long after nearly all other institutions had stopped the practice. And I was on the violent ward! It was a little scary. I tried not to get into too many fights, with this thought hanging over me.

A lobotomy, if you don't know, is a drastic, primitive, desperate surgical procedure formerly widely used to reduce violence and violent thoughts. In a lobotomy, all the nerve connections between the rest (back) of the brain and the frontal lobes, which are the seat of emotion, are severed. The result is that the patient becomes a psychological vegetable, with truncated intellect. But no more violent emotions. No more emotions of any kind. No violence. That's what the hospital administrators were looking for.

Once, at one of our "splendor in the grass" (you better believe it!) picnics with the girls on the Ward's Island Grounds, under the close watch of our keepers, someone was about to introduce me to a girl who had had one of the lobotomies, but I was called away by some other incident. What a pity! I never met another such victim face-to-face, although I did see a frightening PBS documentary years later which interviewed, if you can call it that, lobotomy victims. Horrible! Much better to be dead!

A word about my unfortunate physical condition when I came to Manhattan State. I was emaciated when I arrived there, after a couple of years of living in alleys and flop houses. I had been processed at Bellevue for three weeks, and fed well, before being sent on to Manhattan State. Still, I recall weighing myself on a standing doctor's scale about two weeks after arrival at Manhattan State, and getting a reading of 125 lbs. True, I could have gotten the reading wrong—my mental state wasn't too great at the time. But if the reading was correct, I had lost more than a third of my normal body weight of close to 200 lbs., and I have read that you can die when you lose that much weight. I did have considerable difficulty climbing stairs, I was so weak. I had tried very hard to stay out of the place and avoid commitment. But my Will did not prevail, in this case.

Of course, once I adjusted to the regimen, I fattened up quickly. Too much, in fact. It does seem to be true that your nerves are better if you're overweight, and I believe these psychiatric hospital administrators are aware of this fact. The fat coats the nerve endings, it was said. We got lots and lots of fattening carbohydrates, powdered mashed potatoes, powdered eggs, and U.S. Government Issue roast beef. I don't remember getting a lot of fresh fruit or veggies.

As I was considered suicidal (I had slashed my wrist on the street, doing little damage, only requiring three stitches to close the wound, but evidently it was enough of an effort to frighten the hospital administrators), I was relegated to the violent ward, which was just like a regular ward, except there were twice as many attendants (six, instead of the usual three, for a ward of perhaps 50 patients).

All the attendants seemed to be little guys. It was a fabulous sight, watching three or four of them try to (and succeed in) restraining some huge African-American. There was a good bit of fighting among the patients on the ward, as well. We would all circle around the day room, in time to the piped-in "Easy Listening" music, and occasionally words would be exchanged and fists would fly. Usually, the attendants would rush in, and if it was bad, the perpetrators would be put in straightjackets or the padded cell for a while. And, as I mentioned, there was always the (distant) threat of a lobotomy hanging over you. Of course, if you fought, they would increase your medication, so you would be in a fog all day.

One thing I never understood, until my psychotherapist explained it to me much later. The ward was always well policed by the attendants, EXCEPT that around 4:30 p.m. every day, all the attendants would exit for an hour and the doors would be bolted from the outside. Then, of course, the "bopping" would start in earnest. By "bopping," I don't mean the sounds of blows being exchanged. Rather, I mean the sound a cranium makes when it hits a hard tile floor. A very distinctive noise. Very unfortunate, even to watch.

My psychotherapist explained years later that probably all the attendants left the ward for the regular daily staff meeting. I don't know why I didn't figure this out at the time. It had been a great mystery to me. And the "bopping" could get pretty bad.

I was only in two or three fights myself, but they were not pleasant. Once my nose was pushed halfway across my face (my opponent had been decent enough not to hit me in the teeth.). Afterwards, we became friends, since I had stood up to him. Another time, I tried to silence a chanting Black Muslim, who was working himself into a frenzied trance. His ululating got to my exposed nerves. So it went.

But, other than the "bopping," it wasn't too bad in the psychiatric hospital. The staff left you alone if you didn't make trouble, there was enough to eat and clean bedding, and the variety of people was interesting. After about eight months, I was given day passes, to go out into the City and look for work and a place to stay. Of course, there were no "talking cures" (one-on-one psychotherapy) or anything like that. The hospital just didn't have staff for that.

But I'm still grateful to the place for getting me out of dirty gutters, freezing alleys, sleeping in the bathtubs in abandoned buildings, and strange places like flophouses (which last could be interesting—more about that later). I do have to say that I valued my freedom on the outside and kept it as long as I could possibly stand the terrible conditions of my existence. I had the idea, from family wisdom, that once you entered one of these places, you never got out. This was true until the invention of tranquilizers in 1953. I did know that my maternal grandmother lived out the rest of her life and died in a neurological institute in 1922. My sister was also hospitalized in asylums, on more occasions than I was. And my mother was often hysterical. So, there probably was a genetic component to my madness. I also didn't want the stigma of the asylum on my resume. So I struggled on the outside as long as I could.

From Birth to Puberty
1936 - 1949

I now begin the straight chronology of my life, from the very beginning. By the time most of you, dear readers, come to this document, I will have passed on. So I will start this account of my earliest life with an inscription from a Roman Stoic grave rubbing, which, translated from the Latin, reads:

> I was not.
> I was.
> I am not.
> I care not.

This more or less sums up my thoughts and philosophy on death..

With that said and done, I will go on to recount that I was born, after a difficult labor of 24 hours, at Providence General Hospital, Providence, RI, on June 28, 1936. Shortly after my birth, a hemangioma, or large strawberry mark, appeared on my right forehead. It measured about 3" x 5". My maternal grandfather, Elmer John Lewis, paid to have the blemish removed, thumbnail-sized piece at a time, by dry ice application, at Boston Children's Hospital. My mother made the trip from Providence to Boston and back, with me, once a month or so for two years, until the hemangioma was totally removed and replaced by scar tissue, which was not unsightly. I don't know if this two-year process, up to the age of two, traumatized me at all. I was very young and I have no conscious memory of it.

My earliest recollection is of being put out to play, alone, in a fenced in back yard in Cranston, RI, wearing only a skimpy sunsuit. No underwear. I was embarrassed. I felt the outfit wasn't dignified enough. I was three at the time. My next recollection is of being carried up the extensive wooden green steps of Mount Royal in Montreal by my father. Montreal was where my maternal grandfather, Elmer J. Lewis, worked as a U.S. Customs official. I distinctly remember having sherbet in a little metal dish with my father, in a pavilion atop the mountain. I was three or four. This would have been 1939 or 1940. World War II had probably started (in Europe) by then.

My next memory is of my wonderful kindergarten teacher, Miss (or Mrs.?) Hobson. I don't remember the details, but I know I had a lot of fun in her class and I was very fond of her. Kindergarten was in Cranston, RI. I also had two four- or five-year old pals at this time, Robert Howe and Arthur Larsen. About this time, in late 1941, Pearl Harbor took place. I have a memory that our family heard about it after coming out of a movie (about Hawaii, I believe) in downtown Providence. One other interesting detail was that, at this time, 1940, one of our series of homes had an icebox instead of an electric refrigerator. The iceman came periodically, bringing fresh slabs of ice. I mention this to remind you that all this took place a long time ago.

In 1942, my father, a rubber chemist, got an editorial job writing for *India Rubber World* in NYC and the family moved to Long Island. I was six at the time. So we moved from Cranston, RI, to Bellmore, Nassau County, Long Island (briefly) and then to Merrick (for a longer stay, about two years, until I was eight years of age). In Merrick, we rented a house in a new development that had been started in about 1940 and then construction had been stopped after Pearl Harbor. One street of houses had been finished in the middle of a huge, flat sandy waste, about a mile by a half mile in extent. All the topsoil had been removed prior to construction, leaving only the Long Island sand. The effect was rather desolate, but it was great for playing. With sticks, we kids would draw huge ships or airplanes or city floor plans or whatever in the sand and play our elaborate games there. I would also enjoy handling and playing with the thousands of toads that lived in the sandy waste. I loved small creatures then, later (as with my hamsters) and now. I still know how to call squirrels.

One other interesting incident to report from 1942 (I was age six) was that one curious little girl, Heidi Miller, undressed me completely, but I did not reciprocate and undress and investigate her, even though she offered to comply. I guess I was just backward. In those days I knew nothing about sex, or how it was conducted, and at that time I had no interest in seeing the areas that shit and piss came from.

In perhaps 1943, when I was in the second grade in the North Merrick, Long Island, public school, I was selected to play the role of the school Principal, a Mr. Haig, in a Tom Thumb wedding to be presented in the school auditorium. I dutifully learned and rehearsed my role, and was all set to go, when, on the night before the first scheduled performance, I came down with chickenpox. So I missed out on my first acting gig.

The next topic still troubles me. From about the age of six (1942) to the age of 12 (1948, just before puberty), I amused myself on the floor of my bedroom by playing out famous naval battles, some of them going on right at that moment, with simple paper ships of my own construction, some of them quite elaborate sailing ships with sails, masts, cannons, rigging (thread) and a bowsprit (toothpick). Others, the modern ships, were simply cut out from file cards and named with real ships' names.

Sometimes I would put colored gummed stars or circles (stickers) on these. Oh yes, the aircraft carriers had tiny paper airplanes, white for American and yellow for Japanese. I would act out Trafalgar, Pearl Harbor, the sinking of the Bismarck, Midway, D-Day, and the Battle of Leyte Gulf. I acted out D-Day, among other battles, while it was going on, listening to the radio accounts. I was also an avid reader of naval history and the C.S Forester novels about Captain Horatio Hornblower I would act out with my paper ships on the floor all of Hornblower's fictional, but realistic, adventures in the Napoleonic wars.

Why does this bother me now? Because people were getting killed in these battles, some in particularly grisly ways. And all I could do was make a game of it. Now all I can think of is my friend Paul Steinhacker's harrowing ascent of Pork Chop Hill, when I think of my little war games. About those war games, I read somewhere that U.S. Army psychologists have determined that one man in ten loves front line combat (the other nine look on combat as a very unpleasant, onerous duty, but they go through with it so as not to let down their buddies). It would be a terrible thing if I turned out to be one of those combat-loving men, what with my Quaker education and training. But back to the story line. Finally, a sympathetic 12-year-old friend, Freddie Clark, got me to stop my precocious war games and got me out on the street to play with the other kids. Soap box racing, and such like stuff.

On to my eighth year. The family moved from Merrick to Baldwin, Long Island, in 1944. I entered the fourth grade at Prospect Elementary School in Baldwin. I had a wonderful fourth grade teacher, Mrs. Garbor, who deviated from the State curriculum in marvelous ways. For one thing, she taught us all about the ancient Romans. I particularly recall her telling us of the Roman Legions, how, when they were on the march and came to a stopping place for the night, would build an entire palisade of tree trunks, surrounded by a moat, around their camp, even if they were only staying one night. Always be prepared. *Semper Paratus.* I always remembered that, although it appears from my history that I did not remember it well enough.

Mrs. Garbor also taught us about Roman roads, architecture, baths and regular postal service. I built a diorama of the Roman Baths of Caracalla, of which I was very proud, for Mrs. Garbor's class. There was more. She told us that the ancient Viking men (to whom I can trace my English lineage through "Seemen" in Cornwall and the Danelaw), when they reached the age of 50 or thereabouts, and felt their warrior strength fading, would don full armor and wade out into the ocean and drown themselves, so as not to become enfeebled old men. I never forgot that vignette, either. A modern variant of this tale would be my good friend, noble old Yousof Najibullah, dropping dead quickly in a hospital hallway, at age 62, as he secretly hoped, after moving heavy furniture.

Of course, those were tough times. World War II was in full swing. I believe Mrs. Garbor's husband was killed in that same year, 1944, fighting the Japanese in the .Solomon Islands in the Pacific Theater. A little hard nosed teaching to fourth graders in those days was not out of place.

In the fifth grade, age nine, year 1945, I wrote a play, which Prospect School put on. It was all about a pair of royal twins. The eldest, by a few minutes, was heir apparent. The other twin was bitter and angry. After that, I forget how I played it out. It was a little kid's play but it was a mild success. It was my first and only essay at playwriting.

It should be reported that, at age nine in 1945, I discovered how to masturbate (by accident) Maybe other kids discover it earlier, I don't know. Anyway, it's been my solace in the bad years, when I had no access to the young women in the brothels (see *infra*), and I had no social female friends to oblige me. Incidentally, when young and even when much older, I've had very little interest in "Older Women" (over 35), although I have many older Platonic women friends. But I don't find older women physically attractive. Brothels seem to be pretty much the only way older men can consummate physical contact with young women anyway, unless a man is rich and/or famous. And shouldn't the young serve the old, instead of casting them aside? Many ancient cultures venerate the old, and perhaps this may even be extended to a young woman's favors.

Maybe I just consider younger women to be sex objects. Playmates, Barbie Dolls. So, what's wrong with that, really? I don't know. But I love to look at a beautiful young woman, *au naturel*. As I've said elsewhere, I don't believe in "Love," whatever the word may mean. I've seen too much far out, "funny" stuff to be interested in the transcendental pleasures of Romantic Love. Now, I do "Care" for a lot of people, however, especially for my friends. Martin Heidegger said the first duty of an Existentialist is "care," or *sorge,* in the German. I'm not an Existentialist, but I agree with Heidegger in this. But I avoid going off the deep end about everything these days. There's really NO POINT to it. It's all empty and sometimes even dangerous FANTASY. Anyway, in my old age, 74 as I write this, I'll just go on masturbating as long as I can, until the AIDS epidemic is resolved, if ever, and I can go back to the young women in the brothels (which are illegal in most of this country, by the way, although I believe the Statute of Limitations has run out on these transgressions of mine, which, at least in jurisdictions where prostitution is illegal, ended in 1987).

Incidentally, although I don't care for the transports of Romantic Love, I am interested in better orgasms. There's something called the "Full Body Orgasm," which I may have very occasionally experienced. But most of my orgasms now are clinical and focused in the genitals only. The writings of Dr. Wilhelm Reich say more about such things, more than I care to know. But if you're interested, pick up a copy of *Character Analysis,* Reich's first book, which is still in the Freudian canon, and is read by all beginning medical students preparing to become Freudian psychoanalysts. Reich was an early disciple of Freud, but they later parted company when Reich became interested in orgone theory and cosmic energy. Many people, including the FDA, thought Reich's ideas were completely wacky, but the great Doctor Reich still has many followers. I met many brilliant people at Swarthmore, top intellectuals at elite Swarthmore College, who firmly believed in Reich.

But enough of this Sex Talk. Sex is only a small part of Life, not the be-all and end-all of experience, in my opinion, at least. But it is necessary for me to get some sexual service before I can get down to the real work of my life. Deferred gratification does not work for me. I've only been able to do serious intellectual work in my career at those times that I was sexually gratified. But now let me get back to the unfolding history of my childhood.

At about the age of ten, in late 1945, I joined the neighborhood kids in building and racing soapbox box racers on Southard Street in South Baldwin. Southard Street ran alongside my family's house at 99 Park Avenue, Baldwin. I was pulled away from my paper battleships by my young friend, Freddie Clark, as I said earlier. We built our soapbox racers with baby carriage wheels and axles, sometimes right on the baby carriage frame. We would add a peach basket in the front (where the driver's legs would go, and a soap box in the back, upon which rested the driver's back) Boys who were a little bigger would be the "pushers," supplying the motive power.

We would paint up our racing cars in bright colors, and try to match the driver's racing togs to the soapbox racer's colors. My racer was painted red and black, still my favorite color scheme (as you can see from pictures of my Studio), and was numbered "28," after my birthday, June 28th (1936).

It happens that I was already aiming at the "big time," at the age of 12. I called the City Desk of *The Nassau Daily Review Star,* then Long Island's other big newspaper, along with *Newsday*. The *Review Star* went defunct in 1957, but this was 1948, and getting in the paper was still a big deal. Anyway, I told the paper about our soapbox operation, and they were interested, and sent out a big crew to photograph and write up our operation. I knew just what they wanted. I had little girls with flowers, a gold-painted flower pot for first prize, my big portable radio playing, etc. It was quite a race and quite a show. They gave us a full page (or more) with many photos. The other mothers were angry that the writer said "John Seaman, age 12, Treasurer, is the 'guiding spirit' of the organization." What about their kids? But I did pull this off, all by myself! It was a big ego trip for a 12-year-old. I did many things in my young career that the psychiatrists seemed to be asking me to turn my back on, in analysis and recovery.

A year or two ago, Jane Rose, my ex-model and now my Executor, and I took the train out to a Long Island library (Rockville Center) to try to find the article on old microfilm. The library had the *Review Star* microfilm from 1948, but we couldn't find the article. The microfilm technicians hadn't microfilmed every page of the back issues. Of course, I had lost the original years and years ago, in one of my bouts of madness, probably. Anyway, the whole affair was one of my first small triumphs.

#

The soapbox racing era lasted from age ten to age 12. I then went on to the only private (primary or secondary) school I ever attended, and that for only one year, at age ten, 1946-47 academic year. It was St. Paul's Episcopal Boarding School (although I was a day student) in Garden City, Long Island, New York, perhaps six or seven miles from my home in Baldwin.

I was, in a sense, "privileged," at least to attend St. Paul's. And my mother drove me there and back every, on her way to and from the school where she taught in Merrick, again, six or seven miles away. It was a long drive for her. There were several good things about St. Paul's. They did try to train us to be "men," in the "stiff upper lip" English sense. It was of course, an all-boy school – there was a companion girls' school, half a mile away. We, in the Lower School (First to Third Form, equivalent to Seventh to Ninth Grade) never saw the girls, although I think the boys in the Upper School (Fourth to Sixth Form, Tenth to Twelfth Grade) had Socials with them.

Anyway, my pushy parents convinced the School to enroll me in the First Form at age ten, two years ahead of the other students. Because my parents pushed me, I skipped the Sixth Grade, and I was already a year ahead before this, because Rhode Island, where I was born and spent my earliest years, starts kids in First Grade at age five, a year ahead of most of the rest of the country. When I grew up, I never forgave my parents for accelerating me, because it made my socialization (especially with girls) extremely difficult.

The acceleration didn't matter much, yet, at St. Paul's, because we in the Lower School, or at least the First Form, were still mostly pre-pubescent, and Sex was not yet a terribly big issue. Of course, I had to compete on the playing fields, tough English style, with boys who were past puberty and more than twice my size. But I played tackle football with them and held my own. I weighed 80 pounds and was quite a little gamecock. But it was a struggle.

As far as the Academics were concerned, they were better than most of what I had experienced in public school (Ms. Hobson, Mrs. Garbor, and maybe the Fifth Grade Play excepted). The Upper School boys learned Classical Greek, Latin and Calculus, among other things. All this would have been useful to me later on. But, despite the rigors of the Academics, I was Head Boy (best grades) in the Lower School of perhaps a hundred boys. I was precocious. This lasted through high school, but I did not do particularly well at College. My College, Swarthmore, is admittedly a tough school, at the time rated the best small College in the country, and I was two years' accelerated, but I still should have done better. My academic ranking at Swarthmore was slightly below the middle.

Something should be said about discipline at St. Paul's, which was the primary reason I left the place. The Masters beat the boys when they didn't behave correctly. Yes, they had corporal punishment. Boys were beaten repeatedly across the palm of the hand with a ruler, in a long, swift stroke from behind the Master's back I don't know whether or not they also beat the boys across the bare rump or not. That would probably have been too dicey, even for St. Paul's. Of course, some of the boys had been sent to St. Paul's because they had discipline or behavior problems. But still, corporal punishment, in this day and age! I never actually had a full view of the beatings. They were conducted in a little back room in front of the main Study Hall. But there was a translucent glass door and you could see shadows, etc. It was all very scary. It was supposed to be.

I was never actually beaten, although I was threatened with it once or twice. I was a good boy and I was head boy. I had ambivalent feelings about St. Paul's, with the corporal punishment and all. We had to wear suits and ties all the time. It was a little like a reform school (I think). I liked the graham crackers and milk at 3:00 o'clock (but only if your parents paid a few dollars extra for it), after classes had finished. There was a certain camaraderie in the place. We were all in this together. And the instruction was good. But I was glad to get out, after one year, when I finished First Form (Seventh Grade). I went back to Eighth Grade in Public School in Baldwin.

Entering the Eighth Grade in Baldwin, I was 11 years old. Everybody else was 13. Most boys, in those days, were still pre-pubescent at 13, before the hormones in today's fast foods began to accelerate the sexual development of the young, though the girls were filling out. But puberty was not yet a problem for me, as it soon would be. At Baldwin Junior/Senior High School, in the eighth grade, the only courses I remember are First Year Latin, with Miss Melrose, which was interesting and in which I did fairly well, despite the fact that I have never been adept at languages, and also metal shop, in which I did terribly. But the mechanic who ran the shop course took pity on me, a proto-intellectual, and did most of the work for me, and gave me a decent grade. I wish now that he had encouraged me to try harder to do the work for myself, so that I might have learned something. I've never been particularly good at mechanical skills, although this might have helped me in science (lab, experimentation later on). I do have some art skills, however, and yes, I took an art course at Baldwin, as well, and liked it.

But art was more or less alien to my family's Weltanschauung, even though my mother encouraged me in art. But there were very few pictures in our home, until I put up some of mine. About this time, or perhaps a year or two earlier, my mother enrolled me in Mrs. Leah Hoffman's private art class, conducted in Leah's home, on the back (enclosed with screens) porch. A note about Mrs. Hoffman, the Art teacher in my mother's school (where my mother ran the Special Education class), who always dressed in green and drove a green Studebaker (the model, still remembered, with a fake propeller on the front). I think she had dyed red hair.

Leah Hoffman was a bit of an eccentric. She divorced her husband and then rented him a room in her house. There were no children.

Anyway, I did well in Leah Hoffman's Art Class. Too well. Even then, I suspected that she was playing some strange psychological trick, or telepathically guiding my hand, because I drew so well in her class. It was a long time before I drew that well again. I guess the woman was just charismatic. But I've always had grave reservations about charisma. It's too irrational for my comfort.

What else in this, my eleventh year? I wrestled in Baldwin athletics, in the 80-pound class, and I was good at it. There was a tournament I was eager to participate in, but I got sick. I was very angry about this. Also, at Baldwin, they made me give up my drum classes, which I had begun a year earlier. The Baldwin school authorities said I was too young for percussion, and would have to wait for Senior High. I was very annoyed about this, too.

At about this time, my somewhat remote father and I discovered a mutual interest, or at least something he could tolerate doing with me (a kid). This was bowling. We bowled together quite a few times. I once, at age 12, bowled a 183, which was quite good. I also filled in sometimes for League absentees at the bowling alley, which was fun. Another accomplishment. I learned to set pins, manually. At this early date (1947, 1948), there were no automatic pinsetters. I made a few dollars doing this. It was slightly dangerous. Between rolls, you had to climb up and suspend yourself just above the pin area. A flying pin could hit you hard. I managed O.K., though.

This about covers all I can remember about my eleventh year. Bear in mind that I was masturbating all the time now, but it was all dry runs. That was to change in two years. This was really the last year of my childhood. Puberty would soon follow.

My twelfth year began uneventfully enough. I enrolled in Oceanside High School, Oceanside, Long Island, where I was to remain for four years, until graduation. I came in as a 12-year-old freshman, actually in the Junior High School, which was adjacent to the Senior High School. Oceanside was not my designated high school, by home location, but my parents and I chose it, because we thought Baldwin High School would be a little rough, physically, for me as a 12-year old. So I believe my parents paid $100/year to enroll me out of district in Oceanside. It was a fair sum in those days.

Also at Oceanside, I didn't participate in physical education or athletics. The reasons given by my parents in pushing this through were my extreme youth and also the partial blindness in my right eye (the fovea is completely dark, a sizeable blind spot, due to a birth injury I have already discussed). More important, puberty was upon most of my classmates, the juices were flowing (in them, not me) and I was afraid of hazing and the like. Also, there were "daisy chains" I have been asked to explain what a daisy chain is. It's like this: the boys form a circle, with everybody facing the center. Then each boy reaches over (to his left?) and "jerks off" (masturbates) the next boy. but I didn't want any part of it. It probably didn't help my relationship with my peers that I shunned athletics, and daisy chains, but looking back on it, maybe this attitude wasn't such a bad idea. I resumed athletics, PT, and Varsity Cross Country as a freshman in College, age 16, once the first rush of puberty was past (for ME and my classmates).

But back to my 12th year. Classes were uneventful, and too easy. I understood everything with my Mother Wit. I never had to study and I did all my homework in Study Hall. I almost never took any homework home with me. The exception was first-year French, which I couldn't schmooze my way through. I had to study French, and I didn't do particularly well. I recall my grade one semester was 88, a B+, and I got A+ in everything else. At the end of the year I was Salutatorian, and only missed first place by a few thousandths of a point. I remember I made a scene at the school about this. I had a bad, weak or nonexistent character at the time, for which I blamed my parents. Later, I realized it was up to me to build my own character, and I really worked at it. I couldn't really do this until I escaped from my family at age 15 or 16. There I go, blaming the family again. Anyway, I tried to fix the damage when I was finally on my own. This extended to my resuming athletics in College, the strenuous long hiking trips I organized in College, and even on to my much later skydiving.

My 12th year was just about the final year for the soapbox racing on Southard Street in Baldwin, discussed *supra*. It was also the year I arranged the big writeup in *The Nassau Daily Review Star* for our soapbox racing.

Also in 1948, or thereabouts, I ordered my first pair of Syrian Golden Hamsters from an ad placed by one Herbert Hathaway in Silver Spring, MD. They came by Railway Express (now defunct) and I was delighted with them. I proceeded to breed them (following instructions) and eventually raised a thousand or more, up to about age 15, when the interest in girls ended the hamster phase. The animals were very friendly, the males anyway. You could handle the males in your bare hands with impunity. The females were touchy and might nip you. The Golden Hamster breed at this time was quite wonderful. The animals were larger than they are now, and were uniformly a beautiful golden color. They had large cheek pouches, in which they carried off food and sometimes, when frightened, their young. They had a short puff of a tail. By now, 2010 as I write this, the animals have been overbred, are runty looking, and come in drear gray and white. Not interesting any more.

You would have thought I would have learned a lot about human sex from all my activities with golden hamster sex. But I did NOT. Hamster anatomy is nothing like human anatomy. I was still completely in the dark about human female anatomy and how human sex was conducted, and this held me back in high school (after puberty at age 13, to be described later)

But back to the hamsters. I built all the cages myself, to the most scientific designs. I ordered the lumber and hardware myself. The lumberyard, on request, saved pine wood shavings for me, which the animals loved as cage litter. I ordered 50-lb. Sacks of Purina lab chow. And two, three times a week, I picked up volumes of lettuce trimmings at the supermarket, which I got the market to save for me. No charge for the shavings or the lettuce. The places were enthusiastic about helping the very young entrepreneur.

Yes, I started a little business, called "Hamster Haven," and sold two or three hundred dollars' worth of hamsters every year for three or four years. This was a tidy sum in the 1950s. I had literature mimeographed, which I had written myself, about the creatures' needs, care and habits. Mimeographed because photocopying did not exist in those days.

I took another initiative with the hamsters. I took a booth for three or four years at the Nassau County Fair (now defunct) in Mineola, Long Island. One local sign painter took up my project and made me a big beautiful sign, on masonite. He refused to take any money for it, so I baked him a cake.

At the Fair, I was right on the Midway, hawking my wares, selling my hamsters. There were also agricultural products (biggest pumpkin, biggest watermelon, etc.) and a Circus, with all sorts of interesting characters. My family helped me get my booth materials, signs and the animals, over there, but I was all alone on the Midway. Some of the onlookers were unsavory, or so I was told. One pleasant gentleman introduced himself and said he was a teacher at a private school and said he want to show me his 6" (reflector) telescope. I was entranced but my family was convinced he was a pervert.

Finally, later, my family and I (I was carefully supervised) visited the school and looked through the telescope. I was struck by the fact that the stars were all colored, red, blue and yellow, which I had never before (and have never since) seen through another telescope. All the stars usually appear white to me. I suspected this was some perverted effect the man was having on me. Anyway, my family was convinced this guy wanted to bugger me, and called the Nassau County Vice Squad. The detectives came to our house and interviewed me.

The vice squad cops were so tough and florid looking, they frightened me. I was a callow youth of 12 or 13 years and these guys were like something from Mars (or Pluto). After that, I heard nothing more from the guy. I think now the teacher with the telescope may just have been a good guy and my family caused him a lot of hardship. But I still don't know.

The culmination of the hamster era was my Westinghouse Science Research Scholarship project, carried out with the golden hamsters. The conclusion of this saga took place in my 15th year, so I'll be getting a little ahead of myself.

For four years, I was a top student (but not well-rounded) at Oceanside Junior and Senior High School, an easy and unchallenging place. But the principal and teachers thought I could win laurels for the school, so they encouraged my idea to enter the Westinghouse Science Talent Search (now run by Intel). Westinghouse is now a subsidiary of Toshiba.

Anyway, I decided I wanted to do an intelligence test of the animals. So Oceanside High School Woodworking Shop (other students, under instructor supervision) built a large Hampton Court Maze for me. It was about 6' x 4', and the maze corridors were perhaps 8" or 9" high. We covered it with glass, I think, so the hamsters couldn't climb over the corridor walls. The Hampton Court maze is a standard intelligence testing design, based on a pattern in the Hampton Court hedges in England, dating back to I don't know when. It was the high school's idea that I use a Hampton Court maze. I can't take credit for that, But the idea of testing the males against the females in their ability to run (solve) the maze in the search for food, was mine. In retrospect, it now seems that my project theme reflected my growing interest in the interplay between the sexes, in all creatures, including humans.

The entire project took about two years. I wrote it up, including the chi square test results, which showed what the margin of error was (the use of the chi square test, a statistician's tool, was suggested to me by my Biology teacher, a Mr. Preston or Prentice, I've forgotten now). The results of the experiment showed that the females were slightly quicker in solving the maze, but the results were within the margin of error as indicated by the chi square test.

So, the experiment was complete and I went on to the 1952 Westinghouse Science Talent Search competition. To enter, you had to submit your experiment and also take a long multiple choice exam. The odds weren't very good. 20,000 kids took the test and 2,000 completed an experiment. There would be 40 National Winners and 300 Honorable Mentions. So it was really a 50 to 1 shot. And, lo and behold, I was a National Winner (one of the 40)! Winning meant a trip to Washington to be tested for the highest honors and also a chance to be personally introduced to the President of the United States (Harry Truman in 1952).

This was really my first time away from home. I still sucked my thumb at 15 (covertly). I bet I'm the only person ever introduced to Harry Truman on his (my) own merits who sucked his thumb. I don't think Josef Stalin sucked his thumb.

So, taping up my thumb to break myself of the habit, I boarded the Long Island Rail Road to Penn Station in Manhattan, where the New York contingent boarded a Pullman sleeper train (upper and lower berths) for Washington. Needless to say, we talked all night, and six of us made the decision to attend Swarthmore. At that time, it was rated the best small liberal arts college in the country, and we were all interested in Peace and the Quakers (Religious Society of Friends) as well. We were all good kids.

This was the high point of my life up until this time. Most of the high points in my life, most of the peak experiences, occurred before I was 21. Leading the 30 college kids on mountain climbing expeditions all over the Northeast and Southeast, in all Seasons, was another. And my first lay, I suppose. After these experiences, it was mostly downhill. After the aborted psychoanalysis, I didn't get my initiative back until I was almost 50, in about 1986, just as the consulting psychiatrist who sent me to Dr. Sternschein, Dr. Felicia Lydia Landau (may she rot in Hell, Gehenna I believe, along with Dr. Irving Sternschein), had predicted. Seeing Landau was one of my greatest mistakes, as was (probably) going to Swarthmore.

This was about the end of my fairly happy and successful childhood. The long darkness of my psychoanalysis, repeated bouts of madness, and very slow and constrained 20-year recovery was the second phase of my life. Now, 60 years later, in the third phase of my life, I am reasonably productive and content, photographing young female nudes, writing about my life, studying various topics that interest me, going out to dinners, concerts and plays, and giving my famous Eleutheria Salons. I have written two books and perhaps

200 articles. My hero, Dr. Albert Ellis, wrote 80 books. Goethe wrote 100. What might I have amounted to, with a little more intelligent guidance?

A very wise friend (my Editor, actually) reassures me often that mediocrity is not an unpardonable failing, but I don't agree. By some freak accident, against all the odds of the Universe, we're born into an at least half civilized society with the opportunity to achieve and accomplish all kinds of things. A Great Chance for someone who isn't stupid, and I'm at least not stupid. But I've blown it. Yes, there's no excuse for mediocrity.

Anyway, back in 1952, at the Westinghouse STS Finals in DC, we were put up at the "old" Hilton, which had been built in the middle of WWII to accommodate visiting diplomats and generals. I roomed with a nice young man from Anacostia (also an STS winner). We were banqueted, interviewed for the top prizes, and asked to set up an Exhibit in the large hall of the hotel. My interview was interesting. My interviewer was a Dr. Bart Bok, a famous astronomer, who asked me, "What would I do, if I suddenly found myself in an ant hill, facing the members of the ant colony?" At the time, my thought was too literal for me to be able to answer that, but if I were asked the same question today, I would say, "It would be the same thing as being a very bright student in a run-of-the-mill American public high school. I would cope." As it occurred, though, I had no answer, and I did not win one of the top ten prizes.

The big event, of course, was the visit to meet President Harry Truman in the Rose Garden of the White House. Mr. Truman had an intense, florid complexion. He looked indeed like he had been in the heat of "the kitchen." (It was Harry Truman who said, "If you can't stand the heat, stay out of the kitchen.") He did look very pressured. High blood pressure? But he lasted until 1972. He was very affable. We all filed past him and had a chance to speak briefly to him. Again, I was too young and callow to take real advantage of the opportunity, but a few of the kids asked very pointed questions.

Then a group picture with the President was taken. I lost the original many years ago (in one of my breakdowns. I lost every shred of property twice in those breakdowns.), but I was able to get another one from the Science Service files (did I say that Science Service administered the STS program?) in 1991, when we (a female Russian *émigré* friend and myself, but that's another story) went to Washington and the NEW Hilton for a Reunion and Awards Dinner at the 50th Annual Westinghouse Science Talent Search. The then President, George H. W. Bush, Bush *pere*, spoke at that banquet. In 1991, I had a tux, and cut a little sharper figure than in 1952.

I'm sure the Westinghouse Prize was what got d to Swarthmore College, then (in 1952) the top small liberal arts college and the hardest to get into. My sister, third in her class at Baldwin High School, was denied admission to Swarthmore four years earlier.

So, I've finished with recounting the major events of my childhood, except for the coming of puberty. One day in May, 1949, at the age of 13, a month short of my 14th birthday, while masturbating as usual, I was surprised to produce some ejaculate. I was a little mystified, but I did have a fairly good idea of what had happened. Of course, I didn't tell my family. My parents never discussed sex with me, and I never asked them. It might have helped me a lot, a little later on, but then I might have gotten into trouble early on. In 1949, high school kids were not ALL so experienced in sex as now, and that was true of me, as well.

That's the end of the tales of my childhood. I'll go on to tell the stories of my adolescence and college days in the next section, Section 7.

From Puberty to First Encounter

1949 - 1956

This section will carry my life story from early puberty, through high school and college adolescence, to earliest adulthood, at age 20, and my first "complete" sexual encounter. I treated my freshman year at Oceanside (Junior) High School in Section 12. This was before the onset of puberty, which occurred in May of 1950, at the end of my sophomore year in Oceanside (Senior) High School. I will begin here with my sophomore year at Oceanside, where I was 13 for all of the academic year. My birthday is June 28th, at the end of the school year.

My years at Oceanside (Senior) High School were relatively uneventful. I didn't mix with the other kids much, partly because I was so young and partly because I evaded gym during these four years. I had wrestled in the 8th grade at Baldwin High School, and I went back to physical training at Swarthmore College, where I ran on the Cross Country Varsity, but I avoided gym at Oceanside because I didn't want to be hazed by the older kids. And, as I said earlier, I wanted to avoid the locker room "daisy chains," etc. To me, at least, the daisy chains were a proto-homosexual exercise. I wanted nothing to do with them. So I avoided the indecencies of puberty. The reason my family gave to get the exemption, which was true and a consideration for them, was that the center (fovea) of my right eye was blind, and we didn't want to risk the other eye in projectile games, etc. But I had my own reasons for avoiding gym.

My extra-curricular activities at Oceanside H.S. were limited. Of course, I did a lot of work, with the help of the high school, on my Westinghouse project, with the psychological testing of the Golden Hamsters, as already described in Section 6, "Childhood." I was News Editor of the school newspaper, the *Sider Press,* and worked with Everett Sugarbaker, a rather mild and epicene (though happily married) English teacher. Although he was always cooperative and helpful, acquaintance with him made me decide never to be an English teacher. Not macho enough.

Also on the paper, one year ahead of me, was the Editor-in-Chief, Susan Baudendistal, a tall (taller than me at the time) blonde of German-American extraction, with a beautiful figure. I lusted after her, but she was three years older than me, and I was the class nerd. I never made a move. Once, in my Junior year (I was 14), Susan and I took the Long Island Railroad to the Columbia U. Scholastic Press Association meeting in New York City. I could hardly contain my interest in Susan and her body, but I was afraid (and really didn't know how to) make a move. If only somebody had given me a little instruction in sex, I might have had a better chance. But my family said nary a word to me about sex, and I didn't ask. This trip with Susan was really my first trip to the City without my parents. As to girls in high school, I did have some mild sexual adventures (heavy petting) with one girl (only), Mary Evans, in my Junior and Senior years.

I did have a couple of buddies in the high school years, Richard Cocks and Joe Valenta (or Valente). We all planned to be engineers. I thought of aeronautical engineering or architecture. Of course, this was before computers, and also before sex, art, music, love and passion entered my thinking and changed my life direction (perhaps for the worse).

Anyway, we all took the easy math, physics and chemistry courses the high school offered. Fifty years later, in 2002, after I attended (with my model Jane Rose – more about her later) my 50th Oceanside High School Reunion, and the Reunion was written up in a

Newsletter, I heard from Dick Cocks, who had indeed become an engineer in a large corporation, had five (?) kids and a big house, and was disappointed with me after I told him what I had been doing for all that time. It seems my high school classmates expected me to become a top nuclear physicist. Making thermonuclear bombs, I suppose? But I did well on the Westinghouse Science Talent Search exam (top 2%, at least). All the details of winning the Westinghouse STS are discussed in my "Childhood..." Section, since they are associated with my childhood golden hamster colony. But Swarthmore College (later) was a shock and a blow to my academic pretensions.

I had one other good friend, John Boerner, American-born of a Danish mother and a German father (from Hamburg, always a liberal city). John Boerner was a pianist, but not very good. He practiced and practiced, and finally reached the point where he could give a recital rendition of Bach's, "Jesu, Joy of Man's Desiring." But John realized his limitations and became a musicologist. He had one of the prettiest girls in the high school class as a girlfriend, Diane Lockwood, and I think they enjoyed each other in those early years. I believe Diane danced a version of "Slaughter on Tenth

Avenue," in the high school auditorium, which was rather advanced for Oceanside High School (the setting is a whorehouse). But John Boerner was my first sophisticated friend. After college, he went into the army for two years, and I lost track of him after that. I hope he reads this. He was a good friend, much more mature (and older) than I. I must add here that John Boerner found me, through Facebook, in 2010. We have been in touch since then.

In my high school years, I was really close (not in a good way, more dependent) on my family and did not have the opportunity or stimulus to individuate myself.

I did manage to acquire one girl friend, Mary Evans. We started going out together in my Junior year, when I was 14. She was a class behind me, so she was probably 15. Anyway, all I remember is that she was quite short, about 5'1" tall, and reasonably good looking, with a nice bosom. Her parents (the family was Welsh) were very short, under 4'11'. I remember that for several Christmases I had to decorate the top of their Christmas tree, because none of them could reach it.

So what about SEX with Mary? I remember sitting on her screened-in back porch when her parents were away, stripping her to the waist, and playing with and kissing her breasts. I was afraid to go further, out of ignorance and thoughts of possible pregnancy. Janice several times intimated she would like to go further, but I wouldn't. Too bad. It would have set me up for College, where I didn't have much luck either. But I was very young, and to become a father at 14 was unthinkable. Remember, abortions were illegal until 1977, and birth control pills were not available until the 1960s. This was 1950-52.

Anyway, I ran into Janice again in about 1970, when I was managing a Marboro Book Shop in Greenwich Village. Mary stopped by the book shop and recognized me behind the counter. She was writing for *New York* magazine, had married a stockbroker, and lived in fairly lavish accommodations on Central Park West. She invited me to one of her house parties, but my friend Joan Bennett and I did not make a good impression. I was still recovering from various breakdowns. We were not invited back.

What else happened in my high school years? I acted in the class play one year, but I was far from being the romantic lead. I played a minor role, Mr. Dodge, in

Meet Me in St. Louis set in St. Louis at the time of the 1904 World's Fair. I was adequate.

Summers I regularly went out to neighboring Jones Beach, about 8 or 10 miles away on the bus. I believe my family let me go out there alone after I was 13 or 14. Jones Beach was Robert Moses' great project in the 1930s, and we were all very fond of it. I was, too, until I discovered nude beaches (much later). At Jones Beach, you could swim in the big pool or ocean, walk on the boardwalk, play shuffleboard and other games, roller skate, etc. The food in the concessions was O.K. and cheap (then). I would go out to the beach alone often and sit in the shade and read *Anna Karenina*.

One summer, I worked for Jones Beach State Park, more or less as a locker room attendant. I wore a sailor's uniform with a sailor's hat. Anyway, I was chosen to raise the U.S. flag every morning. That taught me how to fold a flag properly (as a triangle).

Nothing much else happened to me in high school. I grew 6 inches in my Sophomore year, then it slowed down for a while. We nerds had our electric trains, an episode I would like to forget. I could have used the energy I spent on that for more productive occupations.

In my Senior year, I was a finalist for the Grumman Aircraft scholarship, which would have paid for four years of engineering. I didn't get it, I was a runner-up. I'm just as happy I didn't get it, because then it would have been difficult to leave the engineering curriculum after two years of College, as I did. But Grumman did offer me a summer job on the assembly line in their aircraft factory in Bethpage, Long Island, which I was happy to get. It paid well and was interesting.

We made F9F-6 jets for use in the Korean War, then going on. I ran something called an arbor press, a drill press on a long moving overhead arm (the "arbor"), and made thousands of holes in sheets of aluminum intended for jet fuselages. I worked too fast. The regular workers came over to me and muttered, "We're not working piece rate," in a mildly threatening way, to get me to slow down.

I wasn't a pacifist (yet), so the work didn't bother me. And we could lie outside in the lush green Long Island grass watching the new jets take off to be delivered to the U.S. Navy. I wrote poetry about that experience in a writing class in my Freshman year at Swarthmore College. My "jet" poetry was rather limited. I wrote about lying during our work breaks in the lush grass under the bright blue sky, watching the jets we had built fly off (very loudly) to take part in the Korean War. I wrote how the grass was preternaturally green and the sky was preternaturally blue. Was this a foreshadowing of my later perception and hallucinatory problems?

I have just about covered everything that I recall about my high school years. The period was really rather uneventful, compared with the Swarthmore College years that followed, where I really had an adolescence, something from which most of my College classmates were already emerging. I was just 16 when I entered my Freshman year at Swarthmore.

The choice of Swarthmore was entirely my own. I was offered more money by Yale, and perhaps also by Harvard, but my parents were willing to pay for me to go wherever I wanted. I chose Swarthmore because of the overnight discussion on the train to Washington, DC, on the way to the Westinghouse finals, as I have already described. I also chose Swarthmore because it was small (I wouldn't be lost in a huge school), because the administration seemed to look out for the students, especially the younger ones (a little like family), because of its Quaker heritage (I was becoming a bit of a pacifist), and because it was (then) rated (in the *U.S. News & World Report*) the #1 small liberal arts college in the country. Now, in 2010, it's rated #3.

So, in early September 1952, I arrived at Swarthmore to begin my Freshman year, age 16. I was in for several shocks. First, I had taken the initiative of asking to room with one of the other Westinghouse STS Winners, one Mikhel Parlin. That was a mistake. Mikhel was a tough Estonian refugee who had lived in Displaced Person Refugee Camps for most of his life. Don't forget that the Estonians sympathized with the Nazis in WWII because the Nazis had (temporarily) liberated them from Soviet domination. So Mikhel was accustomed to violence. And he took it out on me. He was several years older than me and much, much stronger. Mikhel would fight with me and beat my head against the radiator frequently. It took me a couple of months to get to the point where I would ask the Proctor (a Senior, Frank Sieverts, who after graduation became active in politics in several Democratic White Houses, and who just passed away in 2004) if I could have another room and roommate assignment, but I finally did. I hated to give up and admit failure and that I couldn't cope with this. I will get to the story of my new roommate and my other new friends after a few more paragraphs, about other "shocks."

The next "shock" at Swarthmore was the result of my first Economics exam. I pulled a "D." This was unheard of for me. In high school, I was a straight A student, even A+. Of course in high school, I was never stressed or extended. I had no real study habits. My mind was not trained by high school, even if I had won the Westinghouse STS. So I tried to buckle down and study hard, but all I could manage for the first semester was a succession of "C"s and "B"s. This was all very disappointing to me. A large part of my identity (my "ego"?) was tied up with being a good student. And these results along with getting my head banged against the radiator by Mikhel Parlin made things look very bleak. But eventually, as we shall see later, I found other ways to express myself at Swarthmore.

The poor performance at the outset was one of the reasons I considered, at that early date, getting psychological counseling. It might have helped, maybe a lot, but I knew my family was a little crazy (my mother screamed and was hysterical a lot, my maternal grandmother died in a "neurological institute" in 1922 at age 42). I was afraid the counselors would drive me "nuts," and I would end up in an asylum (as they did, and I did, later on). Family wisdom was you never got out of those places. And nobody did, until the invention of tranquilizers in 1953. So I opted to hold off on the shrink route until I had my B.A. I decided to tough it out for the duration of my college education.

So much for the early major failures at Swarthmore. I knew I was away from home for the first time and I expected a few reverses. Were there any successes? Yes, a few small ones.

The first "good" thing that happened to me was the move away from Mikhel Parlin, the crazy Teutonic. When the Proctor said I could move, I left Wharton Dormitory, which was infested with jocks, on the main campus, and took up residence in Mary Lyons 1, part of an old boarding school, a mile or more from the main campus, that the College had bought and used for student dormitories and faculty apartments. Mary Lyons, Buildings 1 through 4, were off in the woods, or what was left of them in this part of Delaware County. Mary Lyons 1 was the deepest into the woods, several hundred precipitous feet above a sort of waterfall on

Crum Creek. It was really quite beautiful and spectacular.

I found a roommate in Mary Lyons 1, a decent, civil young man who wanted very much to be a doctor, Bernard Sarachek. Bernie's previous roommate had left the College. Bernie and I didn't have much in common, but we were on very friendly terms, and there was no abuse. I finished out my Freshman year as Bernie's roommate.

I should say a word here about my athletics. I've said earlier that I avoided physical training at Oceanside High School, but at Swarthmore, I wanted to participate, eye disability or no. I learned that if you joined a Varsity team, you were excused from the physical training that was otherwise mandatory during the first two years. So I joined the Cross-Country Team. I learned to run the daily 4 ½ miles, albeit very slowly. They let all the runners run in the intercollegiate meets, but I and the other slowpokes would always come in last or next to last. Nevertheless, I learned to run great distances and built up my stamina, which was a great help to me in later life. I could run at least a mile or two until age 65, when my legs gave out with osteoarthritis and tendonitis. Some of us even wanted to train for the

25-mile Philadelphia Marathon, but the coach was afraid we would enlarge and weaken our hearts. I'm sorry I missed the opportunity. Later on, doctors told me there was really no danger.

Another interesting story concerns one other member of the Swarthmore College Cross Country team in 1952 and 1953. This was Michael Dukakis, who later became Governor of Massachusetts and then national Democratic candidate for President of the United States in 1988. Yes, he was right there in the locker room with the rest of us. Most of us later sank into oblivion, but it's nice to know one of us made a run at the top.

But back to other topics. Once in Mary Lyons 1, I began to make many new friends, among the disaffected who lived there and in the other Mary Lyons buildings. I should say that the College staff and students occupied Mary Lyons Buildings 1, 3 and 4. Building 2 was a U.S. Army area, occupied by soldiers who operated a nearby Nike missile base. This was at the height of the Cold War and I suppose the Nikes were defending Philadelphia. Anyway, they and we had strict instructions not to fraternize with each other.

So, who were my other new friends? First of all, there was Barry Silvers, who has remained a good friend to this day, 52 years later, as I write this. Barry and I became roommates in my Sophomore year, but that comes later. Barry was the son of a luggage store owner in New Haven, CT. He had had a good secondary education, at The Hopkins Grammar School. Barry was short, 5'5" tall, and this always bothered him, just a little. In the Hopkins Grammar School, he took up fencing, became very good at it, and became Captain of the School's Varsity Fencing Team. Barry explained to me that it was an advantage for a fencer to be of short stature, since he or she could more easily "get under" the parries of the opponent. Barry was very proud of the fact that the team he captained had beaten the Yale Freshman team the year before.

Swarthmore, perhaps as a Quaker College, then had no fencing team, and Barry had to consider long and hard before giving up fencing and coming to Swarthmore. But the other advantages of Swarthmore weighed more heavily with him, as they had with me, and he elected to come here. Barry had other athletic skills as well. He was an avid bicyclist, with several Century certificates (traveling 100 miles or more in a day). He was also an excellent bicycle mechanic. I believe this last accomplishment was very good preparation for College lab work.

About the same time, Barry and I became interested in the activities of the Swarthmore College

Cutting wood at Randolph Mountain House, now demolished, above tree line in the White Mountains

Outing Club. When we first joined them, they ran local hiking trips, perhaps as far away as Delaware Water Gap (Stroudsburg, PA) and also local spelunking (cave exploration) expeditions. But my initiatives were much more ambitious.

Early on, I led weekend hiking excursions to Delaware Water Gap and similar "nearby" venues, perhaps 100 miles away. I drove the Student Council truck myself, packed with college kids. I was very careful and never had any problems on the road. One young schoolmate, the Quaker Naomi Fox, would sit next to me and be my "spotter," calling out deer and such things, since her eyes were better than mine. Since

Our faithful Student Council truck

College was in session, we had chaperones on these weekend trips. But, when we expanded our range, that would change.

White Mountains scene

Sometime in my second or third College year, I organized an ambitious early "Spring" trip to the Virginia Blue Ridge, in Easter vacation, in March. Again, there were perhaps 30 of us, girls and boys. Nobody wanted to go home to their families, from which they were trying to escape. I managed the logistics, the food, slab bacon, lots of stuff like that, and we were well prepared. I marshaled about three vehicles, including the Student Council truck, which, again, I drove. Others sometimes spelled me. Again, Naomi was my lookout. Best of all, because College was not in session, there were no chaperones. It was a wild, crazy adventure, but I pulled it off without incident.

Except for the weather. We thought, Virginia being in the South, the Blue Ridge would be warm in early Spring, in March. We were mistaken. It was zero degrees Fahrenheit. But we were prepared. We had our

Camping out, boy/girl

double sleeping bags and we paired up, girl/boy. Except I was too shy to attempt any sexual adventures. It was a great missed opportunity for me, on this and later hiking trips. But at least we were warm. We heard from the Rangers that a battalion of U.S. Army mountain troops had given up on the climbing in the Blue Ridge while we were there, because of the cold. But we were fine! We had the Time of our Lives! I thought it was extraordinary that the College let us go, in those days the College played a parietal role over the students, but we had parental permission (from unknowing parents), and College was not in session, so we were free to go.

This and later hiking trips were really the high

John & friends, map reading above tree line in the White Mountains

point of my Life. We were on our own, among close friends, in a dangerous and beautiful situation. And we mastered all the dangers. It was unforgettable! And I had conceived of and brought to fruition these long trips, which hadn't been attempted before. It was a balm for my poor grades.

Before I graduated, I had organized two- and three-week trips to the Virginia Blue Ridge, as already described; the White Mountains, above tree line, in New

Hampshire (we climbed Mt. Washington); the Nantahala National Forest in the Great Smokies in North Carolina; and the Mahoosuc Mountain Range in Maine, 50 miles from the nearest town. I also organized and led a few spelunking expeditions to raw caves near Kutztown, PA, where we crawled through dark tunnels about 18" high, half filled with water. But it was warm and a lot of fun, especially going through the "lemon squeeze." Very chthonian!

Descent in the White Mountains

Anyway, after I started all this, I was elected President of the Swarthmore College Outing Club, in my Junior year. The next year, with a little help from me, the office went to my buddy and roommate, Barry Silvers. We had a lot of fun with this!

But what about my Academics? I started off in the engineering curriculum, and did not do particularly well. I remember especially that I had a terrible time with the Mechanical Drawing class, and spent several all night sessions in the drawing classroom trying to make an exam drawing without inkblots. The drafting equipment was not particularly good in those days, and I believe I had to make 23 copies before I finally made one without inkblots. I had just as bad luck with the metal shop classes. I remember I was unable to successfully use the metal turning lathe, so the instructor finally made the desired piece for me. It all could have been discouraging, all these failures at manual work, but at the time, I didn't care. Now I do.

Ascending Tuckerman's Ravine in the White Mountains

And, more important, there was the calculus. I thought I understood the freshman calculus, but I couldn't do well on the exams. Of course, as always, the Swarthmore instructors marked us on a Bell curve, so hardly anybody received a good grade. It was discouraging. Also, as I was later told, the instructors marked on reputation, so if you came into a second semester or later course with a bad academic history, it was nearly impossible to get a better grade, no matter how well you did. And almost everybody in the Swarthmore class was either a high school valedictorian or salutatorian, and the mean I.Q. at Swarthmore was 145 or 150, so we were all good. I think they should have just given us all "A's."

It didn't occur to me until later that I should have considered transferring out of Swarthmore, to someplace where I would be more appreciated, like perhaps Hampshire College, an excellent progressive school where there were no grades, although student performance there was closely monitored in other ways. I had been 2nd in my high school class, my I.Q. had been tested as a youth at 170 plus, and I was a Westinghouse Science Talent Search winner. I shouldn't have put up with Swarthmore's miserable grading nonsense. But, as I said earlier, it was my first trial away from home, and I didn't want to give up on it in defeat. But I now wish that I had then done something, either seek counseling or a change in academic venue. At graduation, I was so discouraged with my bad grades that I didn't earnestly pursue graduate or professional school. I didn't want to be told any more how stupid I was.

At this time, I was the perfect model of objectivity. I was best at hard or semi-hard science or math. Though they interested me, I could barely function in the liberal arts courses. I had no or very little subjective inner life at all, and never did until after all the psychiatry and psychology. So I suppose I should thank the shrinks for that change. But much of what I acquired from the shrinks was very painful, and drove me quite crazy. Was that necessary? I think not and I think I was in the hands of incompetents who believed in "tough love." Too tough for me! My Freudian psychoanalyst was, after all, a military psychiatrist. It is interesting that I did acquire from this guy the ability to take suicidal chances. More will power, less concern for self-preservation. I believe it was the same sort of thing that they instill into the Marines. This much has been useful. But I could have done without most of this "tough love" and perhaps developed subjectivity through other less traumatic paths

But to get back to the chronology, I believe that after my Freshman year, I worked for the summer at The National Bureau of Standards, then located in

Washington, DC. The institution has since moved to Bethesda, MD. Anyway, I had a quiet summer there. I lived in a huge boarding house near Dupont Circle, taking most of my meals there. At NBS, I worked in an aeronautics lab, reading verniers used in wind tunnel tests. Needless to say, I had trouble reading the verniers accurately, because of my already (always) distorted perception, discussed at length elsewhere. My amusements were Marine Band concerts from a barge floating in the Potomac, and a canoeing expedition up the same river. I remember that we tried to swim in the shallow polluted river and there was two feet of sewage on the bottom. Disgusting. I hope they've cleaned it up some by now. My recollection of that Summer was that I didn't meet any girls (I still looked like a very young juvenile) and that I continued to masturbate, almost daily. Somebody should have taken me to a good brothel. But actually, I couldn't have gotten into one, because I was still under 18. The madams in these places are very strict about not admitting minors. The legal penalties for this are much more severe than for simply selling bodies to adults (18 or over).

#

Next Summer, at the end of my Sophomore year, I decided I did not want to be an engineer. So I switched to my next career choice, a Biology Major in the Pre-Medical curriculum. To be able to make the switch, I needed to take a Summer course in Introductory Biology at Hofstra College, in Garden City, Long Island, near my parent's home in Baldwin, where I spent the Summer of 1954. I drove myself to Garden City, about ten miles each way, every day for classes. I succeeded in getting an "A" for the first summer semester, the Plant Kingdom, but I slacked off a little in the second semester, the Animal Kingdom, and only received a "B" But the "A" was encouraging. And I feel I learned a lot of detailed information about plants and animals in the course, even though the conceptual framework (as taught at Swarthmore) was lacking. Who's to say whose concepts are valid, anyway? But I guess we should at least be familiar with all the varied thinking.

In my Junior Year, now in the Liberal Arts curriculum, I encountered a language requirement. I already had a little French, from high school, but I wanted something different. I enrolled in Russian class, which I continued for the next two years and after graduation. Russian at Swarthmore was taught by Miss Olga Lamkert, a White Russian émigré. She had been 35 years old at the time of the Russian Revolution in 1917, so in 1958 when I entered her classes, she was already well on in years. (Later on, I learned she finally passed away at age 99, at Tolstoy Farms, a retirement retreat for old White Russians in Upstate New York, founded by Leo Tolstoy's daughter). Miss Lamkert carried herself very humbly but she was quite the Aristocrat. Her father had been Minister of Post, Telegraph and Telephone under Nicholas II, the last Czar. Miss Lamkert's fiancé had been killed in the Revolution fighting for the Whites. She never married. She escaped the Reds and went to live in the White Russian community in Shanghai, China. Eventually, she found her way to Swarthmore in Pennsylvania.

Her classes were very small, only five or six students. The classes were conducted in her little second floor apartment, adjacent to the campus. She always served Russian honey cake and tea from a samovar, which we all loved. I met Katrina Murdoch in her classes. Also in Miss Lamkert's classes was Naomi Fox, whom I knew from the Outing Club. Miss Lamkert frowned on my (then) lack of gentility, and, in later years, really got upset when I started flirting with the Communists. However, she always gave me decent grades, "Bs," and said I had a good Russian pronunciation (My French pronunciation has always been terrible.). Knowing Miss Lamkert was a positive experience. Something different for me.

Swarthmore has an Honors Program, which, in my time there, one enters at the beginning of the Junior Year. Something under a half of the Junior Class was admitted to the Honors Program. Honors students take only two Seminars in each semester. Each seminar meets once a week, the students study independently under the supervision of the instructor, and each student writes a short (10-page?) paper for each seminar each week, based on his or her independent research. The Swarthmore Honors Program is based on the principles operative at Cambridge and Oxford, England. I was very bitter that I could not get into the Honors Program. My grades were not good enough. Another reason I should have dumped Swarthmore.

I haven't told you about my other roommate. You have already met Barry Silvers, with whom I roomed in my Sophomore year. In my Junior year I roomed with Gabriel Salomon, a New Yorker from a wealthy family who had graduated from the Bentley School.

Gabriel's father, Oskar, had been an officer in the Czar's army just before the Russian Revolution in 1917. Oskar was very proud of the fact that he had been an officer, even though he was a Jew, in the Imperial Russian Army. Anyway, before the time of the Revolution, during early WWI, Oskar was studying at Liege University in Belgium, and when the Germans invaded Belgium (on the modified Schlieffen Plan), Oskar escaped to London, where he subsequently married, and in visits to Paris, he became a close friend of many of the great modern artists. I know Oskar's son, Gabriel, my Junior year roommate, was very proud of a birthday card he had received from Marc Chagall, a friend of his father. Oskar also may have known Picasso and others. I once found Oskar's picture, with him standing in a group of the famous artists, in a book of Parisian life between the Wars in the Metropolitan Museum bookstore.

Anyway, between the great wars, Oskar and his family emigrated to England and then to the USA. In America, Oskar became quite wealthy importing (and manufacturing?) Grundig radios for the military and then the public. which were good for listening to the classical music of the time. In WWII, Oskar won an "E" from the government for his work. Oskar also became a great collector of famous art works. I was invited to the family apartment just once. It was located on Upper Fifth Avenue, just opposite The Metropolitan Museum, in what was then just about the classiest area in the city. The walls were covered with splendid original oils, among them a marvelous original Renoir nude. Even at the time, naïve as I was, I knew enough to be suitably impressed.

Gabriel had an older brother, Sergei, who was a Yale graduate and took a Masters in mathematics or engineering and then worked for the Sperry Gyroscope Company for three years before joining the Russian Studies program at Columbia U. and taking a doctorate there. Sergei and I are good friends to this day. He supports and comes to my Eleutheria (means "Liberty" in Demotic Greek) Salons and helps me in other ways. He is just finishing his tenure as a Political Science Professor at Barnard College, part of Columbia University. Sergei is very adventurous. Sergei, at age 78, with his wife Carol Moore, was in Ramallah on the West Bank, in the midst of the commotion ensuing after the death of Yassir Arafat. I've been a friend of Sergei's for 59 years, since 1952, as I write this.

Gabriel and I were roommates, as I said, in my Junior year, in Mary Lyons 4. For our Senior year, we all joined together (with Barry Silvers) in an apartment suite, back in Mary Lyons 1. We were quite comfortable there, in ML1, and were beyond most of the College supervision, as we were "deep in the Woods." I had a good English bicycle, which Barry helped me maintain, and I regularly rode the mile and a half to the Upper Campus, where we (then) took our meals, and the other College classroom buildings. In my Junior year, as President of the Outing Club, I authorized Gabriel to keep a car (a Nash Rambler convertible – it ran well, I loved it and drove it a lot). I should explain that cars were forbidden on Campus, unless they were needed by a College extracurricular organization, as, for example, the Outing Club, for trips and excursions.

Gabriel and I were close friends through the College years, and for a several years afterwards. He even let me live in his nice Manhattan apartment, free of charge, during his first year away at Yale Law School in New Haven, CT. But when I lost my mind, I believe I became an "undesirable" person in his eyes, "a dangerous person to know," and he cut me off completely. He visited me once in the mental hospital and that was it. I never saw him again.

Gabriel went on to become a lawyer, then an Assistant District Attorney in New York, and finally a Judge, rising to become a New York State Supreme Court Judge, a high position. Yes, he was a criminal judge. I suppose he thought that maintaining the friendship with me would damage his career. I, for my part, was disappointed that Gabriel took on such an Authoritarian career. But maybe it was in his blood. At Swarthmore, he had taken many English seminars and always did well in them. He also wrote for the College literary magazine. I had always hoped he would become a writer. Incidentally, Gabriel graduated with High Honors (Magna Cum Laude). Barry, who majored in Biology, graduated with Honors (Cum Laude). I graduated in Course, with No Distinction. But Gabriel always used to say, "John is the most brilliant of the three of us." Well, I don't now have much to show for it, if by chance, this was even partly true.

Gabriel did indeed betray me. At first, I was mystified by his action. Then disappointed. Finally Angry. I can only think Gabriel had an irrational fear of mental illness and the mentally ill, and/or that he thought that further association with me would compromise his career. Both reactions are deplorable and, even at this late date, necessitate some speaking out. Gabriel obviously thought of me as a "nonperson." Or can you offer some other possible explanation? Gabriel had been a very good friend.

I remember that I have not filled you in on Barry Silvers' later career. At Swarthmore, Barry was one of my closest friends, and I fill you in on his career because his life meant a lot to me. He graduated with Honors from Swarthmore, and did graduate work for a year at Washington University in St. Louis. He concluded his graduate studies by taking a Ph.D. in Zoology from The University of Pennsylvania, and then went on to a distinguished career in transplantation research (which was just becoming possible during our academic years). He was a full Professor at The Mayo Clinic for a time, and also, seriatim, at several other major universities. He married (sequentially) two of the lab assistants from other labs at his workplace, but never had any children. Barry has said that this wasn't a fit world to bring children into, but perhaps that was just an excuse. I don't know if he had a biological fertility problem, or what. He now lives in Montana (he is still an adjunct Professor at the University of Montana) and he and his wife still hike, climb and ski a lot. Remember, it was I (in the Swarthmore Outing Club) who inspired Barry to take up the Outdoor Life. But I think the urban life is more civilized, and where the future lies. Besides, I skydive. That's enough Outdoors for me, at this stage of my life, anyway.

Now it is time to describe the sex life (such as it was) of myself and my roommates and friends at Swarthmore. In those days (1952-56), the College authorities believed that they must play a parietal role in the development of the students. Dorm visitation by members of the opposite sex was strictly forbidden. The penalties for failure to observe this stricture were severe – suspension or expulsion. If two students married, one of them (I believe) had to leave the College. Off in the woods at Mary Lyons Dormitories, we were not so closely supervised, and could get away with a lot. The faculty couples resident in the dormitories usually winked at our transgressions, but the administration authorities were severe.

Now (2008), things are completely different. The dorms are completely open, the kids are considered to be adults, and visitors of the opposite sex are permitted to stay all night. The College even advises the students with birth control information, and sexual and other counseling. I read in a recent issue of the Alumni Magazine, where one member of the Administration said the College encourages, or at least condones, the students "hooking up," because it "relieves Stress." My, how the times have changed! I could have used some of that. It certainly would have helped me make a better College and life adjustment

One more note on this. As I rewrite this chapter, in 2011, I must report that, at Swarthmore, in the newer dormitories, the bathrooms are now coed. A good thing. None of the students will ever feel ill at ease in the presence of the opposite sex again. Nothing left to the imagination. No more mystification. Great! But I couldn't believe this, when I first learned about it.

Anyway, to get back to the narrative, in my Freshman year, when I moved to Mary Lyons 1, I soon discovered that Roger Thornton, a classmate who was much more mature (but not much older chronologically) was living in the end room on my floor, where he was occasionally visited by his girl friend, Gwen Gwinnett, class of '57. Roger was a dedicated pacifist, and had persevered through nearly a year in the federal penitentiary because he could not even register as a conscientious objector, because he believed that even to do that would support "the military system." Actually, at that time, conscientious objector status was not available to atheists, such as Roger. This has since changed. Roger recently said to me that he "no longer" was the "antinomian" he was in those years. Roger, who was very serious, later became our class Valedictorian (refusing to attend the Commencement for similar reasons) and even later went on to become a famous writer. You may know of him. He and his short stories and novels have been written up on the front page of *The New York Times Book Review*.

We on the floor (and in the building) all conspired to keep Gwen's occasional visits secure. If an Administration member entered the building, on the 1st floor, we would quickly alert Roger (on the 3rd floor) so he and his girlfriend could take precautions to avoid discovery. I learned a lot from this. Incidentally, I believe before graduation, the couple married, and came to live on Manhattan's Lower East Side, not far from where I lived at the time. I was in their place a few times, where Gwen would nurse her baby in full view of the visitors. I of course know now this is a perfectly natural and good thing to do, but at the time (1958), I found it quite startling. This was something else Roger and Gwen taught me.

As to my adventures at Swarthmore, at least until graduation, there was nothing more than a little heavy petting. I've probably forgotten some of the incidents now, but I remember borrowing classmate Bob Ellis' old coupe and driving classmate Angela Thames off into the nearby countryside on a beautiful April or May day in 1953, picnicking with her, with wine I believe (which I'd managed to acquire, though underage) and then undressing her to the waist and fondling and sucking her breasts. I was afraid to go further, though Angela was perfectly willing. Angela thought I was "so sophisticated" for not proceeding further, but I was just scared. Amusing in retrospect.

A year or two later, I asked several girls, on different occasions, to go off with me into nearby Crum Woods at night, but they all turned me down. I remember that schoolmate Kathy Gaposchkin, daughter of a famous astronomer, was one of the ones who turned me down. I don't know if I would ever have been able to consummate the event, anyway. Probably not. Still scared.

Then, in my Junior year, when living in Mary Lyons 4 with my then roommate, Gabriel Salomon, I snuck my girlfriend of the time, Patricia White (not unattractive) into my dorm room and went through the same "undressing to the waist" charade. Patricia was a good friend for several years, even visiting me in the Summer at my home on Long Island, where she gave me the LP, *24 Variations on a Theme of Paganini,* by Rachmaninoff, which I thought was a great gift. I believe the piece is now called *Rhapsody on a Theme of Paganini.*

I saw Patricia years later at Swarthmore reunions on Campus. She did marry, had children (I believe), and went on to become a successful hospital administrator. Of course, I would rather have seen her (also) go on to do something creative. But she was no fool. Too much no fool, I think now.

At this time, in my Junior year, none of the three of us, Barry, Gabriel or myself, had had sexual intercourse. But that was to change. Gabriel and I were 18 and Barry was 20. I think Barry found someone to requite him, either in his Senior year or shortly thereafter. Gabriel's story was more interesting. In our Senior year, Gabriel's father Oskar (see *supra*) sent him to a brothel in Puerto Rico, so that he could have his first sexual experience. Very European. Back at Swarthmore, Gabriel told us how impressed he was with the large crucifix in the bedroom at the place.

In the Summer after my Junior year, I worked as an Orderly in Nassau Hospital, Mineola, Long Island, NY, to try to determine what the life of a doctor was about. I shaved the pubic area of patients (male) before surgery, I gave enemas, I did other simple nursing tasks. I worked in the morgue for a while (my God! – I was only 16 or 17). I was allowed to witness surgery, and watched the irreverent doctors whistle while they worked, performing cancer surgery. I didn't ask to witness a delivery. I should have. Anyway, the blood and gore of it all disgusted me, and I pretty much gave up the idea of a medical career.

Despite the gore, this was a chance to study the human body, then and later important to me in Art, photography, my scientific studies, and of course, sex, in all its many states. But beyond that, my next career trial balloon was graduate school and research in biology, particularly biochemical genetics.

To get back to my sexual career at Swarthmore, I've related most of what happened to me, in a sexual way, up at least until my Senior year. By that time, my good Outing Club friend, also in my Biology classes, then Sophomore (and consequently exactly my age) Beth Bloch, began to take an interest. I believe I relate her story elsewhere, *infra,* but it's pertinent to mention some of it here.

Beth was born into a Viennese Jewish family in 1936. Beth's father, Friedrich, saw the what was coming and brought the family to America in 1938, when Beth was two years old, to escape Hitler and the coming Holocaust. Beth later related to me how she had been told how the family had hid and lived in unfinished basements while making their escape. Friedrich later became a strong supporter of his new homeland America's defense efforts, designing nuclear submarines for the U.S. Navy.

The family was steeped in Freud and sexual permissiveness, I believe. Beth related to me how she was first seduced at age 14 by a journalist friend of her parents, from TIME INC., who was visiting the Bloch family. Beth was very libidinous, and would get off (have an orgasm) merely by riding in a bumpy back seat of the old Fifth Avenue Coach Company busses in New York City.

In about the middle of my Senior year, Beth began trying to get me into bed with her. Once, in Parrish (the main building) Hall, she grabbed me by the testicles (in clothes). But I was very elusive. In the Spring of my Senior year, she tried to come to visit me in Mary Lyons 1 dorm, almost definitely to seduce and devirginize me, but I was unfortunately at the ophthalmologist that day. Most unfortunate. We also had trouble getting together because, at the time, Beth was sexually active with at least one other man, my friend Elliott Daniels.

The big event had to wait until one August day in the Summer after graduation, when I was staying in the Summer home of a Swarthmore Biology Professor friend and his family in Ithaca, NY. A group of us, including myself, Elliott, Beth and others had gathered in Ithaca preparatory to embarking on the last Swarthmore hiking expedition that I would lead.

The Gardner family (the Swarthmore Professor) was away, and Beth took the opportunity to seduce me, twice. It ended with a hot shower together, which was fun. She never performed fellatio on me, though. That probably would have blown my mind completely. But at least I was no longer a virgin. I was 20. I had had to wait until well into my 21st year for this. Maybe the story would have been different if I'd grown up in Europe. I don't know.

More detail. At the time of the above event, Beth was more or less engaged to Elliott Daniels, whom she later married (and eventually divorced), and whom she had also devirginized earlier that year. Beth promptly told Elliott about the event with me, and he reluctantly went along with it (we were all friends), and we all went on our hiking expedition, to the Nantahala National Forest in the Great Smoky Mountains of North Carolina. Elliott knew how uncontrollable Beth's sexual urges were, but he married her, they had two sons, and then they divorced, probably because Beth couldn't stay away from other men Incidentally, later on, Dr. Elliott Daniels (Ph.D.) became a genetics counselor to couples planning families.

One more complication. Also on the expedition was Dr. Indra Raju Singh, a young East Indian Professor who had been teaching Biology for one year at Swarthmore. He was a mycologist (fungi expert), as was Dr. Gardner. Gardner, Singh, myself and other mycologists from Cornell often went on local field trips from Ithaca, and the experts showed me an amazing variety of hidden fungi, in all bright colors and sizes. Also many salamanders and newts, strange insects and flowers, which I had never before noticed in the woods and knew nothing about.

I spent the Summer of 1956, immediately after graduating from Swarthmore, working in the greenhouses and plantations of the Cornell University School of Agriculture, preparatory to entering graduate school there in the Department of Plant Breeding, studying Biochemical Genetics. I planned to study DNA, the spiral helix of which had just been unraveled by Watson, Crick and Rosalind Franklin in England.

To begin the Summer, I bicycled from Swarthmore to Ithaca, setting out the day after graduation, and taking three days to cover the 250 or so miles, over the mountains, to reach the Gardner's Summer place.

Just before leading my last Swarthmore hiking expedition, Indra Raju Singh, getting fired up about my and Elliott's adventures with Beth, exposed himself to her. She was outraged, and had me confront Indra about it. I couldn't see why she took such offense. After all, she had grabbed me by the testicles in the Parrish Hall. But things settled down, and we all went off to the Nantahala National Forest, under my leadership. There's more about the hiking expeditions *supra*, I won't repeat it here.

There were other sexual opportunities during the Swarthmore years, while on hiking trips. I believe I've already discussed these, and I won't repeat those stories here. Otherwise, that's the sum total of it. Very sad!

Oh yes, Barry and I once went into Philadelphia to the TROC, the burlesque house. I believe it was the first time I'd ever seen (and at a distance, yes) a totally nude adult woman in the flesh. I was 17 or 18. Oh, the shortcomings of my upbringing. And I think a lot of my middle class classmates were in the same situation. Consider Barry and Gabriel, for example. The French would be appalled. I DO NOT BELIEVE DEFERRED GRATIFICATION IS A GOOD IDEA, DR. FREUD, ET AL. We need more people who grow up knowing something about sexual life and fewer warped accountants and computer people working in cubicles behind glass partitions.

This about concludes the section on adolescence, "From Puberty to First Encounter." I will go on in the next section to discuss my young adulthood, at least those parts of it I did not cover in previous sections. I should add that in the first years after leaving Swarthmore, I had sexual intercourse with several other female Swarthmore grads. I went with Swarthmore women by necessity: I looked and acted so juvenile (or at least thought I did, which may have been part of the problem) that other New York women would not look at me for another ten years. I thought of getting male hormone shots but I realized this was dangerous, increasing the risk of cancer in later life, so I desisted. I just had to struggle with this. Struggling again!

What was my state of mind in 1956, at the age of 20, at the end of the first Summer after my graduation? I'm a little uncertain about this. I know I was optimistic (foolishly, as it turned out). I wanted to succeed in the Big City, but as yet, I had no idea how to do this. I wanted to learn more about Life, but I thought this would be a gentle process (it was not). And I wanted more experience of Sex, but I did not get this for another ten years. I respected Culture, but I had little.

Above all, I assumed I would be happy. It turned out this was not to be, at least in the near future.

From First Encounter to Crisis

1956 – 1960

I will begin where the last Section left off, after the return from leading my last hiking expedition with the Swarthmore College Outing Club (to the Nantahala National Forest in the Great Smoky Mountains of North Carolina), at the end of my first Summer after graduation, in September 1956.

I returned to New York City and found a Summer share in Greenwich Village with two male friends from Swarthmore, one of whose names I don't remember. The other friend was Ernest Boaten, a Ghanaian and a Black Muslim. Both were very good friends. Anyway, my post-graduation epic in Manhattan started out very happily.

We entertained a lot. I prepared my first and only lamb roast (with mint jelly). And, best of all, I was shacked up in the front bedroom with a constant visitor, Jane Winthrop, Swarthmore Class of '57. I explain elsewhere that Jane was the sometime roommate of my real interest, Katrina Murdoch (later Blackstone). I propositioned Katrina, but she said I would do much better with her roommate, Jane, and Katrina set it up for me. Now, Jane had a much better figure than Katrina (beautiful breasts) but Katrina was more sophisticated, really a young Establishment woman. Her father was Bill Murdoch (Campbell), an adventurer who wanted to surpass the renown of his father, Murdoch Campbell, a maverick writer who celebrated the back to nature life, and such. So Bill Murdoch dropped the "Campbell" last name, took a boat to Russia in the early 1930s, went to the new city of Magnitorgorsk ("Magnet City"), which the Russians were building on the Eastern edge of European Russia. The city was being built as part of a Soviet effort to shift its manufacturing capacity Eastward, to help foil the expected Nazi German invasion.

Anyway, Bill Murdoch wrote about his experiences for *TIME* magazine and eventually became the magazine's Russian Area Editor. He wrote a book, *Behind the Urals,* about his time in Russia. While in the Soviet Union, Bill Murdoch married Anna, a Russian schoolteacher. Katrina was one of the children.

But I have told this story before. Suffice to say here that Jane Winthrop and I were together for about a year, when I tired of her, and threw her out (physically), despite her beautiful body. She bored me. I confess that

Jane, for the most part, had just been a sexual "vessel" for me, as it says in the Bible. But I couldn't find anybody else in NYC. Jane did not have Katrina's sophisticated personality. I kept her as long as I could tolerate it. But it was inexcusable to throw her out the door like that. I can only say I was very young and should have known better. I would never have thrown Katrina out that way. We could have worked out an amicable separation. But Jane wouldn't go!

A little more on that Summer on Charlton Street in Greenwich Village. We were still happy in the afterglow of our undergraduate years (which were not totally miserable). We entertained a lot. As a present on some special occasion, Katrina Murdoch gave me a nice volume of Voltaire's writings, in French. I thought this was a great thing to do. She knew I had very little French, but she was challenging me to rise to the occasion and try to read some of it. Very Establishment, again. That girl always impressed me. I tell the story elsewhere of her several Down's Syndrome children, so things did not work out very well for her, either.

And all Summer I enjoyed Jane Winthrop's body in the front room. The novelty of sexual relations with her had not yet worn off. It was a satisfactory Summer, in many respects.

At the end of the Summer, Gabriel Salomon and I took off in his old Nash Rambler convertible, the same one we had had at College, for a Grand Tour of the American West. Actually, I believe I hitchhiked alone across the country and met Gabriel in Los Angeles, and we took it together from there. My hitchhiking trip was quite an adventure, and I narrowly avoided a couple of bad scrapes. But I got there O.K., and I went directly to Balboa Park in L.A., took my shoes off, and waded out into the Pacific Ocean, which I had never actually seen before.

After leaving L.A., Gabriel and I proceeded up the coast highway to San Francisco. Along the way, we stopped and went down to the beach and each found a wonderful piece of driftwood, which was so sculpted by the wind and waves, as to almost be an art object. I loved that piece and displayed it my apartment until I lost every shred of anything I owned in the aftermath of my first psychotic attack in 1960. But you can read all about that elsewhere.

After seeing the sights of San Francisco, we headed to Las Vegas in Nevada. We met some cowboys and other interesting folk there, but we did not gamble and we did not patronize the legal brothels, for which Nevada is famous. I don't think we even knew about the brothels, and in any case, I thought at that time that brothels, legal or illegal, were only for low types and criminals, so I probably wouldn't have gone to the Nevada brothels, anyway. How my view of this issue changed in later years, when I could no longer attract young women and became desperate for sex with same! You can read about that *supra*. I became familiar with the brothels of New York City, and elsewhere, later on.

After Vegas, we headed for Arizona. Gabriel wanted to visit Joseph Wood Krutch, the famous writer and poet, resident in Arizona. Krutch was one of Gabriel's heroes. I don't know now if Gabriel actually got together with Krutch on our trip or not.

In Arizona now, we headed for Tucson, where an interviewer in the state employment office befriended us and invited us to stay with him and his friends. One thing I remember was that our friend often talked about "muff diving" with his lady friends. This was a new concept for me. Although I was no longer a virgin, I was still very inexperienced in sexual matters. I also remember sitting out alone in Gabriel's car at night, in front of the house where we were staying, listening to "Music Through the Night" on CBS or NBC. In those days, the big radio stations were more enlightened, and played classical music through the night hours. I believe the networks, then, also maintained symphony orchestras. Wasn't Arturo Toscanini the Director of the NBC Symphony for a while? In some ways, those were better days.

Our friend from the Arizona State Employment Service also found me work, doing day labor unloading sheet metal from flatcars. Unfortunately, I neglected to wear the recommended gloves because I couldn't get ahold of the oiled sheet metal unless I used my bare fingers. So I promptly cut my hand open to the bone. But Arizona Workmen's Compensation paid for a doctor who sewed me up (12 stitches, I think) and also gave me a stipend to live on for a while in Tucson with our new friend. So it didn't work out too badly.

I may have become confused now about the sequence of our various stops on our trip. At one point we were in the apple country near the Columbia River in the state of Washington. I should say that West of the inland mountains in Washington, the land is lush and green. East of these same mountains, where we were traveling, the land was mostly cold desert country, though, with irrigation, the apples grew well. We drove into a migrant fruit picker camp run by one Big Jim Wade (his name was stamped on all the blankets). Jim Wade took us on as migrant fruit pickers and gave us a rundown shack with a wood stove to live in. We weren't very good at apple picking. We stayed three or four weeks and made a very few dollars. We had to climb on tall stepladders to harvest the fruit. One old guy said to me, "You haven't been around ladders much, have you, son?"

I was occupied in my spare time reading Bertram Wolfe's, "Three Who Made a Revolution," about Lenin, Trotsky and Stalin. Swarthmore had turned me into quite a Russophile or Sovietophile, at least in those early days. I still keep (a later copy) of the book on my shelf. Anyway, after three or four weeks of apple picking, and "batching out," as it was called (living and cooking as bachelors, I believe), we moved on. We would never have been able to survive for a long time as apple pickers.

We returned to NYC in time for Christmas, 1956, after three or four months on the road. The trip had been a bit of an education for us, since we were so very young, and I had never seen the American West, but we hadn't learned all that much. And it was about the last time I would see much of Gabriel Salomon.

Back in NYC again, staying briefly with my parents in their new apartment adjacent to Gramercy Park (They had been able to move to Manhattan from their last apartment home in Rockville Center, Long Island, after my graduation from Swarthmore and the end of my college bills. My father was making fairly good money as an editor for Bill Communications in NYC.).

My next move was to attempt graduate school, beginning in the Spring semester of 1957. I had arranged this all beforehand, through Dr. Bob Gardner, the mycologist who had spent a year teaching at Swarthmore. I had taken a botanical taxonomy course (interesting) with him, and we had become friends. As mentioned earlier, I had spent the Summer after college graduation (1956) living in his (temporary) home with his family in Ithaca, NY, while I worked in the Cornell U. Plantations. That had worked out well, and I had been accepted as a graduate student in the Department of Plant Breeding, to study Biochemical Genetics with Dr. Adrian Srb as my mentor. Srb had written a genetics text that I had liked and used at Swarthmore. Srb was an eminent man in his field.

Biochemical Genetics was a hot new field at the time. Watson, Crick and especially Rosalind Franklin had just deciphered the basic genetic code of DNA. Watson and Crick and one other had received the Nobel Prize for this work. Rosalind Franklin, who had done the radiological work that underlay the discoveries, was ignored. And she later, at age 37, I believe, died of radiological poisoning contracted during her research work. The cause of getting recognition for Franklin has always been important to me. She may have been passed over because she was a woman or because she was Jewish, or both. In any case, it wasn't fair. She had sacrificed the most, her life, in order to make the discoveries possible. I'm happy to see that now, almost 50 years later, Rosalind Franklin is getting some recognition. I've urged a woman writer, my good friend Penelope Karageorge, to write a play (tragedy) about Franklin's life. I'm sure it would be a big hit on Broadway or in the West End. As you can surmise, I sympathize with tragic situations.

But back to my life at Cornell. I had no instinct for the lab work, and couldn't get reliable results. As discussed earlier, it was a psychological problem with perception. I'd had some trouble with perception all my life, but I'd ignored it. Maybe everybody has this problem, to some extent. But I couldn't handle it. I understand now that there are instruments available that can take the perceptual readings and display them on a big digital readout that anybody can read. But we didn't have this in 1957. The agar-agar plates with my cultures that I was testing looked different from moment to moment. PERHAPS, I tell myself now, it was because I had the eye of an artist, perceiving all sorts of alternate ways of seeing things. Or perhaps I was just beginning to be crazy, seeing things which weren't there. Maybe the two possibilities mentioned amount to the same thing, depending on how you look at it. In any event, I couldn't get any accurate results. It was very discouraging.

So the lab work, the independent research, was unsuccessful. And I was lonely and depressed. I didn't have any friends. I had a couple of classes, but I didn't do all the class work or take all the exams. I think now that one of the reasons for my failure at Cornell was that I wasn't mature enough to do independent research work. Swarthmore HAD been more supportive. In any case, I bombed out at the end of my one semester, the Spring 1957 semester, and was ready to try something else. Incidentally, my friend, Dr. Bob Gardner was, I think, very disappointed with me.

So what did I do next? I didn't want to go back to NYC as a total failure, so I first went to the Agricultural Extension Service at Cornell and located a farm in nearby Cortland, NY, that wanted a hired man for the Summer. I hitchhiked out there and met Ted Carrier, the proprietor of a sizable family dairy farm, and he took me on.

I learned a great deal that Summer from Ted Carrier and his family while working on the farm. Incidentally, the practical life and the regular pattern of farm life prepared me to recognize that a lot of what the bookish shrinks said was nonsense. One example. Dr. Sternschein once provocatively told me that I was "dependent on money." But I learned on the farm that I could work for "found," which is an old Yankee term for room and board. I always knew, when confronted by the anal theories of the psychiatrists, that I could go back and work on the farm, with (basically) no need for money or involvement in the corrupt money economy. I should add that Ted Carrier also paid me $20/week for (incidental) expenses.

I never was particularly interested in money. During these years, in trying to choose a career path, I never pursued money. I have always thought that, if I was happily working at something I liked, the money would take care of itself. As it worked out, that has often, but not always, been the case. And, if I hadn't been derailed by the psychoanalysis, I believe I would have always been financially O.K.

What else did I learn on the farm? The whole family and I worked in the fields, preparing alfalfa and hay for baling, and later for feeding to the cattle. I learned to get up at 4:00 a.m., put on my boots, wade through the knee deep manure in the barnyard, and go into the barn and, on my own, milk 47 cows using the milking machines. I had to learn to spot occasional sick cows, those with secretions and hard udders. I had to put the big milk cans in the cooler. (Once I forgot to turn on the cooler. This was a big scare, but the dairy took the milk anyway, so everything was O.K. except some customers got milk with a higher, but still safe, bacterial count). I learned to drive a tractor. I helped with the threshing of the wheat. I believe we did this when a big ancient steam thresher visited the farm at harvest time.

The farmers let me try out their armamentarium, which included rifles, shotguns and hand guns, including a Luger I visited the local Grange Hall with the family. The Grange is an ancient association of farm families, for social and business purposes. It was a great Summer, but I think I became so "earthy" and "practical" that psychoanalysis would not work on me. These were some of the reasons, anyway. I learned not to tolerate any nonsense. And uncanny, occult, existential experiences are nonsense.

During the Summer, Gabriel and Faith Lewis Greenberg Cohen (discussed elsewhere) drove up in the Rambler to briefly visit me. We went swimming in a nearby Ithaca water hole. My family also drove up to visit me for an afternoon.

After two months of this, though, I was getting a little restless and hankering for the urban life and the cultural pleasures of civilization. So, after eight or nine weeks on the farm, I said goodbye to Ted Carrier and his family and headed back to NYC. Ted liked my work, and urged me to stay on, saying that I could learn to slaughter a cow for meat and also help in a cooperative house raising. But after working in the gore of the hospital one previous Summer, I was not anxious to take part in a slaughtering, and I decided also to miss out on the house raising. In a house raising, all the local farm families get together and put up a house for one of their number in one day. It's a remarkable tradition. The whole Summer farm experience was remarkable. I'm sorry the American family farm tradition is dying. I hate these huge factory farms for the same reason I hate the rest of corporate America.

I went back again briefly to my family in Gramercy Park in Manhattan. It was September 1957. I had I decided to move out and try living on my own. My first independent home was in a rooming house on West 22nd street off Seventh Avenue, not too far from my parent's home on Gramercy Park (East 20th Street and Third Avenue). The rooming house, called "Stanford Arms," or something like that, didn't offer much and I was eager to get a job so I could find a better place to live. Incidentally, last time I looked, the rooming house had become a religious home, 51 years later.

So, what job had I decided to seek for my first "permanent" employment in my adult life? Scientific research was out for the abovementioned reasons. I thought perhaps I could write about science, but that would come later. For the present, September 1957, I was going to attempt to be a newspaperman. Not having any better idea on how to proceed, I resolved to start at the bottom. I heard it was possible for beginners with a B.A. to start with writing jobs at some of the suburban papers, but I wanted to stay in Manhattan. I went to the *Times* to see if I could get anything there, but they weren't even hiring copyboys. So I went to the now-defunct (since the 1960s) *New York World-Telegram & Sun* and Joe Janoff (City Desk Clerk?) hired me as a copyboy for the munificent salary of $45/week. This was about the least somebody could live on, even in those days. It wasn't a great job, but I stayed there for more than a year, and it did lead, indirectly, to something better.

My duties were simple. A copyboy or copygirl would run up when anyone shouted "Copy" and pick up messages or manuscripts to be delivered elsewhere in the big City Room or outside of it. There was also an ancient pneumatic tube system, like the big department stores formerly had, for delivering messages to other floors. We also ran copy to the linotypists on another floor, who operated the ancient Merganthaler Linotype machines, which processed molten lead into slugs of type which printed the paper. This system is now completely obsolete. I felt sorry for the linotypists, who had to breathe the lead fumes all day. Most of the linotypists were very old guys, so I guess they had gotten used to it.

We were also "gophers" ("go for") and we ran for coffee and Danish for everybody who sat at a desk. Coffee then was 10 cents and Danish was 15 cents. I can't remember if we were tipped. I don't think so. For some reason, I remember the names of many of the editors and writers very well. Almost none of them were very polished, but they were all very savvy in the ways of the City. Norman Mockridge was the Editor (he had a little polish), Herbert Kamm was the Feature Editor, Eddie Wakin was the Brooklyn Editor (Eddie was a Lebanese Christian), Paul Meskil was an eccentric fellow who wrote features, I believe. Paul Meskil always wore a beret, which I liked. George Cooper was a clerk who avowed he was a homosexual. He was the first homosexual I'd ever spoken with, knowing I was talking to a homosexual. None of these or the others were sophisticated enough to realize I had talent they could use, or else they felt I was too intellectual. I heard I was being groomed for the Society Page, which I didn't particularly want, but I left before that came to pass.

The other copyboys and copygirls were interesting, but I've forgotten all but two of them. Jack Moriarty had been a lieutenant in the U.S. Army in the Korean War, serving as an artillery spotter. He and a Korean officer companion would ride around in a jeep driven by an enlisted man from place to place up in the hills to direct the artillery fire. It was interesting, and he never told us any horror stories. He went on to report for the *Telegram* on the police blotter and then went on to join the Associated Press.

Another friend was copygirl Susan O'Neal. I had forgotten her for 40 years, but then she spotted me ten or twelve years ago at a party on West End Avenue and reintroduced herself. We've been good friends ever since. She had ended up in a NYS Civil Service job. She loves to come to a lot of the events I organize, including my annual Xmas Eve parties at the Minetta Tavern.

I forgot to say that the *Telegram* was located at 125 Barclay Street in Downtown Manhattan, right on the West Side Drive. I remember that we had a good view from the roof in 1957 or 1958 when the first nuclear submarine, the USS Nautilus, proceeded up the Hudson River on its first visit to NYC. So long ago!

That about covers my experiences at the *Telegram*, except to mention that, to supplement my $45/week, I took on freelance copyediting work with Academic Press, then but no longer located in NYC at 111 Fifth Avenue. I remember editing academic agricultural journals, for the most part. My contact there was the Editor Elizabeth Adams, who I was surprised to later learn was impressed with my work.

Elizabeth Adams was my first post-graduation big break. I had started my career at the bottom and hoped something would happen and it did. I had a call out of the blue from The Columbia University Press because Elizabeth Adams had told her friend there, the Editor-in-Chief Bill Bridgwater, that I was a talented editor and writer. I went up to CUP for an interview and was promptly hired as an Assistant Editor, later to become chief Science Editor. Elizabeth made the call at the end of 1958 and I was hired at the beginning of January 1959, I believe. I was 23 at the time. This was 51 years ago as I write this in October 2010.

My state of mind at the end of 1958 had not much changed since 1956. I had been hoping for a break and I got one. I still knew very little about Art and Culture, or Life, but I knew my science. And I was still having sex exclusively with Swarthmore women, because the mature New York City women would not give me a second look for another 8 or 10 years, I believe this was just because of my youth, although the psychoanalyst would differ, but as I say to myself now, what did he know, after all?

Before I describe my life at CUP, I want to discuss what my housing arrangements had been at this time. When I joined the CUP, I was paid $80/week, then $90/week, enough to pay (then) for decent housing. I rented a 3-room apartment on the second floor of a nice brownstone at 317 West 104th Street on the Upper West Side, for about $100/month. It was a nice place and I moved in. I had to furnish the place from scratch. All I had was my tree stump piece of driftwood from the Monterey beach (see *supra*). But I fixed the place up fairly well.

I believe the apartment was found for me by one Reba Maxwell, a Lesbian who was another editor at CUP, and who lived in the building. I got to know her and her companion, and also the Super and his wife. He was a handsome, rugged Latin from Palermo, who had decorated the backyard to his garden apartment rather artfully, with various plantings. His wife seemed to be a rather randy type, so I guess they enjoyed themselves. These two showed me another life style.

After living on West 104th Street for a year or more, I took a neat little apartment on the Lower East Side, at 71 East 2nd Street, to be near the Bohemian action and also some of my friends and acquaintances who had moved down there. This included Faith Lewis Greenberg Cohen and also the Roger Thornton family. This place was a one-room studio on the second floor, facing a garden in the back. I believe I moved in, in early 1960. I painted the place flat white, had it carpeted with a sky blue used carpet I had found, and put in wall length book shelves myself, with "Molly" screws. The screw goes in and expands the "Molly" so it can bear the weight of the books. I suppose you don't have to be told that "Molly" is a sexual allusion. Penetration, expansion. Cute. I also painted the refrigerator, which was adjacent to the living room, battleship gray, so the whole place would look less like an extension of the kitchen.

I constructed a speaker enclosure from a kit I bought on Cortlandt Street, which was an electronics shopping area before the World Trade Center was built (and fell). I listened to my hifi (LP 33s) a lot. I was quite comfortable in my place on East 2nd Street, at least until the onset of the "Crisis" in August 1960. More about that in earlier sections and later.

The Super kept the place up very well. He was also Super at the Ukrainian Catholic Church next door. There was a large cemetery with a lot of greenery across the street so the neighborhood was very pleasant. Sometime after I left, the place changed hands and I was disappointed to see it had fallen into disrepair and was covered with graffiti. But lately, 45 years later, I was happy to see somebody had cleaned the place up, removed the broken glass and graffiti, and repainted it. It's a nice place again.

But now back to my work and experiences at The Columbia University Press. I was given a window desk on the sixth floor of the Journalism Building on the Columbia University campus, where the CUP offices were then located. I worked directly with the Editor-in-Chief, Dr. William Bridgwater, who was an intelligent, sophisticated, amiable and generous Roman Catholic bookman. Dr. Bridgwater was a bachelor in his early 60s, I believe. He married at that late age while I was working at the Press. Sadly, he died just a few years after I left the Press. Dr. Bridgwater was a great friend to me. He also had an encyclopedic knowledge of everything and I learned to respect Roman Catholics more, after knowing him.

I mentioned encyclopedias. That was my first task at CUP, to write for *The Columbia-Viking Desk Encyclopedia* and bound supplements to the larger *Columbia Encyclopedia*. I was responsible for all the science articles, which was most of my work. I also wrote Russian Area Studies and theatre articles. I was so happy in this work. In my mind, I associated myself with the great French Encyclopedists who wrote just before the French Revolution in the 18th Century, who advanced the Enlightenment and believed in scientific rationalism (and Deism). Diderot, Buffon the naturalist, D'Alembert the scientist and Voltaire were among them.

I worked on the Columbia encyclopedias for about nine months. I believe I did a very good job. Dr. Bridgwater was very pleased with me and wrote up my specific contributions in the Forward (although he didn't mention my name). But my name was in very large letters on the Title Page, listed with the major editors in caps, above a hundred other minor contributors.

What were some of the new topics that I introduced to these editions? Among them were nucleic acids and DNA, carbohydrates, benzene chemistry as the basis of organic chemistry, space travel (this in 1959) and many others. All of the above were accompanied by beautiful and informative plates I had designed.

Although the principal Editors and Publishers of the CUP were Catholics, influenced by the Jesuits, I believe, I was never asked to change one word for doctrinal reasons. I was given a completely free hand. My work was edited for grammar and accuracy, of course, but the corrections were always minor. Dr. Bridgwater knew I was something of a free thinker, and he commented that I had a "Germanic Intellect." I rather liked this. I think Bill meant that I was a scientific rationalist, and an Essentialist, following Plato and Descartes, and not an Existentialist, following Kierkegaard and, say, Heidegger (this last was, yes, a German, but not a scientific rationalist). Bridgwater built up my confidence.

Also, while I was there, there were two Swarthmore Honors graduates from my class working in the hall on menial editorial details. So I had progressed somewhat after the Swarthmore debacle. Furthermore, I had been hired as an Assistant Editor at $80, then $90, a week (a reasonable salary in 1959), but, after six months, Dr. Bridgwater said I could be Chief Science Editor and could put that title on my business cards. Small triumphs!

After the work on the encyclopedias was completed, in Fall 1959, I began to do book editing. I didn't like most of this as much. Some of the authors were difficult to deal with. Some of the texts were too technical for me to completely understand. But I did O.K. One success was the editing of a small Russian language text for Dr. Edmund Stilman, then Chair of the Columbia Slavic Languages Department. For this, I designed and titled the maps (in Russian). Dr. Stilman was very pleased. He was so pleased that he arranged for me to matriculate as a candidate for an advanced degree in the C.U. Slavic Languages Dep't. I only stayed one semester, because the psychological "Crisis" developed soon after, but I received "Bs" in both of the courses.

I tackled one ambitious project which I was not able to finish. I was given the assignment of editing Dr. Margarete Bieber's encyclopedic, profusely illustrated work on *Hellenistic Sculpture*. Dr. Bieber was a German Art Historian, and SHE had a very Germanic

Intellect. We got along fine, after the elaborate introductions were over. Unfortunately, her treatise had footnotes in German and all the other major modern languages, Classical and Demotic Greek, and Latin. I was rather at a loss. I would have had to find an expert in most of the languages (I knew French and Russian, and passed graduate school qualifying exams in both those languages). I guess I could have done it, but the "Crisis" ensued before I could complete the task. I was impressed that Dr. Bridgwater had so much faith in me.

So that about covers my experiences at The Columbia University Press. By January 1960, I was (foolishly, as it turns out) deeply involved with my depth nondirective orthodox Freudian psychoanalysis, and Dr. Bridgwater kindly let me work part time. I cracked up in August 1960 and that was the end of my time at CUP. But it had been VERY WORTHWHILE. I gained a lot from it.

I will add here that, about this time, I had one other one night stand with another Swarthmore girl, one Ellen Greene. Our sexual relations went O.K., but then I noticed, when we turned the lights on, that Ellen had more hair on her chest than I did. This shocked me and I bolted out of the bed and out of the door, and only occasionally saw her socially after that. I was so silly in those days, but I guess I was a purist. In sex, I wanted everything to be perfect.

As a late addition, I'm here including a Rorschach test report, done for, or on, me in August, 1959, when I was still working productively at The Columbia University Press. The report, in my opinion, only gets it partly right. But the tester, Doris Bartlett, was prescient when she said I might have experienced "the terror of my world alone" (this happened later), that I would consort with "women" (she, of course, meant prostitutes, and I did engage in this later), and worst of all, that I was "artistic and esthetic." This has been my damnation and my family's damnation. Many so-called "artists" are half insane much of the time. True of me and my family. And I later began to explore art, partly because of Doris Bartlett's observation. Here follows the Rorschach report:

John Seaman

Rorschach Report

Nathan N. Stockhamer, Ph.D

April 1959

An extraordinary intellect going to pot! is one way of suggesting the disturbances of this patient. Keen, perceptive, artistic and aesthetic, his view of life, of himself, results in a waste and destructive misuse of his abilities.

He is an angry, disillusioned young man, who in his short life has skipped through so much of living and learning, he is burning out. A flash of brilliance has been enough to convince him that he has plumbed the depths; that he knows what there is to know; and, if there is anything more, it isn't worth bothering about. He is relinquishing himself to aberrational practices (in thinking and in functioning with others) partly because there doesn't seem to be any joi de vivre in everyday life. He can drink, take drugs, try homosexuality or excessive masturbation, or "women" – or fool around with esoteric philosophies, etc. – without, any real concern or even active involvement since, in the last analysis, nothing really matters (except to be able to establish that fact). One suspects, though, that a lot of this anger, defiance, and contempt remains within him as phantasy and wish. He doesn't experience others or himself in relation to them as real enough to function directly. His expansions of will and desire whether to create or destroy are leveled off or peter out; fury subsides to an empty shout, passion to a smirk, joy to a grunt of pleasure, hatred to a nasty jibe. This happens partly because he does have to exert much control – and partly because of fear.

He fears reprisal; he fears (and aggrandizes) authority; he fears being hurt and rejected. He fears failure, without recognition that his goals, ambitions and expectations of himself and others are grandiose. He rejects limitations but becomes frightened of the unbounded. He loosens his ties to other people, becomes detached and "free" – but for nothing. In a certain sense he has been close to the state in panic where he has experienced the terror of his world alone. He has fought his way back, but on the basis of having to find that which he can hate, rebel against or deride.

With all of this flair, this grandiosity, this rapidity of knowingness, this sophistication, lurks a boy – hoping no one will crack down too hard, wishing someone would just take care of him a while longer. He would like so much to remain a kind of Peter Pan. The difficulty lies in the fact that he develops strong tensions and his release from them is again based on the unusual stimulus and indulgence that furthers his dilemma.

The problems he faces and has are to a good measure based on his values or philosophy which makes it possible for him to accept and identify with shallowness, an elite position, with prestige and status – and primarily with the attitude that nothing should matter too much because in the long run it doesn't mean a thing. It is a nihilistic, somewhat anti-human attitude which begins to provide a base for asocial activity. However, the unusual intelligence, the active perceptual processes, the capacity to empathize, the aesthetic needs and his yearning to remain in close contact with others (in spite of his destructiveness) may well make for a positive prognosis – (providing he doesn't escape therapy because of his "quick" running through life situations).

Tested by: Doris S. Bartlett
              924 West End Avenue
              New York 25, N.Y.

This ends this Section, "From First Encounter to Crisis" The "Crisis," which ensued on one fateful day in August 1960, is covered in another Section, entitled "Psychiatric Explorations." I'll pick up with the Chronology in the next Section. But I want to add here, that with the onset of my psychosis, I really felt my life was over. Never again could I deal with life on my own terms. It would have to be on someone else's terms. Sure, after hospitalization, I could still have become a professional, but, as I said elsewhere, it would be with the sufferance and condescension of my peers. I didn't want to live like that, with that much humility. I really felt that the old me had died, had been killed, and there was very little left for me. I didn't like the new me which I saw emerging. To some extent, I still feel that way, that my real life ended at age 24. How I PARTIALLY resolved this issue, this problem, is the topic for later Sections. Read On, Dear Reader!

Interregnum
1963 – 1967

My psychotic episodes, which occurred after the events covered in "From First Encounter to Crisis," are covered in the Section entitled, "Psychiatric Explorations." This includes my first brief hospitalization in Philadelphia State Hospital in 1961, and the major hospitalizations in Manhattan State (on the violent ward there) and Kings Park State in 1963 and then 1967. Almost all the raw stuff is in that latter Section.

This brief Section, entitled "Interregnum," will deal with my interesting experiences in the period between the major psychotic breakdowns, 1963-1967. The Manhattan State hospitalization had made me a little less guarded. Strangely enough, I was somewhat more sociable. Do I have to thank the psychoanalysis for that, too? I don't want to give the psychiatrists too much credit. For the most part, they had really messed me up. Perhaps, the answer for my new sociability is that "Misery loves company."

Manhattan State Hospital, in 1963, trained us for and set us up as social workers in the NYC Department of Welfare (Social Services). This wasn't a very inspiring job, but it paid the rent. We worked in the field, interviewing prospective welfare recipients, and then writing up their cases. I made a couple of friends here, too, including one John Sinclair. I moved in with him and his girlfriend and was off the street. I stayed with the welfare job for about a year, but didn't like it. I left when I secured a job as a computer programmer (primitive early punched card computers), but I didn't like this, either. I left after three months.

THEN I landed a dream job, right up my alley. The American Institute of Physics, which publishes *The Physical Review* and *The Physical Review Letters*, the top academic physics journals in the country, and also translations of Russian physics journals, hired me to write précis of the academic physics articles for distribution to newspaper, radio and television journalists. The job was in AIP's Public Relations Department and my boss was Eugene Kone, Director of Public Relations. Kone was a good man and liked my work.

Now, I didn't know that much physics. With Kone's knowledge, I arranged on my own to interview Columbia U. physics graduate students, getting them to explain each article to me. I paid the students $10/hour out of my own pocket and taped the interviews. With this start, it was easy to write smashing précis. Everybody thought I was very ingenious.

I dealt on the phone and in correspondence with astronauts and Nobel prize winners, as well as top journalists like Walter Sullivan, then Science Editor at the TIMES. I made $150/week, then $160/week, not a bad salary at the time, in 1967. Coffee was still 10 cents a cup that year. I had a ball at AIP. I even went to The American Physical Society convention in Washington, DC. President Lyndon Johnson was at the banquet and passed directly by our table.

My spirits were so high (too high, it turned out) that I made a large collage on the bulletin board behind my desk, with all sorts of interesting stuff and people on it. I only remember now that I put up Twiggy (the model) and Lord Curzon, Viceroy of India, in his viceregal robes.

I rented a two-bedroom apartment at 600 West 111th Street, in a nice prewar (WWII) building for $180/month, advertised in the *Times* for a roommate, and found J. Walton Parker, a congenial business executive (purchasing agent) who moved in and paid half the rent. My career was progressing, I had a decent, roomy apartment, and I was to acquire a pretty girlfriend. It seems I had everything I wanted. What could go wrong? A lot did. And I couldn't see it coming.

Then, at a New Year's party, 1966, in the West Village, I met two Vassar graduates who would be important in my life. The party was given by Sally Wood, Vassar grad, graduated some year in the 60s; I'm not sure which. Sally was the daughter of a Brooklyn dentist and herself an aspiring computer programmer. Sally was a very pleasant girl, but she was built like a fullback. She wasn't successful with men and this was to take a toll on her. Lack of success with the opposite sex can get to you. I know. I'd not enjoyed a woman for six years, as of this date. And I was miserable about this. This was, of course, before I began patronizing the local brothels, which helped a lot.

More about my relations with Sally later. Also at the party was Sally's classmate, Rachel Chouxfleur. Rachel and I hit it off right away. This was my first success with a woman since my post-graduation Swarthmore conquests. I had waited ten years for this, until I guess, I matured a little, in appearance at least. Anyway, I took Rachel home to her little ground floor studio at 55 Horatio Street, and we made passionate (lusty, anyway) love while a snowstorm raged outside I'll never forget that night.

Rachel was attractive and intelligent and a good companion. She was unfortunately, very flat chested (like Twiggy, incidentally). Rachel's nipples were different sizes. One side looked like a fried egg. I guess it's cruel to say that, but it's the truth. She wore see-through Rudy Gernreich (designer) soft plastic bras, which I later learned Rudy had thoughtfully designed especially for flat-chested women. I was unhappy over the flat chest, but I never said a word. I was very grateful for Rachel's kindness and companionship. We were together all the way up to Major Psychotic Break #2, and we saw a lot of each other (Platonically) afterwards.

Rachel had had a remarkable assortment of lovers. Recognizing her limitations, Rachel had teamed up with a midget and then a paraplegic. Also, there had been an investigative reporter (for the *Reporter* magazine) and a tennis pro. All this was very colorful. Then there was me, the not completely rehabilitated schizophrenic. Rachel had made us all very happy.

In March 1967, Rachel became pregnant, by me, she swore. Rachel had always used the rhythm method of birth control and thought she had mastered it. But she was wrong. I immediately offered to marry her, and she said yes, and the next day she changed her mind. She wanted to go to law school. I think she loved me, but, knowing me, she probably thought the baby would have two heads. My mind was already slipping a little, but I was able to arrange a safe illicit abortion at a clinic in the Luquillo Mountains of Puerto Rico. Roe vs. Wade was still in the future in 1967. The abortion itself cost $200, a substantial sum at the time. We needed $600 in all, what with air fare and other expenses. I paid $200, Rachel paid $200 and Rachel's parents paid $200. Rachel said it went well and she commented on the attractive Spanish tiles on the walls of the clinic. At the moment of the operation, I went into the interfaith chapel on the main floor of the United Nations Secretariat, just across the street from AIP on West 45th Street, to contemplate.

Rachel came back, we had to abstain from sexual intercourse for about three weeks. At that time, Rachel was reluctant to satisfy me by performing fellatio on me, but later on, she came around to doing this. NEVER, however, would she swallow the cum. She always insisted that I alert her at the last moment so she could withdraw her mouth. I had to wait for the "professionals" to have that complete service performed for me. Nowadays, the women of my acquaintance are more liberal. My models, or at least the few of them that I've later become very close friends with (one is now my Executor), tell me they have no qualms about swallowing the cum for their boyfriends (but not for me – I've never really tried very hard to seduce a model, at least while she was posing. It seems unfair to do this.). And, to allay any uneasiness you may have, dear reader, let me say that I never had such intimate discussions with a model until she had posed for me 8 or 10 times, and when we had become quite close.

So Rachel and I planned our next move. We decided we would go to Europe, the first time there for either of us. My idea. I offered to be a big man and foot the whole bill, which was not a good idea. I signed up for my first credit card to pay for it, thinking my position was secure. It was, until I lost my mind again.

Work was going O.K. and we went ahead and made the arrangements. We flew to Europe in June 1967 on a Pan Am 707. I had tried to arrange a helicopter flight from the top of the then Pan Am Building (now Met Life), after a farewell party with many new friends in the Copter Club in the Pan Am penthouse, but the weather was bad. It was too windy for the helicopter. So, after the party, we went downstairs with our luggage and took a taxi to JFK Airport (or was it still called Idlewild in those days?). We told the taxi driver what had happened with the helicopter, so he said he would try to make the taxi ride "as much like a helicopter ride as he could." New Yorkers are all crazy. Marvelous!

In Europe we visited Florence, Venice, Rome, Paris and London. Really a "Grand Tour." We visited all the museums and chief sights. We dined in cheap bistros and trattorias. We stayed in inexpensive hotels and B&Bs. We traveled on the fine railroads some of the time, rather than flying, so we saw some of the countryside. It's interesting to note that, in 1967, the Italian peasants still carried their live chickens with them into the 2nd class carriages. Best of all on our trip, we made love in every city we visited.

Florence and Venice were my favorite cities. The people there have such dignity and pride. The extreme black-and-white geometric architectural facades on some of the landmarks in Firenze (Florence in Italian), like the Duomo of Santa Maria del Fiore, or the Baptistery, resonated with something extreme that was developing in my own psyche. This resonance was thrilling but it contributed to Major Breakdown #2. In the psychoanalysis, I tried to get down to the very basics, the very bottom of things, the primordial elements. This boiled down to black and white, Boolean algebra, and simplistic elemental modern architecture (not the imaginative stuff like Frank Lloyd Wright), Mondrian, no cuffs on my trousers, and so on. All this, including the Renaissance architecture in Florence, put a great strain on me.

I loved Teatro Fenice in Venice, where we saw and heard Monteverdi's *Vespro della Beata Vergine 1610.* ("Vespers of the Blessed Virgin of 1610"). Fenice later burned down but I'm happy to say it has finally been restored. The original theater dated from the 16th or 17th century. Venice smells everywhere of fish and the sea but the smell is not unpleasant. I rather like it. I often think now about Rousseau's comment concerning the women, and the courtesans, of Venice (Venezia). I mentioned this comment at the very beginning of this tale.

I've been to Europe a dozen or twenty times since then (also to the USSR a couple of times and Japan), several times on business trips as a journalist, also sometimes to visit the legal brothels throughout the Continent, and later on pleasure trips to the naturist resorts in Greece (6 times so far) and France (3 times just to Cap d'Agde). Sometimes these days the accommodations and travel arrangements are much grander. But nothing will ever compare with the thrill of that first trip to Europe with Rachel, even though I lost my mind at the end of it. Rachel was my first long-term lover who had a mind and a sensitivity I could appreciate. Along with my successes at AIP and in my home arrangements, I could almost feel like a normal, successful young man. Too much so. Too successful, as it worked out.

My current good friend, the writer, journalist and poet, Penelope Karageorge, who has helped edit this manuscript, asked me to say something about Rachel, about what finally happened to her. She worked for the City (or was it the State?) for her whole working career, first as a Social Services (Welfare) Caseworker and Caseworker Supervisor, and then, after law school, as a lawyer in public housing administration. Her job was to go to Court to throw people out of their homes in city projects, mostly for drug addiction and/or nonpayment of rent. Not a very desirable job, to my way of thinking.

I was very unhappy that she couldn't do something more creative and rewarding in her career.

But she stayed with it and earned a huge pension at age 55. She left work and dropped out of sight, dropping all her old acquaintances, including me, because she wanted to start a "New Life." Now, I understand she travels all the time, in Europe and elsewhere, and lives well. "Living well is the best revenge," somebody said, but who wants to need revenge? Anyway, Rachel and I have the same lawyer (Rachel directed me to him), and I could get a message to her, if I wanted to. But I don't really care to do that, given her change in attitude. Maybe I should say that perhaps things worked out pretty well for her, after all.

Incidentally, Rachel Chouxfleur never married. None of the (ONLY) three women I ever proposed to ever married. The other two members of the threesome were Joan Bennett, about whom much is said later, and Michelle Dillon, A French woman I met when she was a young secretary at the United Nations. Michelle and I went out, off and on, for 20 or more years. But she wouldn't go to bed with anybody. The story was that, when she was quite young in Paris, someone had got her drunk and forced himself on her. Apparently, Michelle never got over this. Maybe it was all a story. Anyway, I offered to marry her, if she would give me a trial period of sex for six months. She said, "my terms were too hard," and said no. And, as I said, she never married anyone else, either. All this says something about my choice of women. It's that I have always been single and all the most important women in life were single, not drawn at all to marriage.

I want to say a few words about the other young woman that I met at that party in the West Village. Sally Wood was a good friend for a long time, but she had a lot of strikes against her. She was not successful with men. Worse, she'd had psychiatric problems, and the particular tranquilizers they had given her had caused both her ankles to pronate (pronation is the technical term) or turn over, so that she had to walk on the sides of her feet. This made her very awkward and caused her a lot of misery. She was hospitalized for psychiatric problems several times.

She did get a good job as a programmer, and for a time did very well financially, earning $13,500 a year, a great deal of money in 1967. I wasn't physically attracted to her initially, but when I was sick and wandering the streets, she took me in and asked me to sleep with her. I tried, but it was impossible to penetrate her deeply enough. I thought the problem might be me, but later on, another friend, Maurice Sylvester, told me he had failed in the attempt with her for the same reason.

It was probably some simple gynecological problem, an unperforated tough hymen, or something like that. But it made Sally feel terrible. Why couldn't her psychiatrist or gynecologist do something? Perhaps Sally was too embarrassed to talk about it. It was very sad.

All these factors that I have mentioned led to repeated psychiatric hospitalizations for Sally. At one point, she very severely slashed her wrists in the bathtub. She was found, before it was too late, in a pool of blood. Her wrists became covered with thick, deep scars. The doctors were at a loss as to what to do for her. She was an intelligent, even spirited, woman. She wanted Romance and Love. Finally, some doctor suggested she get a dog. This calmed Sally down. She had a creature on which to lavish her pent-up love and affection. What a pathetic resolution to her problems! But I haven't seen her lately. Her particular psychological problems disturb me, when I meet her. Last I heard, she was living alone (with the dog) and was reasonably calm. Probably Stoic, like me.

Sally helped me when I was wandering the streets. She bought a nice overcoat for me from Altman's (a now defunct Manhattan department store). I had to trade it in for credit slips to eat a few good meals in the store's Carolina Tea Room, which kept my body and mind together for a while. I'll never forget Sally. Through her I met Rachel. And there were lots of other good things about Sally. But I still can't stand to be around her. Her psychological problems impinge on my psychological problems.

.So, to get back to the chronology, the conclusion of this document is that in London, the last stop on Rachel's and my itinerary in Europe, I began to hallucinate and have disordered thoughts again. I wandered off from the B&B, got lost, and ended up sleeping all night in a London park. Two huge London Bobbies confronted me but let me go. I had lost my money. The ticket seller in the Underground was sympathetic and let me ride free back to the B&B. That wouldn't happen in NYC.

Anyway, Rachel was waiting for me. She'd refrained from calling the police or the Consulate, because she hoped I'd find my way back on my own. This was a good thing. There would have been all sorts of complications if she'd done so, and I didn't want to end up in an English mental hospital. Rachel immediately sensed what had happened. I was speaking strangely, disconnectedly, non sequiturs, and talking about my many hallucinations. So Rachel just shepherded me to the plane and back to NYC.

Back in NYC, I tried unsuccessfully to go back to work at AIP, but I was too far gone. The frightening, amazing story of my last days at AIP, my unfortunate life on the streets, and my final hospitalization are told elsewhere in this document.

(Very Slow) Recovery and Renewal
1967-1989

It was nearly Christmas 1967. I had just been released from Kings Park State (Psychiatric) Hospital. Readjustment (again) was very difficult. But I didn't sleep outdoors. As I've described elsewhere, some friend directed me to MANPOWER, INC., an agency then located near City Hall, and they gave me work as a day laborer. Some of the work was very light, some was heavy. I couldn't do the heaviest work. I didn't have the shoes and other equipment for it. Or the strength, after what I'd been through.

So, with the few dollars from the day work, I was able to rent a private cubicle, the top of it covered with chicken wire, in a flop house, the Comet Hotel at 80 Bowery, for $1.25 a night. Beds without any privacy were $1.00 a night, but I splurged and spent the extra quarter. The place was clean and had hot showers. It wasn't so bad. I'd seen much worse.

I carried on this way for a few months. I remember walking a lot of cold winter streets. Throughout all of these years, I had become something of a tramp. This stayed with me in later life, when I was physically more comfortable, because for years (not so much any more), I often dreamed of desolate, depopulated, street scenes. And I dreamed of losing the few possessions I had on my person (in the dream). This was, though, just about as it had been in real life. Minimal survival, but survival! Independence!

One lucky day in mid-1968, I wandered into a MARBORO BOOKSHOP (This was a chain of five or six small bookstores that then existed in Manhattan. There was also a mail order business.) I was lucky. I was directed to the main office, located on West 8th Street in the heart of Greenwich Village. Even though I had not yet learned to be quiet about my recurring mental illness, General Manager Jon Zito hired me at once. I was first sent to the 57th Street store, where I worked for a while for Manager Paul Frank, a Jewish escapee from Hitler through India, who was then about 65. Paul told us tales of how he visited the brothels of Bombay on his way from Hitler's Germany to America. Paul still lives, near me in Morningside Heights, or SOHA (SOuth of HArlem). I often see him on the street, with his attendant. He must be at least 100 now.

I then worked for a time in the MARBORO on Third Avenue adjacent to Bloomingdale's. I worked the evening shift. The Night Manager at the time was Liam

Gannon, an Irish actor who had not had a very successful career but who profited for years from the residuals he received from TV ads he'd done, particularly when he played a priest in an Irish Spring soap ad. Liam was friendly and did not preach very much Irish Catholicism to me. I enjoyed working for him. This was still 1968. I was 32 years old.

Noteworthy during my stay at this location was the afternoon when a 55-year-old electrician, working in the shop and hurrying down the aisle, tripped in the aisle while I was ordering books from a book salesman, knocked loose a blood clot, had a stroke and dropped dead on the floor right in front of us. In the space of two minutes, his face turned red, then white and then blue, and then he was gone. I'd seen death before, working in the hospital, but never quite so suddenly. Paul Frank, who was now the Manager at this location, sent me across the street to a Blarney Stone Irish bar, for a drink.

Also at that location, I began reading C.S. Forester *Lord Hornblower* novels again, fiction about the British sea captain in the Napoleonic Wars who had overcome every obstacle to victory. I'd read the Hornblower novels as a child, and had early on used Captain Hornblower as a life role model. I began to do this again. He was altogether empirical and rational. As I've said before, I also wanted to avoid surprises, mysteries and epiphanies in my life. On my dinner break, I would sit at a desk in the store basement, reading Hornblower and eating cheap fried fish from a neighborhood takeout. This combination was soothing.

Finally, in late 1968, I was transferred to the main store at 56 West 8th Street. Here, I was quickly made Night Manager, in sole charge of four or five clerks and a security guard between 4:00 p.m. and Midnight. This was sometimes taxing, as I still suffered from a few hallucinations. Impressions of telepathy, impressions of messages being projected into my mind by passing cars, and so on. But I was able to recognize the hallucinations for what they were, and thus I could discount them.

Of the four or five clerks, several were American homosexuals, several were East Indians, all Gujaratis from Bombay, all with the last name Sanjay, and there were a few assorted others. The usual security guard was Mr. Pinto, a West Indian. The Sanjays were all honest and did not steal from the till. I would sometimes find them in the back room, reading erotic magazines covered (the magazines) with their cum.

Couldn't they have been a little more discreet? Other than that, they were no problem. They were saving money to open newsstands or smoke shops, and waiting for their new wives (arranged marriages, by their parents) to arrive.

The Sanjays taught me a few hundred words of Hindi (the national language, along with English, of India. To learn their own native language, Gujarati, would have been of little use to me.) We would use the Hindi in the shop when shoplifters were detected. Someone would shout, "Admi Dekko," which means, "Watch the Man!" Soon the shoplifters caught on, and would start shouting "Admi Dekko" to each other. It was very amusing!

One of the Sanjays, Kanti, was more original. He started acting in sex films (porno). He would give us interesting reports on his experiences.

Among the other clerks, some of the homosexuals made me nervous. They would ask such penetrating, intimate questions. There was one straight, white clerk Gerry Grant, who, it turned out, was a small time drug dealer. He was later killed, with his wife, in an auto accident, while fleeing (half out of his mind) New

York State's (Nelson Rockefeller's) Draconian drug laws.

But Gerry Grant did one good thing for me. Still in 1968, he introduced me to one of his wife's friends, Joan Bennett. Joan was an attractive schoolteacher. We went to bed right away, and continued to do so, off and on, between fights, until 1975. We have remained good Platonic friends (again, between occasional fights) until the present day. We traveled all over North America together. There will be more about Joan later. I want to finish with MARBORO BOOKSHOPS first.

The Day Manager was my immediate boss. We worked well together. His name was George Spath. He was married and a photographer. He was also an Army veteran. Later on, after I left MARBORO in 1974, George contracted a neurological disease, which left his feet, and then his shins, without any sensation. George became very bitter and left his wife and moved into a cheap hotel. I don't know what finally became of him. In later years, I tried to contact him, perhaps to help him, but he refused all contact with everybody. Very sad.

In 1968, while at MARBORO, I began my Christmas Eve Dinner tradition. We would meet for dinner in a classical old Italian restaurant in the Village. These dinners, Dutch treat, were followed by a visit to Ascension Episcopal Church in Greenwich Village, just for the carol service. I have continued this tradition up to the present day. 2010 was the 43rd meeting without a break. I hope to make it 50 or more. All this is described in a separate section, "Holding to Tradition (?)."

Also, in 1968, I met my first post-breakdown friend, Ralph Bentley. Ralph wandered into the MARBORO near Bloomingdale's, struck up a conversation, and we agreed to meet later for a drink at the then nearby "Sign of the Dove." We hit it off and became good friends.

Ralph sprang from a wealthy St. Louis family (breweries and Red aniline dyes, not the deadly ones, he assured me). He had graduated from the University of Chicago, with middling grades (about like mine). He had matriculated at The Polytechnic Institute of Brooklyn (Brooklyn Poly) for a Doctorate in Physics, but never finished, because, being temperamental, he had fought with his academic committee. Ralph WAS temperamental, proud and touchy, but he'd never lost his mind, due perhaps to his well-rounded sophisticated upbringing. He was prepared to anticipate and deal with the problems. At least that's how it looked to me, coming from where I was coming from.

Ralph's family didn't help him when he started out in New York. For a while, he drove a taxi. And he's not a good driver. Then, when I first knew him, he was working as a computer programmer for about $15,000/year, in 1968. Ralph's father had died young, before I knew Ralph. Then, in I'm not sure what year, his mother Elsie Bentley, passed away. Elsie and I had become friends. Ralph wanted company at the funeral, so he flew me out to St. Louis with him. Then I learned that he had inherited two million dollars.

Ralph immediately stopped working (he hated working for bosses, because he was so touchy and temperamental). He proceeded to live on the income, and to do his experimental researches in "Classical" Physics. Ralph did not think much had been accomplished in Physics since Newton. Ralph believed the speed of light was not an absolute limit. He proceeded to carry on elaborate experiments, with expensive equipment, to support his ideas. He even started a journal, *The Journal of Classical Physics,* to promote his ideas. Among his supporters and fund sources were the Creationists. I did lament this. Anyway,

Ralph made our mutual friend, Otto Koch (biographical sketch much later in this document), the nominal Editor of the Journal. I wouldn't do it. Too retrograde.

Despite all these very conservative inclinations, Ralph was a very good friend. He had an informal society of friends, which I was invited to join. There were about thirty of us, men and women (maybe more later), and we gave singles parties, entertained and dated each other, kept each other informed about outside singles events and parties, and kept ourselves going in hostile Manhattan. I can't recall what we called ourselves. Maybe it was "The Group" (Mary McCarthy, please excuse me.).

There was another aggregation, similar to our "Group," with which we maintained ties. This was the "Circuit," consisting also of about thirty people, in this case mostly ethnically Jewish. The "Group" and the "Circuit" exchanged invitations all the time. Our "Group" had members of all nationalities, including many Greeks, WASPS and a good number of ethnic Jews.

So the "Group" and the "Circuit" kept me active and amused, and kept me from thinking too deeply about anything, until, in 1974, Otto Koch took me to my first brothel, Patricia's. This was my introduction to professional, satisfying sex. It became no longer necessary to dance attendance on the lot of women I met socially, mostly neurotic 30-year-old women. I had the real thing. But all my experiences with the (New York) brothels are covered elsewhere, in the first Section of this Memoir, entitled, "To Begin a Tale."

Back to Ralph Bentley. After Ralph came into his millions, he helped me considerably, in a financial way. But that help began in the early 80s, and we haven't reached that point yet. Ralph did other things for me, too, early on. He taught me to dress acceptably to go to "Social" occasions. Following his model, I bought a blue blazer and gray slacks. With a shirt and tie, it's standard "Eton" garb. You could go anywhere with it, even to meet the Queen of England. I wear a modified version of this outfit every time I go out. However, I have now replaced the shirt and tie with a black crew or turtleneck, as befits the artist in me. It's just another version of the uniform.

But Ralph could be very touchy at times. Much later, in 2010, Ralph refused to speak to me for 10 months because I had inadvertently given away his age at a Thanksgiving party. He also would be peremptory with store clerks, taxi drivers, and other people he met in his world.

But Ralph was my friend. And Ralph became my steady beer drinking companion. After locking up MARBORO and dismissing the help every Midnight, I would meet Ralph at the infamous, now defunct, Cedar Tavern, on University Place and 12th Street, for a couple of hours of beer drinking and conversation. Sometimes supper. Ralph and I pissed ten years away in that place. Now I regret the lost time, but at the time, it kept me going.

The Cedar Tavern, at its earlier location on 8th Street and University Place, had been the hangout of the most famous of the Abstract Expressionists, including Jackson Pollock and Willem de Kooning. Al Pacino also held court there. By the 1970s, though, most of this Glory was in the past. The Cedar finally, at its 12th Street location, was mostly populated by paparazzi and flacks. They talked a lot, but none of it was serious conversation any more.

Another "treat" for me at this time was frequent shore dinners (actually, a fried mixed seafood platter) with two martinis at the Howard Johnson's Restaurant then just across Sixth Avenue from the bookstore. The meal was greasy, but I loved it. And, with the two martinis, I would fly through the remaining hours from about 7:00 p.m. to Midnight, when I would lock up the store, send the staff home, and repair to the Cedar Tavern to meet Ralph Bentley and my other drinking buddies. I had a better capacity for alcohol in those days. My stomach and my head can't take it any more. And I've started to think about my health (dying healthy?). Actually, I never was a really heavy drinker. The martinis were occasional then and never now.

On ONE occasion at the Cedar, a young woman invited me to go to her home for sex, late at night. She left first, and I came along a little later to the appointed address. The girl was lying in the bed with her legs spread, clothed only in a peignoir, and I was surprised and shocked. Too available. I backed out the door and never saw the young woman again. Other than that incident, I was never very successful at picking up women in bars, at least then. And anyway, nowadays, with AIDS everywhere, it's too dangerous to mix it up with women you meet in bars, women that you don't know anything about.

#

That about covers my time at MARBORO. I still thought I wanted to be a science editor and writer, and I regularly answered ads in *The New York Times* Classified. Finally, in 1974, I was offered a job as Associate Editor of a small magazine located in Valley Stream, Long Island, NY. The magazine was *The Data Communications User*. So I ended my marking time at MARBORO, we had a little party with the Gujaratis and the homosexuals, and I was off to my new job. I'll pick this up later. Right now, I want to begin to describe my long relationship with Joan Bennett, which began while I was at MARBORO.

As I mentioned earlier, I was set up with Joan by Gerald (Gerry) Grant, a small-time drug pusher who was later killed with his wife in an auto crash, fleeing Nelson Rockefeller's Draconian drug laws. Joan was a friend of Gerry's wife. Both women were schoolteachers. Joan had had some of the same psychiatric experiences as I had. But she stuck to her Civil Service job, eventually earning a very substantial pension. Joan couldn't handle classroom teaching, she couldn't discipline the students, so she switched to Special Education, and taught the developmentally or emotionally disabled on a one-on-one basis in their homes. Some of these homes were in NYC Housing projects, and Joan was assaulted in the halls and on the stairs more than once. On one occasion, she was thrown down a flight of stairs and her nose was broken.

Joan also had to spend a good deal of her own money on teaching materials. The Board of Education was very stingy in this respect. But all of this was compensated for in the great pension she received, which enabled her to buy (much later, perhaps 1988), with my help, a cooperative apartment in Morningside Gardens, where I have lived since 1983. I think I can say that I've helped a lot of my friends, at least in little ways, even when I was not totally sane. But I'm getting ahead of myself. Back to Joan and me in 1968.

We made love at once. Some of Joan's constraints on our lovemaking were a little onerous to me. For some reason, she did not want to take birth control bills. So I always had to wear a condom, and besides that, pump her up with a spermicidal douche before coitus. It made things rather less romantic for me. To top that, in fellatio, she also wouldn't swallow the cum. This irked me, but I must say, despite these reservations, we got on pretty well in bed.

At the time, I was living in one of Maurice Sylvester's furnished rooms near Columbia U. I lived in these places, off and on for 15 years, instead of paying high rent for an apartment. I saved my money for concerts, dining out and travel. I remember that when I first rented a room from Maurice in 1963, the rent was $9/week. Now such places are $700 - $800/month. New York real estate is so crazy and exploitative. Big Dog Eat Little Dog. If I didn't have my Morningside Gardens cooperative apartment, I would still need to live that way. Maurice was a strange character. I'll get back to his story and my relationship with him later. But right now, back to Joan and me.

Joan would visit me in the little room and we would make love. I had my marginal bookstore job and a passable girl friend, so I guess I should have been content. But I was not. I wanted a better life. Of course, in 1968 – 1974, the bookstore years, I was still slowly recovering from my breakdowns. I was still hallucinating sometimes, but I recognized the hallucinations for what they were, and could discount them. The hallucinations finally ended about 1974 or 1975. It had been as if my nerves were totally exposed, and I had to rebuild my "shell" or "character armor" before I could effectively deal with Reality again.

Of course, some might say, the conclusion of a successful analysis might have included the ability to function WITH nerves somewhat exposed, so as to be more sensitive and passionate and "tuned in to the universe." Maybe so, but I wanted no part of it. The religious and other hallucinations, and the uncontrollable trembling and shaking, even if it all was "thrilling," were not what I wanted. I wasn't prepared to be totally dysfunctional for 30 or 40 years in order to arrive at some "emotional cure." I liked myself as I was, neurotic or not. At least, I decided I liked myself better when I saw what the alternative was.

To make up for our rather plodding lives, Joan and I saved our limited funds and traveled quite a bit. First, we went locally, to Atlantic City and Block Island. Then we became more ambitious, and went to the province of Quebec twice, to Montreal and Quebec City and also to a resort in the Laurentian Mountains. I must say we were more like comrades in adversity, not lovers (notwithstanding the sex). But the resort was very fine. It was really a ski resort. The resort made most its money in the Winter, but they kept the place open in the

Summer, and the rates were very low then. The food was very good, French or at least Quebecois cooking, and also there were lots of Summer resort activities. I especially enjoyed the horseback riding, at $1/hour.

One little treat I gave Joan at that time in Quebec was a pousse café. That's a liqueur drink made from three or more different cordial liqueurs, each of a different color and specific gravity. If, in making the drink, you carefully decant each liqueur down the inside of the drinking glass, the liqueurs will form varicolored layers and not mix. I believe it was my friend Dr. Sergei Salomon who taught me how to make it. A pousse-café is very pretty but a little recherché. Joan liked it, the maitre d' was impressed when I told him how to do it, and it added to our evening. But the women I know now would laugh at me if I offered them a pousse café today. Have we all become so jaded?

Joan and I also went for a couple of weeks to Mexico. We took the usual first time tourist route, flying to Mexico City, staying a week, then a comfortable bus via Taxco to Acapulco, then a week in Acapulco, then flying home to New York City. I should say, that on all these trips, Joan paid her own share, which I greatly appreciated. I remember lying on the beach at the resort in Acapulco, listening to the Vietnam War news broadcast over a loudspeaker from the hotel, and thinking how lucky I was not to be there. I hated the Vietnam War, thought it was stupid politics, as I now hate the current Iraq War. Foolish war-making politicians, causing all kinds of suffering.

Joan agrees with me in opposing these unjust wars and we think now that her phone at her retirement home is tapped because she gives a lot of money to the (Quaker) Friends Committee on National Legislation, which vehemently opposes the Iraq War. Also, when she was an undergraduate at Cornell, she was a Trotskyite. So today, there are a great many clicks, buzzes and whistles on her phone line, which I get nowhere else, and we suspect an FBI tap.

The final trip that I took with Joan when we were lovers was a windjammer cruise on the "revenue cutter" "Shenandoah." This was my idea. I was very enthusiastic about going to sea on an exact duplicate of a partly square-rigged 1830s (?) revenue cutter. There was no engine. Propulsion was by sails alone. The only concessions to modernity were modern navigation equipment, including radar, for safety, and a few electric lights. Otherwise, everything was exactly as it had been in the 1830s. (If the ship was becalmed, the captain could put out the motorized whaleboat, which could tow us, but the Captain rarely did this.) The entire voyage was quite an experience.

The "Shenandoah's" homeport was Vineyard Haven on Martha's Vineyard. On the cruise, we visited and went ashore in the evening at Block Island, Point Judith, Newport and several other places which I cannot now remember. We were rowed ashore and back, late at night, in the dory. We had one big storm, which the cutter navigated nicely, except I got seasick. I didn't care. I thought it was thrilling. Joan did not get seasick.

Oh yes, the food! It was wonderful. The cabins, for 29 passengers and nine crew, were the size of horizontal phone booths, but there was a great salon, with stained glass windows, where we ate. The New England chowders and stews (oyster, etc.) were among the best foods I remember ever eating, and they were prepared in the tiniest of galleys. It was perhaps 1974 or 1975 when I took Joan on that ill-fated windjammer cruise. I loved it, but Joan hated it, and blamed me for her terrible experience. She broke up with me about this time, partly because she was mad over the windjammer. I should have known better than to take her on such a rough trip. I knew she loved luxury. But I like roughing it sometimes. Anyway, the relationship was over, at least physically, though we became very good Platonic friends again later on for many years, up to and including the present (with some more breakups along the way). Joan helped me a lot financially later on, but I'll get to that later.

At about the time of the first breakup with Joan, my friend Otto Koch, discussed earlier, introduced me to the pleasures of the New York brothels. This was really quite wonderful, a selection of pretty 18-year-old girls who would do anything you would want, in a sexual way. But I have discussed all this in the first Section of this Memoir, entitled, "To Begin a Tale." Anyway, the brothels occupied me from 1974 to 1987, when I quit going because of fear of contracting AIDS, which by then was just becoming an epidemic. Well, with great trepidation, I had an AIDS check, and I was O.K. I've stayed away from commercial sex since then, totally (in New York, anyway – I've had a couple of forays since then to the legal, inspected brothels of Nevada and Europe). Too bad! I really enjoyed this part of the New York scene. And I'm fairly confident that the statute of limitations has run out on any penalties for my legal malfeasance, which ended in 1987.

#

As I said earlier, I left MARBORO in 1974 to become an Associate Editor on *The Data Communications User*, a computer management magazine with editorial offices in Valley Stream, Long Island, New York. I worked out of a three-person office. At the time, I thought this was what I wanted out of life. I only learned much later that I could do other things with more zeal and enthusiasm, such as creating my nude photograph portfolio. But the Editor of this small magazine was one Morris Edwards, a youngish Englishman who was married with a pretty wife and two kids and maintained a home in a nice suburb of Boston, I forget now which one. He was very proud of his home and his upscale Mercury car.

Morris was a considerate, intelligent fellow to work for. He could tell when I was writing well and when I wasn't. I had to write about various computer management topics, about which, initially, I knew zilch. But I embarked on a crash-reading course and was soon up to adequate speed. The computers in those days were simpler than the ones we have now, anyway

There was one other person in the office, the Secretary, a pretty young married woman. We got along fairly well, but I was occasionally tactless in dealing with the Secretary, sometimes giving her too much work at once. I could never completely master corporate office etiquette.

Once a year, we covered the big INTERFACE data communications show, which the year I was there, was held in New Orleans. Our office may have had some role in running and managing the show. I've forgotten the details. But there were thousands of people there. I don't know how we could have had the resources to manage it.

While in New Orleans, the editorial staff was taken to dinner, by the Publisher, to the famous Antoine's. It was very expensive. I still remember that I had *Pompano en Papillote,* fish in a pastry envelope. It was exquisite!

The aforementioned Penelope Karageorge, the writer, on hearing the story of my "Dinner at Antoine's" and of some of my later hosted luxury trips to Europe and beyond as a journalist, has commented on the "Dickensian" contrasts in my life, between absolute squalor and a measure of luxury living. I find the contrast interesting, too. I think it has stimulated me as a writer and artist. But what a price to pay!

To get to my regular workday in Valley Stream, I commuted on the Long Island Rail Road. I remember that I would ride in the smoking car, just to smell the smoke. I had smoked briefly during my first hospitalization, when I was very upset, but I had discontinued the practice, for health reasons, when I felt better. But I still remembered the pleasure it had given me and I liked to smell the smoke in the smoking car (there are no more smoking cars on the LIRR today).

I was making fairly good money for 1974, $14,500 and then $15,000. I took a nice modern studio with a picture window at 145 East 29th Street and began to entertain. Entertaining, and my Eleutheria (means "Liberty" in Demotic Greek) Salons, became very important to me, later on. But I started simple. All this came to an end when the magazine folded in mid-1975, after I'd been there for about a year and a half. I had to give up my nice apartment. First, Rachel Chouxfleur put me up for three months (that was the time limit, and no sex). Then I moved in the famous or infamous Hotel Chelsea on West 23rd Street for a while, and then I had to eat humble pie and move back into one of Maurice Sylvester's furnished rooms again.

The next writing job (1975-1977) was with *Electronic Products* magazine, located in Garden City, Long Island, New York, again on the LIRR, an even longer commute. This magazine was a property of the Cox Broadcasting Empire headquartered in Atlanta, GA. It was my first experience with a really big corporate enterprise. (I learned later that I worked better and fit in better in intellectual environments, like The Columbia University Press and The American Institute of Physics, but all that was lost to me now. I couldn't really shine in corporate settings.)

I had been hired by the Editor, Bill Giusino, who was a dark complexioned Italian (Moorish blood) from Sicily. He was the first person I ever knew who wore expensive, custom tailored suits. Bill was very stylish. He was a good editor and a good friend to me, but he was fired by the Publisher for his sexual peccadilloes in the office. The new Editor, Frank Egan, and I did not get along as well. He eventually fired me. But the experiences with *The Data Communications User* and *Electronic Products* had substantially improved my command of the craft of writing.

But before I was fired, my new friend, Allan Brown, a Brit who was Second Secretary (a junior ambassadorial rank) in the British Mission on Third Avenue and 52nd Street in New York City, arranged for me to travel, all expenses paid by the British and French governments, on a three-week tour of the respective electronics industries in those two countries.

It was quite a tour. For two weeks in Britain, I had a private car and driver, and a pretty U.K. Foreign Service guide with a hyphenated name, Susan Smyth-Postlethwaite, shepherding me to all my various appointments at electronics companies around the country. I toured (London and environs) companies with Susan, furiously taking notes and pictures, and then we embarked on our tour to the South of England (Brighton, I think, among other places), and then on to the North and Manchester. We stayed and ate in lovely, upscale English inns. The food rated with the best I'd ever eaten, once I accustomed myself to handling the seven or eight pieces of silverware on either side of the plate. This was high class English dining. I'll never again subscribe to the myth that English food is bad. This trip included more luxury than I'd ever seen. And this was a

SECOND-CLASS journalist excursion, according to the U.K. Foreign Service.

I believe Susan propositioned me, but I was too backward and scared of what the Foreign Service would think of me if I seduced their guide. It happened like this: after a busy day of junketing, Susan and I were having a drink in a hotel bar. I noticed she was lapping up the scotch, so I suggested she have a double. She quickly said, "If you're trying to get me drunk, I don't mind!" If that wasn't an invitation, I don't know what would be. The lavish pleasures of the rich and successful are enviable, much better than lying in a gutter. But I quickly retreated into silence and then into my hotel room. I had missed another opportunity! And, now that I think about it, the U.K. Foreign Service would probably have thought better of me, if I'd seduced their escort.

Except for that missed opportunity, I had a wonderful time on the trip, that my new friend Allan Brown had arranged. Alan Brown was a big, burly fellow who had been an officer in the Royal Army. He was about 45, and had accepted the fact that he might never reach Ambassadorial rank. But he did make First Secretary, before he retired, years later. I had met him at some U.K. Government function for British industry, given in Manhattan. We took to each other right away. He lived in a nice apartment maintained by the British Government on East 72nd Street.

Allan was my first and only contact with any diplomatic or foreign service. This was important to me. It's a part of society I knew little about. I valued Allan as a friend.

Allan was married to his second wife at the time and had a son by his first wife, who (the son) was in boarding school. Allan liked to entertain, as I did. I went to many drunken parties at his place (although I didn't drink much). He came to the parties I gave, when I had a place to give them. Sometimes, incidentally, I would rent artists' lofts, so I could give a party. Allan later married a third wife, whom I didn't like His second wife, after the divorce, stayed in NYC, working at the Libyan UN Mission, while Allan moved on to other assignments in other countries. Allan Hird's second wife later propositioned me, but I wasn't interested.

The story of my relationship with Allan Brown had a sad ending. Although for years he arranged trips for me and took me out to lunch in fine French restaurants, we finally had a falling out. I was traveling in Spain one year, much later, and Allan offered to put me up in his digs in Madrid. It was there I met his third wife. This was during the Soviet era. His new wife was a Georgian (Stalin's birthplace) and she had managed a difficult escape from the USSR police state. I didn't find her at all feminine. In fact, she was big and tough.

At dinner with the two of them, one night in a Madrid restaurant, I casually suggested that, "Communism, AT LEAST IN THEORY, is a humane philosophy." That was it! I never heard from either of them, or the British Foreign Service, again. I'm sure that now I have a terrible security dossier with the U.K. Government, as I probably do with the U.S. Government. So what? I'm rather proud of that fact. I learned later that over 100 million Americans have security dossiers with the U.S. Government. A badge of honor! But still, the incident with Allan and his wife taught me that comments that seem innocent enough to me, are terribly offensive to some other people. But then, you can't please all the people all the time. I think Lincoln said that. I think it's better not to try to (please everybody all the time).

After about two years, the *Electronic Products* job ended when Frank Egan fired me. I wasn't very happy there, anyway. My coworkers didn't think very deeply, and I had no luck with the girls on the staff.

But there was the problem of earning a living. I guess I went on Unemployment Insurance for a while, and then I was hired by Lorry's Bookstore, a technical bookstore then facing City Hall Park. In a short while, I was Night Manager again, and I hung out here for about a year and a half (1977 – 1979). I don't remember anything especially notable about the place. More marking time for me!

Next, I passed seven months working for The Association for Computing Machinery (ACM) as a section editor on their journal, *Communications of the ACM*. This was a highly technical journal that I did not completely understand. But I soldiered through, and was able to do most of the work. About this time, and previously at MARBORO, I suffered from narcolepsy. I just couldn't stay awake. If it hit me on the street, I would have to hurry home and throw myself on my bed. If it happened in the office, I would need to sleep at my desk, and my cubicle mate would alert me if anybody was at the door. Narcolepsy is a great annoyance. It didn't help any that I hated my boss, Alan Corneretto. I don't know what it was between us. Our personalities just clashed. I got out of ACM as soon as I could, I think early 1980, when I was hired as Associate Editor at *Computer Decisions* magazine, then located in Rochelle Park, NJ.

A few words more about my time at ACM. It was an intellectual office, and I liked most of the people there, except Corneretto. A sad note. My 29-year-old cubicle mate, pretty Alicia Gutman, had a positive Pap test while I was there, and had all her internal sexual parts removed. This was very tragic for all of us. Alicia took it hard, and never married. I've been unable to get back in touch with her, even though she's still in the telephone book. I believe she's still bitter, 25 years later.

I left ACM as soon as possible, mostly because of Alan Corneretto. In 1980, as I mentioned, I received a job offer from *Computer Decisions* magazine, then located in Rochelle Park, NJ. In the beginning it was a small outfit, and I got along O.K. The Editor was Jack Jones, a divorcé about ten years older than me. Jack was all right, but he had the defect of always trying to surpass everybody else in everything. He was very proud of his tennis game, his driving and his success (at his age) with the young ladies of his neighborhood. He wasn't lying about this. I'd seen the girls at his home door. Jack was also very proud of the fact that he was a "Mustang," that is, a (Navy) officer who had been promoted from the ranks in the field (or at sea, in the case of the Navy), instead of having attended Annapolis or OCS (Officers' Candidate School). He was also rather imposing, 6' 4" and lean and lanky. Sometimes Jack was insufferable about all this.

My duties at *Computer Decisions* included writing almost every month a long feature article about computer management, about 5,000 words, and getting the photographs for it, doing the interviews, etc. I also, after a while, was asked to write a bylined "Data Communications" column, which had my photograph at the top of the copy. I also had to write some occasional shorter pieces. It turned out to be quite a lot of work. Besides all this, I had to travel a lot, perhaps twice a month, usually by air, to visit computer installations all over the country. More about that later.

At first, I wrote on a typewriter, but I was finally pushed into using an early word processor. This was about 1982. We only had a couple of the word processing units, and we wheeled them around the office to whoever needed to use one. I managed to keep up my end of the writing for almost six years, although the deadline pressure was sometimes very heavy, until in the end I made a big mistake. I'll tell you about that later, as well.

In the beginning, as I have said, the office was in Rochelle Park, NJ, about 15 miles from the George Washington Bridge in upper Manhattan. I tried getting out there on the bus, from the Port Authority Bus Terminal in midtown, but it was impossible. So I took on credit, and bought a lemon of a used car. Because I had liked Gabriel Salomon's American Motors Rambler in College so much, I bought a used American Motors Hornet, for about $1,100. This one was a wreck. It had drum brakes instead of disk brakes, and the drum brakes were useless when it was wet. I had to become very skillful in operating the car.

It began to break down almost immediately, and I took out more and more credit to be able to keep it running. The car wasn't much good. Jack Jones would gleefully speed past me on the way home. The car broke down constantly. I used it very little, except for the commute. And I had to "garage" it, on an outdoor deck at Morningside Gardens, where I lived. More money.

In retrospect, I could have purchased an (almost) new Japanese car. And financed it (I was making about $36,000/year at the time, in 1980) and spent less on the payments than I spent for repairs on the Hornet, and I would have had a considerable asset. Another life mistake! But I was a car owner, like lots of other sane, normal human beings.

About the travel connected with my job. About twice a month, I had to fly somewhere in the U.S. for a convention, a trade show, or to visit various computer electronics outfits. In the beginning it was fun. I stayed at nice hotels, all expenses paid. But I had to drive alone in rented cars, which I picked up at the airports, all over hell and gone. I'm not a confident driver, and it was quite a strain to drive alone on the twisted, winding roads of the Boston area, or the fast freeways in California. I almost came to grief several times, but I was lucky. I always avoided disaster at the last moment, and I never damaged a rented car (running over curbs, etc.) enough that it became an issue.

I often wondered if, with my past propensity to hallucinate, if I should be driving, but this was never a problem. Reality was all too vivid when I was driving. I did, however, have to get an O.K. from a Manhattan State Hospital Aftercare psychiatrist before I was able to get my driver's license back.

I went to all the major (electronics) industrial areas. Mostly, I remember traveling repeatedly to the Boston area, Texas, Atlanta, and Northern and Southern California. Orange County was an important destination. It's the richest county in America. Anyway, "travel is broadening," but it exhausted me and I eventually tired of it. Did I say that I sometimes had to speak to large groups of a thousand or more at some of these meetings, which initially terrified me, but I eventually got the hang of it? I never spoke with much feeling, though. I was usually quite stiff.

I did manage some even grander trips during my tenure at *Computer Decisions*. In about 1983, I flew at my own expense to the USSR, as a tourist. I passed a week in Moscow, a week in Kiev and a week in Leningrad (now, St. Petersburg again). I remember being very impressed with the Kirov Ballet in the Maryinsky Theater in Leningrad. I thought the Soviet actors did the royal gestures and protocol in the Tchaikovsky ballet, "Sleeping Beauty," better than I had ever seen it done in the West. Since this was a Communist state, I thought this was remarkable.

Looking to the future, I tried to research progress in Artificial Intelligence (AI) in the Soviet

Union. I asked the USSR Academy of Sciences to find me a contact with expertise in AI, either an academic or a journalist. Nothing turned up in Moscow or Kiev, my first two stops, but in Leningrad I had a call from a Dr. Viktor Aleksandrov, a professor at a Soviet AI think tank in Leningrad. Viktor and I met and talked about AI and our life situations, and I thought that would be the end of it.

But a year later, back in the U.S., I had a call from a U.S. Government Agency that was helping host foreign visitors to the U.S., and I was asked if I would host Viktor on his forthcoming visit to New York City. I said, of course, but that I couldn't put him up, but that I would make all arrangements for him in NYC. So Viktor arrived, and I took him around, to meet my friend the Russian expert, Dr. Sergei Salomon, and to hear jazz at the infamous West End Café near Columbia University. I also drove him out to *Computer Decisions*, now much enlarged and moved to corporate headquarters in Hasbrouck Heights, NJ, to meet Jack Jones and to see how we worked.

Viktor and I have remained friends through to the present day. He, on occasion with his family, has come to the USA several more times. He has spoken at my Eleutheria Salon, given in my Studio, and also at one of the Colloquia I have organized for the Computer Group in my Morningside Gardens Cooperative. Viktor spoke on how visual images, rather than words, can be used as the operating basis for AI. A panel of priests of various stripes then commented on the philosophical and theological implications of the developments Viktor discussed. The Colloquium was a success.

In the Soviet era, Viktor was a member of the Communist party, although this was apparently for the success of his career. He was married (to Margarita, or Rita, who spoke only Russian and German) and had a daughter, Valeriya, who was an artist specializing in representations of horses. Valeriya was not especially strong, and stayed with her parents, possibly up to the present. She did recently publish a book on computer imaging. Viktor had a Doctor of Science (D.Sc.) degree, which is earned in the hard sciences in Europe only after you have acquired the Ph.D. It is a more advanced degree. Viktor had a couple of Ph.D.'s working for him in his Institute.

Viktor had a great time when he came to NYC in 1985 and promised to get me a journalist's visit to the USSR. This was duly forthcoming within the year. The

USSR Academy of Sciences paid all my expenses in the USSR, and on the strength of this, a visit to study AI developments, I cajoled *The New York Times* into giving me an assignment to write an article on "AI in the USSR" for the Sunday Magazine Section, and the *Times* paid my airfare to and from the USSR. (Unfortunately, the *Times* did not like the article I wrote, and I only received the $250 kill fee and the airfare. But that was later.) This was in about 1984. This failure with the *Times* was a big disappointment to me. I'd always wanted to write for the *Times*, and now, I never would. But I'd made the Russian trip into a success, anyway, even without selling the article. At least, I'd made a lot of new friends.

In 1984, when I was in the USSR on my sponsored trip, Viktor drove me around Leningrad in his Volga sedan. Not many individuals owned private cars in Communist Russia. Viktor drove me to the famous sites and memorials to the siege of Leningrad, in WWII, when the Nazis invested the city but could not take it. Viktor lived through the siege as a child. At the time, he lived in a 4-building apartment house complex. Three of the four buildings were destroyed by German shelling.

Only Viktor's building survived. I believe Viktor's father was killed in the siege.

Almost a million Leningraders died in the siege, mostly of starvation, but Leningrad did not fall. I was given a pin commemorating the "Hero City of Leningrad." The siege was indeed a terrible, remarkable saga. The recently deceased Russian Editor of *The New York Times*, Harrison Salisbury, whom I have met, wrote a book about the siege, entitled, *The 900 Days,* which I recommend to anyone who might be interested in this great event of WWII.

Viktor Aleksandrov was important to me because, among other reasons, I had never known a real Soviet intellectual, and meeting and knowing Viktor.helped me build and adjust my fantasies about the Great Soviet Experiment. I'd always wanted to go to the USSR and meet Russians. And been very jealous in earlier years when Swarthmore student friends, with a better command of Russian, got to participate in various Soviet-American trade fairs and such like.

Before I leave the subject of my trips to the USSR, I want to add that one of the Soviet Government representatives, seeing I was 48 years old and had no wife, offered to find me one in the USSR. I considered it, remembering Lenin's apocryphal, reputed dictum, "From each according to his abilities, to each according to his needs." Maybe it was an innocent, well-intentioned offer, but maybe they wanted to plant an information-gathering contact in the USA. Anyway, I was impressed by the offer, but I thanked them and said "No." I was at that time having too much fun with the 18-year-old girls in the Manhattan whorehouses, to give it up for the responsibilities of a Soviet wife.

My successes with Viktor and the Soviets were important to me. I had grown up, unhappy with the educational system and the social development of my youth, and I had always been a little sympathetic with the Russian Communist experiment, notwithstanding the Gulags. Seeing it all in person let me get a better idea of what the strengths and weaknesses of the system were, and to get some of the romantic idealism out of my psyche.

Then, in 1985, I managed a trip to Japan. I was hosted by MITI (the Japanese Government bureau that supervises industry development) on a 3-week tour of Japan. I was only "hosted," meaning they set up introductions and appointments for me, and bought me a few meals. Mostly, I had to pay for the airfare and the expenses in Japan myself. I rode all over Japan on the very fast Shinkansens, or bullet trains. While there, I visited Tokyo and also Hiroshima and Hakone National Forest (where Mount Fuji and some sulfur hot springs are located). The Peace Park in Hiroshima is remarkable. There are still thousands of origami (paper folding) whooping cranes tied to many of the statues there, as good luck charms, affixed by those afflicted with radiation sickness or birth defects resulting from the atomic bomb.

In Tokyo, I stayed in a Ryokan, or Japanese inn, very cheap, frequented only by Japanese and Europeans, where I slept in my private room on a futon (with a beanbag for a pillow. Hard enough. But if you're a Samurai, you sleep with a curved wooden block under your head.). The walls of the Ryokan were decorated with original Japanese art and there was communal bathing. The manager spoke no English and I had to negotiate using the Japanese I had learned before the trip. The manager also had a talking parrot on his shoulder all the time. The inn was of modern construction, and had both Levantine and Western toilets.

My Ryokan was located in Edo, the Old City of Tokyo, with all Japanese wooden construction. I believe Edo had been burned down in the fire raids of WWII, but the district had been rebuilt exactly as it was before the war. At night, religious processions of big burly men, naked to the waist, chanting and beating huge drums, would wind through the streets. There were also excellent museums of Japanese art in Edo. I recommend that, when anywhere in Japan, you try to stay in a Japanese Ryokan, to experience the "real" Japan.

In Tokyo, I also visited Rappongi, the entertainment and sex district. I visited a nightclub, where we were encouraged to dance with the (almost) nude dancers. They wore only G-strings. Actually, Rappongi is pretty well policed. The Japanese do not allow full frontal nudity (hence the G-strings) and prostitution is entirely undercover, run by the Yakuzi, or Japanese crime families. Most Japanese refuse to admit that prostitution exists in the country, but it does.

Incidentally, before my departure, I took 36 lessons in basic Japanese conversation from a brilliant young Irish-American woman, Kathleen Connolly, who had graduated summa cum laude in Japanese from Harvard and was at the time I knew her a law student at

Columbia U. I had asked the employment service at Columbia U. to send a Japanese native instructor, but Kathleen showed up instead. I was about to turn her away, when she offered me a free lesson. I was hooked and studied with her for the better part of a year.

Kathleen also became a good friend and protégé. I also came to know her wonderful family. Later, I attended Kathleen's wedding at the Waldorf-Astoria, to a brain surgeon who quickly decided he could not tolerate my nude photography or naturism. I lost touch with Kathleen after that.

Eventually, I returned to New York and *Computer Decisions*. As I mentioned, the magazine had moved to much larger corporate headquarters in Hasbrouck Heights, NJ. The organization was now run as I big corporate machine. I didn't like it at all. And, to make matters worse, the Publisher jumped a young junior editor, Ed Schultz, up to Managing Editor. I now had to report to Schultz, who was a hard-nosed young man under thirty years of age. I didn't like working for him one bit. All the humanity was gone out of the organization.

Working conditions were so bad, that at lunch, I would repair to a nearby tavern/inn, and have a mostly liquid lunch of two martinis and three beers. This would put me in such a good mood, that I was able to smile and nod assent to Ed Schultz's insults, without losing my temper.

One important event that I have not yet mentioned took place while I was at *Computer Decisions*. Under the direction of the Publisher and the Editor, Jack Jones, a collection of my major articles, passably written for the magazine, was compiled into a sizable book, *Data Communications – A Manager's View*. I wrote most of the articles included, about 80%, but there wasn't enough usable copy to meet the Publisher's requirements, so about 20% of the material was by other contributors to the magazine. I was annoyed that, on the cover, it only says, "Edited by John Seaman," even though I wrote 80% of the book. I agitated for a change to, "By John Seaman, et al.," or "Compiled by John Seaman," but to no avail. In any case, the book sold several thousand copies and I received about $2,000.

Now I must tell you about one of the bigger mistakes of my life. Not the biggest – entering the Orthodox Freudian depth psychoanalysis was the biggest mistake, as you can see from this Memoir. But what had

I done this time? Rarely, in my writing career, I had borrowed a line or two or even a short paragraph from something I had read. This happens, I don't know how often, among other writers. But it was never more than 1% or 2% of my output. Morris Edwards had said, "If you use something, change the beginning and end."

Anyway, one afternoon at *Computer Decisions*, when I had been pumped dry of my writing creativity by too many deadlines, and I wracked my brain but could think of nothing to write, I borrowed a couple of paragraphs from another magazine. I was caught (by Ed Schultz) and immediately terminated. I'm not making any excuses for it. The plagiarism was a very bad thing to do. But I will say that I was under a great deal of pressure, and the working environment was no longer congenial, so I was not unhappy to get out. I had discovered that I liked writing in an academic milieu much better than writing in a corporate environment. Why had I done what I did? As my friend Faith Greenberg Cohen had once said to me, "You have to keep going somehow."

I was not sure how I would manage financially without the *Computer Decisions* job. But I learned from the magazine that I would still be eligible for about

$13,000 in retirement benefits, for my almost six years' work there. This, I believe, was in a 401(k). There was no pension, even if I had not been terminated. The magazine was very cheap.

With the $13,000, I had enough to live on for a few months. However, I could no longer meet my credit card payments. I decided to see if I could possibly declare bankruptcy. I went to Budget Credit Counseling Service, on East 23rd Street, which was run by Luther Gatling, an African-American whom I heard was also a Marxist. Maybe not. For a few dollars, Luther fixed me up with the bankruptcy forms, which I filled out myself, and I successfully declared bankruptcy *pro se,* which in Latin means "for oneself." The court-appointed trustee was very impressed with my skill in filling out the bankruptcy documents and said a paralegal couldn't have done better.

I was very lucky. The old bankruptcy rules said you could keep your home, if it was worth less than $10,000, and my tax abatement cooperative apartment in Morningside Gardens then had a resale value of $8,000 (this has since gone up to $240,000, and will double again in the next year or two because of changes in the resale evaluation rules). Likewise, these ancient rules said you could keep your car if it was worth less than $2,000, and the book value of my old Hornet was $800. So I didn't lose anything, and credit card and other debts of about $35,000 were voided. I got a new start in life!

But the $13,000 wouldn't last long, I knew. Here my old friend Otto Koch again came to the rescue. I couldn't get another editorial job at the time because I now had a bad reputation. So Otto suggested I get a job as a messenger in a big law firm, to make $200 a week, enough to tide me over until the bankruptcy went through and until I found something better.

So I did this. I found messenger work with the law firm of Cleary, Gottlieb, Steen & Hamilton. This was sometime in 1986. I worked with the mostly black kids, just off the streets. My own experiences on the streets, after the breakdowns, helped me here. I rode around in limousines, dressed in a blue blazer and gray slacks, delivering documents, some of them checks for many millions of dollars, and I even delivered one SEC filing to Washington, DC, via the air shuttle.

After three months of this, and after some agitation from me, Cleary Gottlieb offered to train me as a legal proofreader, which paid $15 - $20/hour. I learned the basic skills in three weeks, and I found I had a new job. I decided to work the third, or "graveyard," shift, usually 12:00 Midnight until 8:00 a.m., because it paid better and because I wanted to be free in the daytime to consider new options, perhaps, finally, an "artistic career," despite all my philosophical reservations about that. What else could I do? Concerning a writing or editorial career, I'd shot myself in the foot at *Computer Decisions* with my "big mistake." Furthermore, what career can a known ex-mental patient, a "pariah" in some circles, undertake with any hope of major success and recognition, other than an "artistic" career, where there are so many eccentrics and deviants?

On another subject, about this time, I made the first of my five trips to Greece. I spent some time in Athens, and then I took a bus tour of the Peloponnesus, and on to Thessaly. I had audited some Classics courses at Columbia U., so I sometimes knew more than the guides. Then I went on to the Greek Islands, Crete and Knossos, volcanic Santorini, and finally, Mykonos. In Mykonos I hunted up the (optionally) nude beach, Paradise Beach, and marveled at my first naturist sights. The first I saw was a statuesque, attractive young woman who paraded proudly through the thatched roof taverna, totally nude, without a care in the world. Then I went down to the beach, where I saw more, including young pubescent girls, playing happily, totally nude in the Sun. I was hooked immediately and decided then and there to become a Naturist. This was an important part of my "Renewal."

I did so very soon, and even wrote articles for the naturist press on my experiences, one on Lighthouse Beach near my home and one on Cap d'Agde, the huge naturist resort (65,000 naturists in Midsummer) in the South of France. You can read these illustrated articles elsewhere in this Memoir. I visited Paradise Beach on Mykonos five times, but I shifted my destination allegiance to Cap d'Agde when I discovered that Cap d'Agde enforces total nudity for everybody in some areas. At Mykonos, nudity on the beach is only optional.

I organized many bodypainting beach parties for my friends, mostly at nearby Lighthouse Beach on Fire Island, NY. The deceased Yousof Najibullah, the deceased Gil Philiba and also the deceased Rae Karel were regulars in my group. We sometimes had as many as 15 participants. We used water-based theatrical body paints, which easily washed off in the sea, after we were finished taking photographs of our paint jobs. Sadly, most of the regular participants in my bodypainting expeditions in the 1990s have passed away or moved away. The good die young. As we all get older, I'm finding it harder and harder to round up enough participants. But I'm still eager! And all this was part of the "Renewal" I mentioned in this Section's title.

Another big change in my life took part in 1983, a little earlier in this chronology, but I didn't want to interject it into the discussion of my life at *Computer Decisions*. I bought a tax abatement cooperative in Morningside Gardens, a planned community, taking up a full city block between Broadway and Amsterdam Avenue, bounded on the South by West 123rd Street, and on the North by La Salle Street, which is really equivalent to West 124th Street. The neighborhood is near Columbia University and is in the North part of Morningside Heights, and lately the trendy restaurateurs in the neighborhood have started calling the area SOHA, SOuth of HArlem, a play on the more famous district name SOHO, in Lower Manhattan.

I didn't want to take out any more credit in 1983, so Ralph Berntley loaned me the $3,500 cash necessary to buy the tax abatement cooperative studio apartment. By the time I left my relatively well-paying job at *Computer Decisions* in 1985, I had repaid about a third of this. But there was no way I could continue the payments after I left the magazine. So Ralph took a bad debt tax write-off, and saved another $1,200. He was content that he only lost $1,100, and he was genuinely happy for me that I had a nice place to live.

Morningside Gardens turned out to be a wonderful place to live. We have six buildings on our landscaped 11-acre campus. It's really something of an arboretum, with lots of flowers and flowering trees in the Spring and Summer. Very beautiful. The people are very friendly and there's a real cooperative sense to the place. I have been active in the Computer Group, giving four Colloquia for them. Other members of the Computer Group helped me buy a computer for very little, and help me all the time with hardware and software problems, for nothing or next to nothing.

Morningside Gardens is a NORC, or Naturally Occurring Retirement Community. Because of all the services provided by Management and also by Morningside Retirement and Health Services (MRHS), it's not necessary for most of us to leave our homes and enter retirement or nursing homes. Most of the necessary services are provided here. I have spoken and shown videos and slides at MRHS, of my skydiving and of the young classical female nudes that I photograph. More on these topics later, in the appropriate time frame, but I will say now that these activities have become an important part of my "Renewal."

At MG, we have a well-equipped Workshop with computer room, dark room, ceramics kilns, woodworking area, and, thanks to me, a well-equipped area for the life sketch groups, every Tuesday night, which I have led since about 1999. I also use the darkroom a lot.

MRHS has also sponsored classes in French, Spanish and Mandarin, various exercise and meditation techniques, etc. I have attended all the language classes. There are also theme dinners and excursions to museums and other places of interest. The overpriced cooperatives on the East Side have nothing like we have

All in all, I'm very happy here. As of this writing, in January 2010, I am in my 28th year here. I will not leave unless the Republicans win in 2012, and I need to move to France). I live in a fairly large studio, the main room about 20' x 17', with an adjoining kitchen large enough for a small table, there is a bathroom and a long foyer. I have carefully decorated the place in a basically red and black color scheme (an old Chinese color scheme), with an Oriental rug on the floor. I have hung pictures everywhere, mostly classic nudes and bodypainting beach party scenes, everywhere. I photograph my classic nude models here, with much moving of furniture and hanging of backdrops. I also entertain a lot, especially my semiannual Eleutheria Salons and other holiday gatherings. I can pack up to 35 guests into the Studio. But that's a Squeeze!

Since I own the cooperative apartment, I pay only maintenance, which is low, less than half of what the rent for an equivalent rental would be. It's only because of this that I can maintain myself on my limited pensions here in Manhattan.

To mention another activity I was interested in at this time, I must say that my relations with Swarthmore College as an alumnus have been irregular. For some years, I came regularly to the College Alumni Reunions every June, bringing half a dozen friends from the "Group" and the "Circuit" with me. Then, remembering all the things the College had NOT done for me, I would completely cut off my contacts with the College. I was quite ambivalent about the place. Then, in about 1984, I became active in the Swarthmore College

NYC Connection, an Alumni group which arranged events and excursions for NYC Alumni.

I can't recall all the excursions I organized, but two come to mind. I led two different trips to Paradise Nightclub, a Russian émigré place in Sheepshead Bay, Brooklyn, and I also arranged a trip to Project Access, an operation, then as now, at the Mid-Manhattan New York Public Library, where the Futurist Ray Kurzweil's "reading machines" were installed for the use of the blind. A person could put a book in the machine, and the machine would read it off aloud in a clear, properly pronounced and accented, voice. The technology to do this is available today, in 2008, to do this, but in 1984, it was thought to be impossible. IBM and XEROX had laughed at Ray Kurzweil when he proposed the idea, so he went on to start his own company and do it himself. It was a great technological tour de force. Ray also built another machine, which would turn spoken passages into clear, grammatically correct, printed text. Ray is a great Futurist. I especially like his book, *The Age of Spiritual Machines*, about the future era when computers will be more intelligent and capable than we are.

Ray also says than in "20 years" he'll be able to transfer a person's intelligence and a replica of his or her consciousness to a supercomputer, using nanobots (tiny computer devices) in the blood stream to map all the neurons and synapses, and then extract all the nanobots and transfer their information to the supercomputer. I don't believe Ray really offers immortality. The original human would eventually pass on, and the supercomputer would be "only" be a replica, but its mind would be just like the original human mind, with all its memories, education and imagination. A really Big Dream! I hope something comes of it. Ray is really brilliant, but I don't know if he's brilliant enough to pull this off. I've even considered volunteering for the experiment. Heidegger's "emotional" existentialism offers nothing like this.

I happened to meet Ray's mother, Hannah Kurzweil, at a meeting at The Explorers Club, one of my favorite destinations here in Manhattan. She was a member of The Explorers Club, not an easy club to join, and she told me stories of Ray's brilliant youth and of Vienna, from which she had escaped when Hitler came to power there.

My successful activities in the Swarthmore College NYC Connection garnered me an appointment as Connections Representative on the Swarthmore

College Alumni Council, an advisory group to the College. The appointment was for the academic years 1985-1988. I enjoyed going back to the College for the meetings. I received a little more respect from faculty and administration than I had received when I was a student there.

One of my fellow Alumni Council members was a physician, an epidemiologist, whose name I now forget. I confided to this fellow that I was still spending a lot of time in the NYC brothels, despite the new threat of AIDS, and he warned me in no uncertain terms to quit. I took his advice seriously and made my last trip to a NYC brothel in 1987. Ending this was a great loss to me. I was then too old to seduce young social acquaintances or models, and I wasn't interested in sexual relations with older women. I just don't find older women sexy or esthetic, though I'm happy to maintain Platonic relationships with them. So I had to go "cold turkey" about sex and go back to masturbating a lot. At my age!

I tried to become a sperm donor in the early 1990s, but I was turned down because of my age and my lower than normal sperm count (a little low for my age, 40 million instead of 60 million per cc), and also because of my psychiatric hospitalizations. The clinic generally liked my qualifications, Westinghouse STS Winner and all that, and would have overlooked a short psychiatric hospitalization, but my year or more in various hospitals was too much for them. They also gave me an HIV test, and I was greatly relieved to discover I was still clean. So the epidemiologist had spoken up in time! But I wasn't able to enter the gene pool.

My proofreading career continued apace. From 1986 to 1989, I worked as a third shift legal proofreader in the offices of Cleary, Gottlieb, Steen & Hamilton, one of the top ten law firms in the country, then located at One State Street, near the Battery in Lower Manhattan. I received about $35,000/year for my work, including a lot of overtime. This was certainly enough for my needs in 1986-1989. I was picked up outside my home by a black Cadillac or Lincoln limousine every night at about 11:15 p.m., and driven down the West Side Highway to work. It wasn't that we were so important that we required a limousine; rather, the firm wanted to avoid any liability from mishaps of whatever kind that might occur at that late hour.

Once you learned the general principles, the work was usually relatively easy. Once you were experienced, going over legal documents for grammar, style, spelling and punctuation errors did not require your full concentration. I listened to classical music on WQXR and my cassettes while I worked. There were frequent periods when there was no work, but we were kept in the office because we needed to be on call, and we would order deli food in and have long philosophical conversations, often about Bertrand Russell and such like. The other proofreaders, usually but not always younger than me, were actors, dancers, writers, artists and musicians. A very interesting, Bohemian group.

All in all, the work was a pleasant change from the deadline pressure of *Computer Decisions*, although I also recognized that proofreading was not a career job. And, in the daytime, I was free to pursue my artistic interests. Of course, I had to sleep in the daytime, but if I was busy with my activities, I found I could skip a night's sleep, or on rare occasions, even two, without too much trouble. Of course, I don't know what effect all this has had on my health in my later years. But I still feel O.K.

What were my artistic interests at this time, about 1985-1989? I had been studying at the century-old (older than that, actually) Art Students League on West

57th Street since 1974, and I became a Member in 1987 and a Life Member in 1997. I studied with Richard Barnet, a well-known artist in his own right, and son of the famous artist, Will Barnet. Later, from about 1985, my friend the artist Carl Ashby asked me to be his Monitor in his painting and drawing classes during the Summer Sessions at the Parsons Division of The New School, located on lower Fifth Avenue. I learned a great deal from Carl and we became even better friends and remained so up until his death at age 90 in 2004. But something else quite remarkable happened in 1989, which I now believe was the most important part of my "Renewal."

This happening came about in 1989, when my wealthy friend Ralph Bentley, after looking at some of my much improved drawings of young nudes, done with Richard Barnet at The Art Students League and Carl Ashby at Parsons, offered to buy me a good camera so that I could photograph young (female) nudes in my Studio. Ralph let me pick out a $400 Minolta 370x camera, a (30 mm-200 mm) zoom lens, and a flash attachment at a big camera store in Chelsea. I was all set, and very grateful to Ralph for getting me started. I couldn't have possibly afforded all that.

In 1989, I started putting up notices for models at Barnard College and Columbia U., and at the local art schools, dance studios and drama academies. I received a good response. Professional photography models would have cost way too much, but students were eager to pose for $60 for 3 hours photo, or $30 for 2 hours life class sketch. And I paid less in 1989, when I started this. What follows is the text of my current ad. It draws well:

FINE ARTS/PHOTO MODELING

Avant-garde artist seeks college women, 18-28, for life modeling (nude and seminude), esthetic photography, watercolor, pen & ink, pastel, charcoal. Dancers, athletic preferred. No experience necessary. Photo, $60 each 3-hour private session; painting and drawing sessions for a cooperative sketch group of 4-7 persons, $30 each 2-hour session. Standard rest breaks. Maximum 3-4 photo sessions per each model per year; frequent sketch groups. Morningside Heights location (near Columbia U.). The artist will give a small portfolio of photos and a few sketches (copies) to the model, gratis, if this would be of interest. The artist is a Life Member of The Art Students League of New York and a graduate of Swarthmore College. He has assisted in painting courses at The New School (Parsons Division) and can supply other references as well. He has won a number of prizes and has exhibited in a variety of venues. If this sounds like something you might want to do, call John Seaman at (212) 866-4360 or e-mail him at johnseaman28@juno.com. You can view John Seaman's photographic work on his web site, http://jseamanclassicnudes.Artspan.com . Click on any thumbnail. John Seaman's bio is included in the 57th Edition of Marquis' *Who's Who in America* You must be at least 18 years of age to respond to this ad. Leave message or call over the weekend, when the artist is more likely to be in the studio.

The ad, and word of mouth, were quite successful. Over the years, I enjoyed working with dozens of beautiful, nubile Barnard and Columbia U. undergraduates, as well as lots of others. It was a real privilege and I made a great many excellent photographic prints. These photo shoots were the best part of my "Renewal," and I'll say a lot more about my photographic and art work in the next Section. At this point we are up to the year 1989. I conclude this Section here, at the inception of the most important part of my "Renewal."

From Renewal to (Some) Self-Realization
1989 – 2010

In the last Section, "(Very Slow) Recovery to Renewal," I wrote how my friend of many years, Ralph Bentley, had been impressed with my sketches of young female nudes, created at The Art Students League, and gave me an expensive studio camera so I could also photograph them. I don't know whether the initial idea for the photography project was my idea or Ralph's, but it doesn't matter. I was started on what turned out to be a very fulfilling endeavor.

I have decided to put the story of my experiences photographing and drawing young female classical nudes, along with other material, in a separate topical section of this Memoir, entitled, "My Life in Photography and Art." You will find the whole story there.

In 1989, I left Cleary, Gottlieb, Steen & Hamilton to take up similar work at another New York City "top ten" law firm, Sullivan & Cromwell. Working conditions and pay were much better here. I continued to work third (graveyard) shift, and, with overtime, earned over $40,000 a year, this in 1989. I passed many pleasant shifts at S&C, working some of the time, listening to classical cassettes on my Walkman, reading philosophy, eating and drinking, and conversing with my new, mostly younger, friends. These new friends were, mostly, writers, artists, musicians, dancers and actors, so I obtained an even deeper look into life in the arts. The middle of the nights could occasionally be very mysterious, for example, when listening to such music as Rachmaninoff's choral "Vespers."

Every night (I often worked six or seven nights a week, to make extra money. I don't know where all this money went.), I was picked up by a black Cadillac limousine or Lincoln Town Car to be whisked to midtown or downtown to my 3rd shift gig. The drivers all knew I liked to listen to WQXR (The New York Times 24-hour classical music station) during the ride, and that station was playing when I got in the car. The rides were luxurious, but we didn't get them because we were VIPs. The law firms simply didn't want to risk any liability.

In 1992, at Sullivan & Cromwell, the firm wanted to cut staff, and they wanted to do it in a decent way. They offered us, if we were 55 or older (younger persons were allowed into this later), the opportunity to take a lifetime pension calculated on our term of service plus five additional years. I had been there 3 ½ years, so

I would get an 8 ½ year pension. This was too good an offer to refuse, although I was happy at Sullivan & Cromwell and making $40,000 - $45,000 a year, this in 1992. So I opted out, and received about $325/month for the rest of my life. This was a great help to me later on, and enabled me to (semi)retire in 1998 and take Social Security at age 62 in 1998.

After reluctantly leaving Sullivan & Cromwell in 1992, I worked for one year (permanent) at White & Case, another big law firm. Work here was not satisfactory, and I left after one year, and began working as a temporary. As a temp, I would be taken on by various agencies throughout the City, and they would parcel out the work to me and others. Temping was all right, it gave me flexibility in my schedule, I could work when I wanted to. I bought a beeper, and would get calls, often at 9:00 p.m. or 10:00 p.m. in the evening, for work in law offices (and banks and printing houses) all over the City and even in nearby New Jersey, to report at midnight or 1:00 a.m. for a night's work, which could run late into the morning hours. I made $15 - $20/hour, more later on, so I was doing all right. There was even overtime at time and a half and double time on Sundays.

I would learn to sleep in the daytime. If I had activities in the daytime, I could sometimes go two days without sleep, and, on rare occasions, three days. I felt all right, but I don't know what this did to my health, later on.

After a while, I began showing in the various offices the naturism articles that I had written for publication on Cap d'Agde and other places, and also the classical young nudes that I had photographed. My work was well received and I was encouraged to do more, in some places, particularly Sullivan & Cromwell, but later, in other venues, after about 15 years of temping, it caught up with me, and there was sometimes a strong negative reaction. I was banned (DNU status, "Do Not Use") at a number of places.

The DNU status, combined with the fact that the computers were beginning to be able to do the proofreading without our help (with spell check and grammar check, the legal secretaries could finish it up) eventually ended my temp proofreading experience, in about 2001. But I'd had a good run of about 15 years at this pickup career. I confess I did feel rather like a Luddite, eager to smash the big computers, for dispossessing me.

Listening to classical music on cassettes and FM radio (on my Walkman) while temping in the various (law) offices enriched the appreciation of classical music that I had first developed in my College days. I never heard a note of classical music as a child or high school teen, so I was completely unaware of how wonderful (to me, at least) classical music was. When I arrived at Swarthmore in 1952, the 33-rpm LP (Long Playing Record) had just been invented, and the more sophisticated students had early hifi systems on which to play their marvelous collections. I heard their music and was enthralled. The first classical record I ever purchased had Handel's "Water Music" on one side and the Mozart "Haffner" Symphony (#35) on the other.

As a student at Swarthmore, I soon began traveling into Philadelphia on weekends to hear The Philadelphia Orchestra, still conducted at that time, I believe, by Eugene Ormandy. I couldn't read music but I soon knew the essential repertoire and recognized many of the themes. Incidentally, I also took up ballet attendance and the grand opera, but these were less important to me. Classical symphonic music was my new love, and I soon had a good LP record collection.

All this made the difficult early years at Swarthmore more bearable.

I even interested my Father in classical music (he'd had no experience with it, either). For himself, early in the LP years, he bought a "new" 78 rpm record player, and would sit close to it (with his bad hearing) to hear his multiple-record Tchaikovsky symphonies, etc. I was unable to prevail upon him to get an "up to date" LP player, as I did. But I was pleased he had found something, through my experiences, that he could appreciate and enjoy.

After graduation, when I returned to New York City, I began to regularly attend The New York Philharmonic. In 1975, I took out my first pair of subscriptions, third tier box, the cheapest seats, but one hears and sees well from up there, hearing particularly the brass and percussion. I believe the high box seats, or the people in them, are called, the "Gods," in Europe. I've renewed my subscriptions every Season up to and including the present, the 2010-2011 Season, a 35-year span. Regular attendance has given me great pleasure, and I enjoy introducing my dates and other friends to the musical experience. When I can, I combine the music with a good dinner (usually after the concert) at a fine Lincoln Center vicinity restaurant.

I also enjoy the Mostly Mozart Festival in Summer at Lincoln Center. I try to be in town for the 4-week MM Festival. The Mostly Mozart Festival Orchestra (The Philharmonic does not play for the MM Festival) was conducted for many years by Gerard Schwartz. He was very good, but the new MM conductor, a Frenchman, Louis Langrée, is equally good. MM is a high point of my NYC Summers.

About 20 years ago, I gratuitously put The NY Philharmonic in my Will (my Estate consists of the value of the cooperative apartment, now about $240,000, but it may be revalued much higher, if the coop's rules on this change). I was surprised to learn that I was now a member of the Philharmonic's "Heritage Society," and would receive a regular pass to the Patrons' Lounge, where free drinks are served and the elite swells hang out, and also (occasional) free tickets and sumptuous dinners, served by black tie waiters. This was the Life! Another Dickensian leap.

I inquired further, and found that The Metropolitan Opera and The NYC Ballet, along with the umbrella Lincoln Center Administration, all had similar charitable societies. I joined them all, with moderate bequests, and now receive wonderful perks all the time. I have paid nothing up front for all these benefits, and I felt a little guilty about that. I knew I might not die suddenly, and that terminal medical expenses might exhaust my small Estate, and there'd be nothing left for Lincoln Center. I discussed these feelings with an administrator of the benefit programs at Lincoln Center, and he quickly reassured me, "That's all right! We'll speculate!" So everything is O.K. with my arrangements!

There was one hitch with all these charity perks, however. Perhaps eight or more years ago, at a Heritage Society luncheon, a young matron working in public relations for the NY Philharmonic, expressed interest in my work photographing young nudes and gave me her card. I promptly mailed her a small portfolio of Docutech (good quality) photocopies of my work, and she didn't like it (receiving erotic nudes in the mail). She complained to the Administration, and I lost some of my NY Philharmonic perks (I lost attending the dinners; I was able to keep the Patrons' Lounge privileges).

Then I complained, saying I could not suppress my Art, and was told I could come back if I apologized and said I would never do it again. I was outraged at this bunch of Philistines and would NOT apologize. In fact, I demanded an apology from the NY Philharmonic, which was not forthcoming. That's where the matter rested until last year, 2007, when I again began receiving invitations to Heritage Society dinners, without my having made any apology or promise. Whatever prompted them to reconsider? So I have all my perks back. And I just signed up for my 35th year as a continuous subscriber (with the 2010-2011 Season).

On to other topics. As I mentioned earlier, it was about 1985 when I became an active Naturist. I went to Paradise Beach on Mykonos, a Greek island in the Cyclades, a clothes-optional nude beach, five times in the late 1980s, always alone. I couldn't get any of my woman friends to come and foot half the bill. I had a good time anyway. I also visited local (to NYC) nude beaches, particularly Lighthouse Beach on Fire Island, where I organized bodypainting beach parties, sometimes for as many as 15 people. Eventually, however, I discovered Cap d'Agde in the South of France. Here, total nudity, on the beach at least, is enforced. This was more to my liking. I spent a couple of weeks there in each of 1996, 1998 and 2000. I wrote this all up, also, in my article, "The Nude Gastronome," which is also a Section of this Memoir. Sadly, now that I am semi-retired, I can't afford to go there anymore. But perhaps my fortunes will change.

Living here in Morningside Heights, for several years in the 1990s and 2000s, I audited courses, from about 1990 to 2002, at Columbia U. and even Barnard College. Initially, I paid the adult education auditing fee of about $300 for each course, but then I discovered that, if properly approached, some of the professors would let you sit in on their classes, without paying a fee. They just wanted to be sure you could or would contribute something to the class discussion. There were no formal grades for auditors, and no class work requirements, but I usually tried to do all the readings, write the papers, and take the examinations. Most professors allowed me to do this, and would even give me a "grade" (which of course didn't count for any credit) if I asked. I always received A, A- or B+. Maybe they were humoring me. Maybe I'd learned something from all the psychoanalysis (becoming more subjective, for example). Or maybe the terrible Swarthmore grading WAS unusual. I'll never know.

Anyway, I learned a few things, .got to know some interesting professors, and wrote some interesting stuff, some of which I was able to use in my writing later on. I sat in on graduate and undergraduate courses in Philosophy, Classics, Art History, and particularly, with Dr. David Albert, Philosophy of Science courses, where I learned that time and space are interchangeable parts of the same reality, and that quantum mechanics teaches that there are multiple realities and that some physical events don't happen until they are perceived. All this helped me make sense of what I had experienced in and after my psychoanalysis. And I met a lot of brilliant young women, including the aforementioned Rivka Kfia.

Some of the courses I sat in on were concerned with Classical Greek Philosophy, Nietzsche, Wittgenstein, Heidegger, Kant, Hegel and Spinoza, Ancient Greek Art and Modern and Contemporary Art History. All of this was very engaging, but I eventually decided I did not have an academic temperament (despite the good grades) and that I would try to develop and express myself more creatively. My hero in all of this, in the matter of what temperament one should strive for, in my early years and until this day, is Ernest Hemingway.

Another element in my ongoing relationship with neighboring Columbia U., besides as a place to audit excellent courses and as a source for models, has been the Columbia University Faculty House, where I have been a member for at least 40 years (maybe more). I first visited CUFH in the Spring of 1959, at a cocktail party given to announce the Columbia University Press's Spring List for that year. You'll recall that I was Science Editor of the Columbia U. Press in 1959 and 1960, before the onset of major psychosis. I was fascinated with CUFH, the excellent bar lounge and the fine buffet lunches given at moderate prices in the 4th floor De Witt Clinton Dining Room.

I also liked the tweedy professorial ambiance of the place, all the professors hosting young female student companions ("arm candy"?). CUFH also has run an adult education dinner seminar program for 100 years, with many, many subjects, including "The Arab World" and "Shakespeare," for example. One has to establish that one has the right credentials or in some way can contribute to the seminar discussion before joining. I have occasionally sat in on the seminars but have never been a regular attendee. Not quite suited to my temperament. There are also Wednesday luncheon chamber music concerts and many other interesting activities.

I was able to join Columbia U. Faculty House as an affiliate (cheaper annual rate) because of my previous affiliation with the Columbia U. Press, 51 years ago. Once or twice a month, I take a date or a friend (perhaps a model who has charmed me) to CUFH for drinks in the bar lounge at 5:00 p.m. and then the buffet dinner at 6:00 p.m. It's all very elegant and makes a great impression.

To summarize my activities and interests since 1989, there has been the Classic Nude photography, the writing of this Memoir, regular attendance at the NY Philharmonic (I am a 36-year subscriber, as of this writing in 2010), the NYC Ballet, and, occasionally, orchestra standing room at The Metropolitan Opera (you almost always get a seat by the first intermission). I also regularly attend the no longer free but still inexpensive orchestral concerts at The Manhattan School of Music, conveniently located one block from my home in Morningside Gardens. And I go to the plays that my friends (e.g., Stanford Pritchard, Stephanie Sellars) have written, and others in which other friends are acting. We always party up before or after these events, sometimes at the aforementioned CUFH.

Since about 1999, I have led the life sketch group here in Morningside Gardens. This gives me a chance to "try out" prospective candidates for my photography. I have also tried skydiving, and want to do more, when I can afford it. I've planned a group jump this year, 2010, if I can find the money for my own solo jump. I went to Paradise nude beach on Mykonos in the Greek Islands, five times in the 1980s and 1990s. In 1996, 1998 and 2000, I visited Cap d'Agde naturist resort in the South of France, and had a wonderful time. Unfortunately, I can't afford to go again, in my pensioned retirement. Maybe my fortunes will change. I also run bodypainting expeditions to the local free beaches, such as "Lighthouse Beach" and Gunnison Beach in New Jersey, for mixed groups of as many as 15, usually every Summer.

In the 2002-2003 year, with very little outside income coming in, I had to find some kind of job to tide me over. But I was 66, and it was very hard to find anything. I ended up, after reading the ads in the VILLAGE VOICE, in taking a job as a messenger, or, more grandly, a courier, for a small company located on

Maiden Lane in Downtown Manhattan. I had done similar work before, for a law firm, and I believed the outdoor work would be good for my health. The other messengers were either Inner City African-American kids, or retirees like me. So, for a year, I walked ten miles a day, and climbed perhaps forty flights of subway stairs every day, all for the munificent sum of about $85/week, more or less. It got me through my financial crisis. But my legs gave out (tendonitis in the anterior and posterior tibial tendons, and then also in my patellar tendons). I was able to get one settlement for this from the Workers Compensation Board, a NYS state agency, and, a few years later, a second settlement.

Except for the leg problem, I did become very healthy. I lost about 20 pounds, which I have not regained. I worked in all kinds of weather, heavy Summer rains and deep Winter snows, often in remote locations, such as on the West Side of Manhattan by the docks or in remote areas of Brooklyn. I'm not sorry I took this job. I did learn a few things.

I continued to pursue my group therapy with Hilde Grey, LCSW, every Tuesday evening, except in August, until June 2009, until I became concerned that the group was digging too deeply, and I felt chaos again just beneath the surface. So I quit and have been fine since. But I've been in some form of psychotherapy or psychoanalysis since 1957, fairly constantly, 53 years now. It doesn't do much good in the way of improvement, but it now helps me maintain myself without much further damage to my psyche.

The question is, I seem to want depth from my therapists, but not too much. When the very structure of reality begins to shift, it's too much. And, try as I might, I can't dismiss it all, totally, as a pack of hallucinations. Some of it was too vivid for that, and there are those "multiple realities" in physics. The Buddhists and some of the Western philosophers ("idealists") maintain that reality is a product of the mind. However, I still believe in empirical science, but that may not be the only reality. But I'm careful now to stay in touch with "ordinary" reality and to eschew the "artistic" and other visions. If anything starts, I just take another tranquilizer. And I've been "normal" now for 40 years, more or less. If I'm missing something, I don't need or want it.

Actually, now in 2010, I've been living without psychotherapy for about a year and a half. I seem to get along without it all right. I have a few weak moments, like everybody else, but I'm O.K. Maybe, I've finally learned to live without it (psychotherapy). I would go to REBT (Albert Ellis) Workshops, if there were any, but Al has passed on. His young wife, Dr. Debbie Joffe Ellis, a fine psychologist in her own right, says she will eventually start and run the Workshops herself, but she is not ready.

I've become friends with Debbie, and she has spoken at Eleutheria. Her friendship also helps hold me together. My friends and my readings in psychology and philosophy help me go deep into my psyche, but not too deep. Heidegger, the existentialist, writes approvingly of Van Gogh and his light visions (*lichtung* again). But Van Gogh ended his life in an Asylum and cut his ear off. I don't want that and I didn't want 30 plus years in an Asylum working out some damned Existentialist "emotional" cure. I say to my analysand friends, "You have a rich Inner Life, I have a rich Outer Life."

I've run my Eleutheria Salon, twice a year, regularly since 1990. I wear my tux and put on a good show, with three or four presenters, including myself. It's a lot of fun.

Most of the different events described in this closing summary are written up in detail in separate sections of this Memoir. See the Table of Contents. I now (2010) look forward to another 20 years of enjoyable life, with its ups and downs, if I am lucky. But I won't feel I've missed much if everything ends before then!

Some Friends

Madness is a very lonely experience. Since I put that all behind me, I have made many friends, although a good number of them have died off. In this part of my memoir, I am going to relate vignettes about some of my more remarkable friends. At the time of my first psychotic break in 1960, I had very few friends. Almost nobody visited me when I was locked up in the Manhattan asylum. But after my second major psychotic break occurred in 1967, and I was hospitalized again, in Kings Park, on Long Island, I had many friends, who often visited me during my brief confinement there. I guess the first breakdown and recovery had, as a side effect, socialized me somewhat. Perhaps I owe that to the psychiatrists. I believe the constant flow of visitors impressed the hospital administrators and was a factor in my quick release, after six weeks, because the administrators knew I had friends to encourage me.

In 1999, my friend of about two years, Rae Karel, had a bout of abdominal sickness and was taken by her friends to Beth Israel Hospital here in New York City, where she was diagnosed with terminal abdominal cancer. Rae could not keep any food down. Five and a half hours of surgery on May 4, 1999 were supposed to remove the obstruction but did not. Dr. Paul Liu, the resident surgeon, told me however that he removed 90 to 95% of the malignancy.

A week later, Beth Israel was preparing to give Rae chemotherapy in hopes of "melting" the obstruction. This treatment, of course, would greatly debilitate Rae. Her relatives and friends were told that if the chemotherapy was too tough for Ray, they would just let her go (as I understood it). Oh yes, after the surgery, she was given 17 to 37 months to live, more than we had expected. But that was when we thought the obstruction had been cleared. But, after the surgery, Rae could still not keep any food down and continued on UIV. We didn't know what to expect.

Throughout all of this, Rae had a pretty good idea of what was going on, though she may not have known the details. She cracked jokes before and after surgery, and never seems to lose heart. She was unable to eat or drink anything for 3 weeks. One day she asked me to take myself to a classy bar, and order a fresh lemonade with gin and anisette. This is what she'd been dreaming of. I did this, and when I next saw her, she had the experience vicariously through me.

Additional surgery to remove her stomach and more chemotherapy were rejected by Rae. She wanted no heroic measures. She had lived a full life the way she wanted and she recognized that it was finished. She signed the papers to leave the hospital and enter a hospice. At this point Rae was very clear-headed, calm, and without a tremor of fear. If I believed in such things, I would say she looked radiant and transcendent.

Rae Karel passed away a day or two later I visited her in the hospital a few hours before her death, but she was sleeping, and I didn't want to wake her. I heard from the doctors that they had given her enough morphine to kill the pain and give her some rest, but this, it seems, was a lethal dose. A kindness. I have been told that hospitals are permitted to give enough anesthetic to ease the pain, even if it turns out to be a lethal dose. I don't know. But she went out very easily, for which I am glad. Rae was a very good friend to me.

But who was Rae Karel? I met her perhaps in 1996 at one of Gil Offenhartz' famous Halloween costume parties. She was in an off-the-shoulder iridescent sari, I was in my tux. She was very spirited woman of perhaps 76 years, born in Bessarabia (Rumania? Moldovia?), family came to the USA before

WWII. I'm told Rae was a rare beauty in her youth and up to the age of 40 or so. In WWII, she joined the U.S. Women's Army Corps (WACs) to escape all her romantic entanglements, and, I think, for the adventure.

Rae was sent by the Army to Paris in May 1945 and served there at least until V-J Day. She tells me the French V-J Day party at the Arc de Triomphe (Or maybe it was the Eiffel Tower) was the greatest party of her life. Rae said she had many romances in Paris, and that the Frenchmen were charming, unlike the Jewish boys she knew when younger who would chase her around the room.

Rae's other friends have told me she didn't like the army much, but she always only told me the good side of it. She did rise to Technical Sergeant 4th Class (that's 4 or 5 promotions) by asking to be promoted, she said.

Rae was always something of a Red, a Communist, and she was hounded so much in McCarthyite days she legally changed her name to Rae Karel.

Rae's lifestyle was to go to all the galleries and receptions she can get into, for the food and drink and glitz. She had press credentials from some Brazilian newspaper and she used these to good effect. This isn't what I like to do, but more power to her, if she got a kick out of it. I know some wealthy people who do the same thing. Perhaps that's one reason they're wealthy—they free load when they can.

Rae loved my bodypainting beach parties at Lighthouse Beach and my Eleutheria Salons, and always took part and helped out. We also went to bistros together and each of us would try to pick up young companions of our own sex to introduce to our "hunting" partner. This trick worked quite well. In this way, she found for me, this time in the famous Saturday standing room line for The Metropolitan Opera, Ms. Lucy Yates, a 28-year-old opera singer, who has become a good friend to both of us.

Rae often propositioned me, as many older women have, but I can't do it with them. Too squeamish. Rae took this like a good sport and helps me in the "hunting" for younger women.

I learned at the interment from the family that Rae's young mother was killed in a pogrom (in the twenties?). Rae's mother's father comforted the bereaved husband, Rae's father, by offering him another of his daughters in marriage. I'm sure it was consensual all around and it struck me as a very compassionate way of handling a very bad situation and its aftermath. That's about all I know about Rae. It's not much. But I'm still very fond of her. She was a fighter. I'm sorry she didn't get her 37 months or more of full life.

My second friend that I want to bio is still very much alive. This is Grace K. (not her real name – she now works with children and she is sorry to say she must now remain anonymous), who also is a very free-thinking and brave woman and lets no one else do her thinking for her.

Grace comes on my nude bodypainting beach parties, though she doesn't partake in the bodypainting. I believe she thinks the painting is frivolous. She has also spoken and sung at one of my Eleutheria Salons, describing her very remarkable work as a sexual surrogate under medical supervision, helping dysfunctional men lead some kind of full sex life. She related with great good humor how the men with delayed ejaculation were much more work for her than the men suffering from premature ejaculation. Grace told me her Roman Catholic priest endorsed her work at the clinic.

Grace is also an animal rights activist, chaining herself to furriers, getting arrested repeatedly, and singing animal rights songs (are there such things?) overnight in jail. More to the point, her angry letters to cosmetics companies have been instrumental in eliminating the hideous Draize test from several cosmetics laboratories. In the Draize test, cosmetics in thousand-fold concentrations are applied to the large, clear eyes of thousands of rabbits. I helped her prepare some of the letters.

She is also a vegan, a strict vegetarian who consumes no animal or even dairy products, and uses no leather. I dined with her at Greene Vegan Restaurant in Brooklyn Heights and was very impressed with the meal and also Grace's thoughts on the topic.

Grace also sings in church choirs and as a soloist cabaret singer, particularly at Judy's, a cabaret formerly on West 44th Street adjacent to the famous Hotel Algonquin, locale over the years for many other independent-minded women.

Grace's story doesn't end here. She's bisexual and once stole the girlfriend away from a guy I know. I thought this was hilarious. She also had a long heterosexual affair with one of the best-known, and best-hung, porn stars in New York City. It's interesting to note that he later became a born-again Christian, perhaps partly as a result of Grace's influence.

I first met Grace when we were both legal proofreaders. She smoothed the way for me in several firms. Now she's gone beyond proofreading into an animal-rights position, which makes her very happy.

I knew most of Grace's story early on, and always kept quiet about it for fear of embarrassing her. But one day Grace told me she was proud of everything she had done, and that she wouldn't mind if I spoke or wrote about it. So, eventually, she gave a wonderful presentation at Eleutheria Salon about her work in the sex clinic, and her generous and open attitude toward sex impressed me and my other friends very much.

In this take, I will reminisce about a friend who has been gone for many years, Mr. Otto Koch, killed in a tragic hit-and-run auto accident on November 1, 1990. I first met Otto 30 years ago, in the social circle Ralph Bentley introduced me to. I'm also going to write about some of the people Otto has helped me meet, including the redoubtable Gunnar Frost.

Otto was also a bit of a mystery. He was born the same year as I was, 1936, and grew up in Nazi

Germany during WWII. He came to the United States shortly after the war, whether with his family or not, I don't know. His only higher education was a year or two of business school, but for all of that, Otto was a very learned (and also wise) man. More about that later.

Somehow, Otto was drafted, and went into the U.S. Army. How long was he in? We don't know. First Otto told me that he sorted laundry for two years, then he said that wasn't true, and that he had spoken up from the ranks when his unit was told it was going to Korea, and that he had said something like, "I'm not going to Korea! I don't know anybody in Korea!" He then told me he had been given a psychiatric discharge. I don't know what to believe about this, but I do know that his discharge was honorable, or other than dishonorable, because the U.S. Army sent a flag for his casket at the funeral and buried him in Calverton Military Cemetery out on Long Island.

Back in New York City, Otto had an affair with an Ecuadorian woman. The woman became pregnant but Otto would not marry her and recommended an abortion. But the Ecuadorian woman was a devout Roman Catholic and would not do this, so Otto had an out-of-wedlock daughter, who grew up to be a handsome young woman who unfortunately shared the tight religious views of her mother. After Otto's death, I invited the daughter to one of my Eleutheria Salons, but she walked out indignantly when the slides of my nudes were shown. I have had no contact with the daughter since then, regrettably.

In New York City, in Morningside Heights where I live, Otto found work as an assistant librarian in the Columbia University libraries. He worked there for 17 years, with a specialty in musicology. Otto knew classical music very well—professors would call him up at work or at home for detailed information about a particular composition or composer. Otto knew off the top of his head how long each of the Bruckner symphonies ran, for example.

Everything went well in the libraries except when Otto was drunk or hung over. Otto had a penchant for spirits, which he could not quite control. Otto loved everybody, but sometimes, when he was drunk, his childhood Nazi indoctrination took over. One day, when Otto was badly hung over, a homosexual superior was harassing him, and Otto burst out with, "Leave me alone, you Jew faggot!"

That was the end of Otto's library career. The authorities put him in a drunk tank at St. Luke's Hospital for two weeks, I think just to humiliate him, he always sobered up quickly, and then fired him. Otto was never quite the same afterwards.

Otto told me he was a nihilist, but late in life, he began to go to church suppers and pick up fat little old ladies who gave him a lot of pleasure in bed. I remember, at the funeral, there were several of these chubby little ladies adjusting the flowers, the vestments, and so on. All of them were in tears. We all loved Otto.

About those chubby little ladies, Otto's taste in women differed radically from mine. I have always preferred young women with champagne-glass breasts (not very big) (there is a probably apocryphal story that the first champagne glass was made from the shape of an impression of one of Marie Antoinette's tits), while Otto preferred buxom women with tits that hung down to their knees, or thereabouts. And most of such women are very glad to be appreciated! But *chacun a son gout!*

Otto helped me, in his quiet way, in many ways. First, he introduced me to the pleasures of whoring, in 1974. He introduced me to the delights of young girls who would do anything you asked, without getting squeamish like my social acquaintances, and without making any demands on me, other than for a few dollars. There's lots more about my happy days in Patricia's bordello elsewhere in this memoir. But Otto was the start of it, and for that I will be eternally grateful. Unfortunately, Otto couldn't afford to go much himself. I hope I at least treated him to it a couple of times, but memory does not serve.

Otto also introduced me to a wonderful German-American retreat in the Berkshires. It was run by one Norbert Hinze, a then-youngish German-American business executive who ran the place, summers and winters (for the skiing) at cost for his friends and his friend's friends. The expense was something like $30. for a three-day weekend, with wonderful food, the best cuts of meat and good wine, that Norbert purchased and that we cooked up in a group ourselves, under the supervision of those of us who really knew how to cook. We ate, outdoors or in, German-style, at a long table with Norbert at the head.

#

Of course, there was the lake, and tennis, bicycling, Tanglewood and, within walking distance, Jacob's Pillow Dance Festival, excursions to theatre in

Pittsfield, trips to Lee and Lenox, mountain climbing where we watched the hang gliding on Mt. Greylock (like talking to angels as the flyers hung still in the invisible updrafts), the drinking parties at night in the basement, and skinnydipping off the float in the lake at night. Wonderful times!

Most of the people there, Germans included, were young and emancipated. A lot were veterans of the American army, like Norbert. However, they had respect for their elders, there were a few old Wehrmacht men around, and sometimes it got a little like the Bund. One of these Wehrmacht men, who now goes by the name of Gunnar Frost, served as liaison to the Wehrmacht in the Finnish Army during the siege of Leningrad during WWII. I'll speak of Gunnar when I finish with Otto.

I can remember one more great thing Otto did for me. In late 1986, I was thrown out of my high-paying (for me, then, $35,000 a year) job as a writer and editor on a leading, 200,000 circulation computer management magazine, the now defunct *Computer Decisions* . At that time, my survival skills were not too good and I was totally at a loss as to how to make my living. I couldn't get and didn't want another editorial job just then, so I didn't know what to do.

Otto came to the rescue. He suggested I get a job as a messenger with a big Manhattan law firm, making $200. a week, easy work which would tide me over, while I declared bankruptcy and until I found something better. So I worked with the young black kids. My former times on the street served me well here, with the black kids.

After three months, the law firm, Cleary, Gottlieb, Steen & Hamilton, trained me as a legal proofreader, also not too hard and work which I enjoyed.

After that, I worked as a legal proofreader, permanent and temp, for 47 law firms, brokerage houses, advertising agencies and printers. I worked third shift (usually midnight until 8:00 a.m., more or less) because this left me free for my new photography and art career (more about that elsewhere herein) in the daytime, and because on third shift you met a lot of other interesting musicians, writers, dancers, actors and actresses, and so on. It was a lot of fun and these kids kept me young. I made a lot of good friends in this. We exchanged our life stories, or in my case, parts of it. And I made as much as $43,000. a year doing this. Enough for me!

But now, the story of Gunnar Frost. Gunmnar told me he took part in the famous siege of Leningrad, which lasted from 1941 to 1944. Specifically, he knew Spanish and German and worked with Franco's Blue Division, which also took part in the siege. He was a medic (carried weapons) and proudly told me the mortality rate for medics in that situation was six times higher than that for front-line infantrymen. Gunnar was a volunteer, too. He was really Swedish and had joined the Finnish Army to help "stop Bolshevism."

At the end of WWII, Gunnar was put in a concentration camp under joint Russian/American administration. There was nothing much to eat, they were given 500 calories a day, a starvation diet. But Gunnar, with his excellent survival skills, found a way to get by. In an all-night poker game, he and a friend won the carcass of a dead horse, buried and hidden in the frozen ground. Whenever the hunger pangs struck, Gunnar stole off at night to the spot where the horse was buried, and shaved off a few slices of frozen meat with his *pukka* (Finnish close-quarters knife which Gunnar was allowed to keep for the needs of camp life). This dead horse enabled Gunnar to survive the concentration camp in good shape.

For all our differences in politics, Gunnar and I became good friends. He lives near me on the West Side of Manhattan. He must be at least 75 now but he carries himself like a virile young man, and has lots of young women friends. He's had a lot of medical problems in recent years but he toughs it all out and comes out as good as new. I'm convinced he's indestructible. He's let me help him with his hospital arrangements. Gunnar spends one-third of the year in New York City, one-third with his family in Sweden, and one-third in Chile, from the latter of which he imports the young girls who keep him happy and going strong.

In Chile, Gunnar owned for a time, a "strip-tease" hotel, where the girls after the show could take the men to a room, but Gunnar insists it wasn't quite a brothel, because the girls were not supervised. Perhaps it would have been better if they had been. Anyway, the hotel wasn't making money, the employees stole liquor from the bar when Gunnar wasn't around, so Gunnar sold it.

Gunnar also told me about the *Chocolatieras* in Chile. These are girls as young as 14, the age of consent in Chile, who offer themselves to local men and especially to tourists for free or for a bar of chocolate, in order to gain experience. All types are available, blancas, mulattoes and blacks. The older, local working prostitutes for pay hate the *Chocolatiera*s because they ruin the business, by giving their favors for free. Gunnar told me Chile is "heaven on Earth" for a man and urged me to come down to visit him. He swore he himself never took a girl younger than 17.

Gunnar told me he didn't really, really enjoy life, even with all his life experience, until he got to Chile when he was in his seventies. He warned me earnestly not to lose any more time before I get any older. More on the *Chocolatieras:* Gunnar told me that when the U.S. Navy ships are in town, the U.S. Shore Patrol went around arresting any sailor who took a girl younger than 17, even though it was legal in Chile. So you can't escape American morality anywhere.

Furthermore, Gunnar told me, in Latin America, girls are brought up to be very aware of a man's "Necessity," or urgent need for women and sex all the time. So the girls tend to be more helpful in taking the first step than happens here in the States. Maybe we need to inculcate such an attitude in young women here.

Gunnar gave me a lot of other good advice and information and I had a lot of respect for him. He'd come through the most terrible times and managed to do it all with good heart and optimism.

A LITTLE MORE ABOUT GUNNAR. A COUPLE OF YEARS AFTER THIS SECTION WAS FIRST WRITTEN, GUNNAR PASSED AWAY AT AGE 71. WE LEARNED AT HIS MEMORIAL GATHERING THAT HE WAS TOO YOUNG TO HAVE TAKEN PART IN THE RUSSO-FINNISH WAR. HE WAS A SWEDISH SAILOR WHO MADE UP MOST OF THE ABOVE, AT LEAST, ABOUT THE WAR. A SAILOR'S YARNS TO FOOL AND CHARM US ALL. I BELIEVE HE DID HAVE A SUCCESSFUL ELECTRONIC WIDGET BUSINESS, SELLING TO THE NAVY, AND THE CHILEAN PART OF THE STORY IS PROBABLY TRUE. THE REST OF IT, HE MADE UP. MORE POWER TO HIM! I AM LEAVING IT ALL IN THE MEMOIR BECAUSE IT IS SUCH A GOOD STORY, EVEN IF HE MADE UP SOME OF IT.

Another close friend, now deceased, was Perry Anastos, my friend and closest confidant since Ralph Bentley married (?) and moved away. I met Perry through Ralph, perhaps 40 years ago. Perry was of course a Greek, as many of my friends are. From the Jews I first met at Swarthmore College, I got my intellectual education, and from the Greeks, I learned how to live. Both are very ancient traditions that I am proud to have been associated with, if only through my personal friends.

Perry and I were not close in the beginning. He has told me that he first thought I was very badly adjusted (psychologically), then after a time, he changed his mind and thought I was better adjusted than most. Now, I don't really know what he thought, since I subsequently showed him parts of this Memoir and he then knew some of my history.

Perry was an interesting mix of liberal, even radical, ideas and also very conservative thinking. This is partially explained by the fact that he was a Reichian, i.e., a follower of the great radical psychoanalyst, Dr. Wilhelm Reich. Some people say Reich was completely looped, but as *The New York Times* said in one of its several front-page Sunday Book section reviews of new biographies of Reich, no matter how crazy any of his new ideas seemed, he did nothing without imbuing it with at least a touch of genius.

I first encountered Reichians at Swarthmore College, where I learned about "character armor" and "orgone boxes," more properly designated as "orgone accumulators." Reich believed that the universe was filled with something he called "orgone energy" and that by sitting in an orgone box for an hour or so, you could charge up on this orgone energy and have better orgasms in your sex life and, I suppose, be more energetic and more in touch in your whole life. An orgone box consisted of a wood box about the size of a phone booth with steel wool in the walls, nothing more. For the believer, the boxes were very effective.

For such a wild philosophy, Reichianism was very successful. Many of the highly intelligent liberal or radical parents who sent their children to Swarthmore swore by it, and so did their children.

There are other points in the Reichian philosophy that appeal to me as well. Reich does not subscribe to the theory of that staple of Freudian psychoanalysis, the Oedipus complex. I heartily agree to this—I could never let myself be dominated by another male, my own father, an analyst, or anybody else. I believe such a resolution would crush the autonomy of the young spirit and will, and forever doom it to carrying out the tasks of others, instead of its own work. Also, Reich believes that the (orgone) energy between any one man and any one woman dies after a year or two, and a new source (partner) must be found. Perhaps this is the reason many Reichian analysands never marry.

Incidentally, about the Oedipus complex, I read somewhere that 9 out of 10 young men who had unresolved Oedipal complexes were total failures, but the tenth man, unconstrained by the father figure, became wildly successful.

Another concept of Wilhelm Reich's that has been very important to me is that of "character armor." According to Reich, if you're neurotic, your muscles are held in a rigid way that blocks the "streaming," or flow of orgone energy. To some extent, the concepts of character armor and streaming (without the orgone energy) are accepted by orthodox Freudian analysts. But the Reichian analysts work on their patients, now mostly or totally nude, male and female, by kneading their muscles to break up the character armor. From my own experience, I have a pretty good idea what Reich is talking about when he speaks of character armor. He's right about a lot, but the concepts of orgone energy and streaming are too occult for me to accept, even if it is true. I prefer to remain a scientific materialist.

Anyway, to get back to Pericles, or Perry, Anastos, he was a Reichian success story. Women fell all over him, even in later life, and he claimed to have had 127 affairs and a lot of one-night stands (I learned later this was hyperbole). Now, quantity isn't everything, but it sure helps. He always seemed to say the right thing to women. At 75, however, he no longer partook. I don't know if his prostate was gone, or what. I couldn't get this out of him. All he would say is that he was afraid of AIDS.

There is another aspect of Reichianism that was reflected in Perry's attitude. Like all Reichian analysands that I have met, he was politically conservative. He went to Norman Vincent Peale's church every Sunday. He agreed with me in being a good democrat (Democrat?) but we differed in that he said, if he couldn't be a democrat and had to choose between a dictatorship of the Right and a dictatorship of the Left, he would take the former. Reich himself flirted with Communism when young, but ended up in America, more than conservative politically.

Incidentally, Reich went beyond psychiatry on a few occasions. At one point, late in his career, he built the "Cloudbuster," a rainmaking machine, to help the American Indians in the Southwest. You can still find plenty of Zuni and Navaho who will swear the thing worked.

Perry lived his life on a schedule like clockwork. He got up every morning at 7:00 a.m. without fail, had black coffee, toast and marmalade at a neighborhood Greek coffee pot, went home and puttered with his papers until noon, when he again went out every day for a slice of takeout *spanakopita* (Greek spinach and cheese pie—very tasty—I sometimes eat it myself but certainly not every day), back in by 1:00 p.m., whereupon he puttered with his papers again until 4:00 p.m., when without fail every day he went out for his constitutional, a stroll patrolling and surveying the neighborhood to catch up on the latest doings therein

Then, in the evenings, he went to poetry readings every Monday and Wednesday (in the Winter), and a "religious" dinner every Thursday with a few like-minded friends in a fine restaurant, even the Plaza sometimes, to discuss topics of religious interest. Occasionally he went to a French movie on the odd nights. When nothing else intervenes, he went to the local bar, "Benjamin's" to dine and have three or four glasses of (only white) wine.

Saturday nights, about once a month, I got him tickets to The New York Philharmonic at Lincoln Center, either in a group or just the two of us. Sundays, without fail, he went to hear the hucksters at Norman Vincent Peale's church at Fifth Avenue and 29th Street. On holidays, he went to the Greek church of his forbears.

Perry's regular schedule has always bemused me. I try to do something different every day and not fall into any predictable patterns. But then, I thought that, living that way, I'd probably die young and Perry would live to 120. His mother died not too long ago at about age 96.

Perry was drafted into the Army at the beginning of the Second World War. His eyes were bad, so he was sent to noncombatant duty in Iran, operating a huge port crane to unload mostly Dodge trucks to be sent up through the Caucasus to help the Russians withstand the German onslaught. Often, a Russian officer sat next to Perry in the crane cab. The war was uneventful for Perry, relieved only by occasional trips to the whorehouses of Khorramshahr, the nearest place that was at all exciting. Just before V-E day, Perry was sent to Marseilles and instructed to drive a jeep to Antwerp.

He says the French and Belgian women along the way were very good to him.

After the war the Army offered to make Perry an officer, but for indoor office duty only. Perry declined and took his discharge, whereupon he returned to the States and entered Teacher's College at Columbia U. to become a teacher of French and English. He also entered his Reichian psychoanalysis which has already been mentioned.

Perry pretty much stayed in New York City, mostly in his own neighborhood or midtown. He quoted Ralph Waldo Emerson on the evils of travel. Perhaps he saw enough in WWII. He noted that the Army trained him in California, shipped him across the Pacific to Iran, sent him to France and Belgium, and then brought him home across the Atlantic to muster him out, so he has been "around the world," in troopships anyway.

Perry was always a good buddy to me. I respected his advice and I appreciated the $50. or so he lent me every month when I was short. I always paid him back at the end of the month without fail.

I could never get Perry to come along on my summer bodypainting beach parties. Too bad he couldn't unbend, but Reichians are conservative in such matters. He hid behind his Paul Stuart clothes while we had all the fun.

Notwithstanding what I said earlier about Perry's aversion to travel of any kind, he did make several fairly lengthy trips every year, on the holidays of Greek Easter, Thanksgiving and Greek Christmas, to his birthplace in Manchester, New Hampshire. His parents established themselves there on their arrival from Greece to work in the Manchester factories and mills, which made shoes and I think, textiles. Perry worked in a shoe factory summers when he was young.

It's interesting to note that Perry's mother was born under Turkish rule in Greek Macedonia, which was not liberated from Turkish rule until 1912, long after most of the rest of Greece had been freed. Perry was very proud of the fact that his maternal grandfather played an important role in driving the Turks out of the ancestral village.

Perry told me that Manchester, to this day, is mostly inhabited by Greeks, French Canadians and Irish, all of whom came to America to work in the mills. All the Greek children were given elegant Greek names, like Socrates, Plato and Pericles, and the other kids teased

Perry on the playground when he was little about his pretentious name. So my friend "Pericles" decided to go by the name "Perry." Only in recent years was I able to get him to use his wonderful original name, when he declaimed poetry in English, French and Greek, in his own translations, at my Eleutheria (means "Liberty" in Demotic Greek) Salons.

When Perry occasionally pissed me off, I would repeat Demosthenes' admonition to the Greeks of the City States, when they were threatened by the Macedonians under Phillip, that "Macedonians are not Greek." Phillip's blandishments had weakened Greek resolve, and Demosthenes was trying to rally the city states to resist the Macedonian Empire. Unfortunately, he was unsuccessful. But anyway, Perry was a blond, like the ancient Greeks, and most modern Greeks of Greece proper are now dark and Slavic, after all the migrations since antiquity.

Perry was an excellent translator of Greek, French and English poetry, as I have said. I hope he wrote some original poetry—he was certainly capable of it, and he might have done it—but he never let on whether he was so involved. Perhaps, also, he worked on writing a memoir. But I am afraid his natural humility kept him from doing any of this. It's a shame. I'd like to have something to remember him by, he has been such a good friend.

In about 2002, Perry became slightly disoriented and was taken to a hospital, where the diagnosis was dementia. After a short while, when it became clear he would not recover, he went back to New Hampshire to live with his sister. A little later, he entered a Veterans' retirement home in Tilton, NH. I'm told by his sister that was quite content there, reminiscing with his new army buddies, and that he was himself, clear in his head, two-thirds of the time. He had a private room and a little kitchen, where he made do for himself. I'm happy things worked out as well as they did. And we found out that he didn't have Alzheimer's Disease, which can kill you quickly. He only has a milder form of senile dementia and was expected to live a long time.

I must report, here at the end of my story of Perry, that he finally lost his will to live and starved himself to death in the Veterans' home in about 2004, at the age of 84. Yes, the Veterans' home is no place for a true New Yorker and boulevardier and who would want to continue living with dementia? Perry, we all still love you!

More Friends

I now lead a rich an immediate life, with many remarkable and rewarding experiences. But I will add that I also live somewhat vicariously, through the lives and experiences of my good friends. I could not have survived, especially at the beginning of my recovery, without this. My friends' life experiences, especially when they are beyond the norm, help me build my character. It's reciprocal, as well. The many remarkable things I do help bolster my friends' developing characters.

Before my first psychotic break in 1960, I was, as I have mentioned, engaged in an intensive nondirective orthodox Freudian psychoanalysis, perhaps with existential overtones. I went to the Freudians because I had spent the previous year with a friendly, supportive but aimless psychologist, and nothing had been accomplished. I wanted to get deep into this. But I got more than I bargained for. But in pursuing this, I dropped all my friends. In the psychoanalysis, I learned to empty my mind, which is not a good idea, despite what the psychoanalysts and the Buddhists say. I expected to find a desert or empty void. Instead, I found a void filled with incapacitating, bizarre, uncanny, occult and Religious phenomena. I could not cope with it. I couldn't think straight. I lost the ability to function normally. I couldn't support myself and eventually ended up in the asylum.

Forty years later, I am more or less cured and sane, thanks to my tranquilizers and my friends. Now I stay well and avoid the void by filling my life with projects, activities, art work, photography work, writing work, concerts, dinners and friends. All these help kept the crippling Religious Subjectivity at bay. I never want to experience anything like that again.

Another friend, Yousof Najibullah, deceased in 1998, had a remarkable life that contributed to my own and helped me reestablish myself. An Afghani, Yousof was born in 1935 or 1936 (he was not sure which) into the extended Afghani royal family, the Najibullah clan. His grandfather was an Emir who had 50 wives, so Yousof has lots of relatives. His father was a prominent diplomat at the United Nations.

Unfortunately, Yousof's education was interrupted by all the wars in Afghanistan so he was never able to attain such prominence. But he did something better. He became one of the best artists and caricaturists that I have ever known.

Yousof first came to the United States in the 1960s, with his father. I don't know too much about Yousof's first stay here, except that, around this time, he married a pretty English girl. The marriage did not last and there were no children. At one point, on his return to Afghanistan in the 1960s, Yousof and his wife drove alone from London to Kabul, and had several interesting experiences along the way, including a knock-down fight with a Customs inspector in Bulgaria who wanted baksheesh.

In the 1980s, the Communists and the Russians took over Afghanistan, and the Civil War began. Yousof tried to get out and ended up in a concentration camp in Pakistan. The Pakistanis were going to shoot him because they thought he was a Communist, but he was able to demonstrate his Royal Family connections, and they let him get on a plane to New York. Yousof arrived at Idlewilde without a cent—he cadged a token and got to Times Square where he immediately began drawing charcoal portraits on shirt cardboards to make a little money. Yousof explained the turf battles he had to wage to get a spot to draw in Times Square. Some of it was pretty rough.

Of course, he could get money eventually from Afghanistan, but in the beginning, he did not have access to it, and getting started here was a hard proposition, as it is, of course, for most people. After an indeterminate period of struggle, Yousof found a job of sorts at the United Nations, through, I think, his family connections. Since his formal education didn't qualify him for anything else, Yousof ended up driving a fork lift truck in the Documents Section of the U.N. But it really wasn't such a bad deal—some years Yousof earned in the neighborhood of $50,000, plus all sorts of U.N. tax, health and other benefits.

There were, however, other problems at the Secretariat. Most of Yousof's co-workers in the Document Section were African-American and Hispanic, and many of them resented what they took to be Yousof's arrogant and lordly ways. Yousof had been, please remember, in the Afghani Royal Family, and was accustomed to being treated decently. So there were fights, but Yousof was a good boxer, a good fighter, and survived all this. And there were troubles with the administration.

Finally, towards the end of his life, after many years at the U.N., Yousof was put on psychiatric disability, drawing full salary and benefits and not required to put in an appearance. Really a good deal for Yousof, I think. And he wasn't in the least crazy, to my way of thinking. As I have explained, I know about such things from personal experience.

Like quite a few of my friends, Yousof loved to crash parties, buffets and receptions. He could talk endlessly and interestingly about Life and Art. And he was, of course, a Very Good Artist, but he never made the right connections, or was able to display or sell his work, other than to his appreciative friends.

Yousof was always a faithful friend to me (although we almost came to blows a couple of times), loved my Eleutheria Salons, at which he spoke and gave carefully prepared presentations (about Gandhara Buddhist art from his native part of the world and other topics about which he was equally knowledgeable) several times, and also was a stalwart at my Bodypainting Beach Parties at Lighthouse Beach on Fire Island. He always provided transportation in his wonderful 4x4. Yousof's 4x4 was always available to us, his friends, on our many expeditions, and was a great help to us.

Yousof was in good shape for a man in his sixties and always looked good nude on the beach. He had a great natural dignity, even with his clothes off. Even more so, with his clothes off. And of course going nude was extremely unusual for a Muslim, although Yousof told me the Nudity taboo was really more an Arab thing, not quite so much applicable to Afghanis and much of the rest of the Muslim world, particularly in the case of those individuals who were comfortable in the Western World, like Yousof. But it was still a big cultural leap for a Muslim.

For the last few years of his life, Yousof had an English ladyfriend here in America, one Hilary James, a widow with one daughter. More about the mother and daughter elsewhere, but here, suffice to say, Hilary's behavior would become outrageous without Yousof's restraining hand. Hilary would get insufferable unless she had Yousof to , yes, slap her around a little, after which she was fine and socially agreeable. I can only equate Yousof's firm hand with the restraints I had to accustom myself to in the asylum. It did work for Hilary, and she was not hospitalized. After Yousof's death, I couldn't cope with Hilary. She was totally unmanageable without Yousof. Incidentally,

Hilary was also a competent artist, technically a little better than Yousof, in a variety of media, but she couldn't match the imagination and spirit of Yousof's caricatures.

Toward the end of both their lives, Yousof and Otto Koch roomed together in a nice little apartment in Astoria, Queens, with a cat they were both very fond of. I wonder what ever happened to the cat? Yousof and Otto were compatible, if in nothing else than that they both loved a good party. Yousof was the soberer of the two. He related to me how Otto would often come home late after an extended drinking bout, be unable to get his key through the lock, and be found in a little heap in front of the door by Yousof on his way out in the morning on the way to work.

Yousof's end was quick. Like so many men I know who are in their 60s and 70s, they continue to do heavy work occasionally and move furniture in the secret hope that they will drop dead suddenly and not linger for months or years stuck full of tubes, somewhere. That's exactly what happened to Yousof. He was moving furniture for a friend one afternoon, when he suddenly felt badly.

He thought he was having an asthma attack, though he'd never had asthma. Well, the attack passed and Yousof went back to moving furniture. A second attack struck and Yousof was taken to White Plains Community Hospital. Yousof walked from the ambulance to the emergency room. The hospital must not have tested him thoroughly, because they found nothing, and decided only to hold Yousof overnight for observation. That night, Yousof got up from his bed to walk to the bathroom and dropped dead on the way. The first "asthma attack" had been a first heart attack, to be followed by the second and then the third in the hospital which killed him. A great loss to all of us who knew him. But Yousof had the quick death he wanted, far from his ancestral home but not far from all the many good friends he had made in New York City. I don't see any reason for an active man like Yousof to linger, incapacitated, at the end.

Paul Steinhacker is another friend who has made a great impression on me. I don't know much about Paul—we keep our distance and he is a very laconic person, unlike most New Yorkers that I know. But we respect each other from a slight distance and occasionally have long phone conversations.

For many years, Paul operated his own art gallery here in Manhattan, on East 71st Street, where he showed his collections of Eskimo, Aleut and also Tibetan art. Paul spoke about this work on several occasions at my Eleutheria Salon, with wonderful slides, to great acclaim.

When Paul was about 18, he was drafted into the U.S. Army for service in the Korean War. Paul is something of a hero to me –he took part in the infamous Battle of Pork Chop Hill, which, Gunnar tells me, was a Pyrrhic victory for our side, in that we took the hill, but our losses were so heavy that it may not have been worth it.

Paul's description of the battle was chilling. He says, as he ascended the hill, "there were pieces of people all over the place and bullets whizzing everywhere." But Paul survived.

After the Korean War ended and Paul was released from the Army, he returned to New York City where, for want of anything else to do, he took a job in advertising on Madison Avenue. But this was too bland and insipid for Paul, who, after a short time, on the advice of a shrink (I think), began to educate himself in the intricacies and fine points of Eskimo and Aleut

Indian art, and soon was in a position to open his small gallery on East 71st Street to deal in these materials. I believe he educated himself totally on his own in how to do this.

Paul was no fool, but a very brave and resourceful man. He began making trips in the Summer to the Bering Straits region of Alaska, with Nome as a base of operations. Soon he became friends with the Eskimos and Aleuts on the isolated islands in the Bering Straits, and he made arrangements with them to buy any walrus ivory artifacts they managed to dig up from the ice. Some of the artifacts Paul obtained in this way were a thousand or more years old, and worth ten thousand dollars or even more. Paul knew exactly what was valuable and what was not.

Paul was always fair with the Eskimos and Aleuts. He paid them half what he thought he could get for the pieces. He seldom made a mistake in evaluating the work, and so he soon had an effective network of suppliers (the Eskimos and Indians), dealers and customers, and a thriving business.

He bought land in the wilderness not far from Nome, and began gold prospecting on the side. He was eventually able to sell several large plots to the big gold exploration companies at a considerable profit.

Anyway, the years went by and Paul got older. But now, in his seventies, he still spends part of every Summer in Alaska, flying to the islands in the dangerous bush planes, and keeping up his business. He did sell his gallery in Manhattan, however, and, a couple of years ago, he moved to Seattle.

Paul and I speak on the phone every month or so, and we get together for lunch or dinner when he is in town. I'd say he was the strong, silent type, except he's just a wiry little guy. He finds Seattle congenial, nearer his work in Alaska, but he says the Seattle natives are even more laconic than he is. He says the locals apologize when they order a cup of coffee in a coffee shop, so as not to put anyone to trouble. It's not entirely true that Paul is laconic—over the telephone with me he can become positively garrulous when discussing politics (he is to the right of me—he is a Republican), a topic which I've learned to avoid with him.

Paul made successful presentations several times at my Eleutheria Salon, describing his work and showing beautiful slides of his artifacts. I'll always be grateful to him for this. Paul has always been an example to me of what you can accomplish on your own, without special advantages or formal training. And his independence and love of the wild have been an inspiration. I love his stories of eye-to-eye contacts with grizzly bears in the wilderness, which, due to Paul's restraint and care, never became violent. You can love a grizzly bear as a creature of the wild even when he's menacing you, I learned from Paul.

Paul went to Alaska last Summer. Every year he says it will be his last year there, but he always goes back. I hope he never stops.

Eleutheria

1989 – 2010

I have always liked to entertain, but I became systematic about it sometime around 1989. It was then that I sponsored my first Eleutheria Salon in my Studio apartment in Morningside Gardens Cooperative. "Eleutheria" means "Liberty" in Demotic, or popular, Greek. I'm almost certain that I learned the word "Eleutheria" from my good old friend, Perry, or "Pericles," Anastos.

"Eleutheria" is correctly pronounced "ELEFTHERIYA," with the "leu" pronounced like the British "lieutenant," that is, "LEFTENANT." I don't know if the derivation (of the pronunciation) is the same in the two instances. I chose the word because, as I matured, I became something of a philhellene.

I admired the Ancient Greek idea of a man being able to do just about anything passably well, without becoming a specialist in anything. Anyone who did have a specialty was usually a "metic," or "foreign" artisan, not really a part of the community. I have always been a Generalist, and follow science, math, computers, music and art with equal avidity. I also like the outdoors and sports (skydiving?) and have worked at a great many kinds of jobs. I'm probably a damned fool for thinking this way in the Modern World, but I never wanted to be shut away in a cubicle in a huge office somewhere, practicing my "specialty." Of course, maybe all this just ties in with all those Gentleman's "C's" I earned at Swarthmore College. But then, I've also worked as a day laborer and at other lowly jobs, so maybe that last part isn't right, either. The Dickensian contrast between these lowly jobs and my limited moments of a better life, again. Maybe the Dickensian ups and towns have saved me from a mediocre life in an office cubicle.

Another consideration is that, because of my psychological disturbances, even prior to the failed psychoanalysis and the breakdowns, I couldn't concentrate too intensely on most things or everything would start to spin and I would be confronted with rapidly multiplying realities, or something like that, which were very difficult to cope with. I would get a dose of Chaos, my Recovery would be reversed, and I would be back to Square One. Or maybe Square Zero! Yes, all very existential, but not for me. Maybe the disturbances were of a sort that would be good for artists! That's a laugh! A Dumb Irony!

Anyway, being a host was something I could do comfortably. I began to invite my friends and acquaintances, some of them fairly prominent, to talk about, recite, or show their creative work. The Eleutheria sessions, generally held on Sunday afternoons, beginning about 3:00 p.m. and lasting until past 9:00 p.m., would begin with two hours of eating, drinking and sociability, and then there would first be two or three presenters, professors, poets, playwrights, artists, musicians, explorers, world travelers, etc. Finally, I would show slides of my classic young female nudes. Then there would be a couple of more hours of eating and drinking, and we would call it a night.

Before I describe some of the presenters, I'll tell you what we ate and drank. Originally, I provided all sorts of rich food, like smoked salmon, pate and quiche lorraine. This went over well with the gluttons, but it was too much for most of us. So I switched to lighter Mediterranean fare, which most of us preferred. This has come to include *taramosalata,* a Greek fish roe dip, served with small torn-up pieces of pita bread; *skordalia,* a garlicky Greek dip, served in the same way; *dolmades,* or the popular stuffed grape leaves (stuffed with rice and oil); *spanakopita,* or Greek spinach and cheese pie, served warm; and finally the ubiquitous baklava, a delicious dessert pastry, rich with honey and ground walnuts, from Poseidon Bakery, the best Greek bakery in Manhattan. Incidentally, baklava is not a Greek invention, whatever else they might have accomplished. The Greeks got baklava from the Turks, during the Turkish conquest.

There were other delicacies, as well. I served the huge, black Kalamata olives. One of my guests and a sometime presenter at Eleutheria, a member of the prestigious Explorers Club, a very sophisticated man with ordinarily meticulous manners, would spit the olive pits out on the floor, on my beautiful (acrylic) Oriental rug. When I complained and asked for an explanation, he said that's what the explorers do, when they're in the Middle Eastern back country, and are consuming Kalamata olives in huts with dirt or mud floors. So, apparently, spitting out the pits on the floor was the "sophisticated" thing to do. I still don't believe it, however. Maybe I'm not sophisticated enough!

Other treats at Eleutheria include dried apricots, seedless white grapes, pepperoni (yes, you can buy it in Greek delis), sliced artichoke hearts, crackers and assorted good cheeses, and finally, Greek cookies to accompany the baklava. Brewed coffee is served.

As to drink, I have a couple of interesting stories. I eschew hard liquor at my gatherings - it ruins people's heads. I serve wine and various aperitifs. I do serve grappa, which I find in my dictionary is classified as a brandy. Grappa is a very old European drink. In the Middle Ages, the lord of the manor would make his wine from his grapes, and then give the leftover *pomace* (or grape husks) to his peasants, from which they would distill a very clear, very intense liquor which was grappa. Usually, all the different varieties of *pomace* were thrown in together

Grappa became the drink of the peasants, and a little later, because it was (then) cheap, it became the drink of artists and Bohemians. I first encountered it in the studio of an Italian artist woman friend in the artists' colony of Williamsburg, Brooklyn. I took to it at once. Nowadays, because it was associated with artists, grappa has become very popular with the cognoscenti. It is now made in a number of different specific varietals, which have become very expensive. But you can still find the original mixed up stuff, reasonably cheap. I buy it in my favorite Greek liquor store in Astoria, Queens, an ethnic neighborhood.

Another of my special offerings is Kourtaki (brand) retsina, a Greek flavored white wine. Kourtaki retsina, from Attica, is ordinary white wine flavored with pine resin. Why do the Greeks add the pine resin? Three thousand years ago, in the early days of Greek winemaking, there were no glass bottles with metal screw tops in which to ship large amounts of wine. So the Greeks shipped the wine in amphorae, ceramic vases which could be handled easily. The Greeks sealed the amphorae with skin, and closed the seal with pine resin. Eventually, the resin got into the wine, and the Greeks developed a taste for it that way. Nowadays, you either love retsina or hate it. But it's an acquired taste, like beer. You can learn to love retsina, as I have done. And it's quite inexpensive.

That about covers the food and drink. Did I mention that I usually need to take up a collection (donations in advance) to cover the $400 plus the event costs me to put on? But my friends and attendees are very supportive. I usually do not have too much difficulty in coming up with the necessary funds. Earlier on, I had to pay another $80 for a party helper? Now, regularly, my good friend Julia Poulos (yes, Greek) helps out with the cooking and serving, just for love. I really appreciate her help.

Did I mention that once, 25 years ago, Julia propositioned me, but I turned her down. I was happier with the pretty 18-year-olds in the brothels. Julie, then about 40 or 45, was very proud of her body, and claimed she had the body of a 25-year-old. She was a NYC Marathon (carrying on the Greek tradition) runner and had won a lot of prizes. Well, I saw the body on a nude bodypainting beach party to a free beach on Fire Island, and I, at the time, I gave her credit for a body of 32 or 33 apparent years. Anyway, Julia has never held my turning her down as a bed partner against me, and we continue to be close friends. I should add that other friends also sometimes help out at Eleutheria, including Eugenia Dimitriadis (also Greek, but now, sadly, deceased).

We move on now to the stories of the presenters at Eleutheria, of whom there have been at least 50 (some repeats, on new topics). I try to sponsor Eleutheria, semiannually, usually near the Vernal Equinox and the Winter Solstice. Some years I have only been able to hold the affair once. But I've kept Eleutheria going with some regularity.

What follows are excerpts from some of the many Eleutheria Salon Flyers, giving you some idea of the range of my presenters. Giving the Eleutheria Salons has been a very worthwhile endeavor for me.

The Eminent Columbia University/Barnard Professor, Russian Studies Expert, Peace Activist, Writer and Television Personality (WNET Charlie Rose Show, Etc.),

PETER JUVILER,

Will Speak about his New Book, "Freedom's Ordeal," which is about the fate of democracy and human rights in the 15 countries that have emerged from the breakup of the Soviet Empire. Dr. Juviler explains that History has shown that states emerging from collapsed empires rarely achieve full democracy on the first try. He analyzes these successor states as crucial and not always unpromising tests of democracy's viability in post-communist countries. As a long-time observer of this important region, Dr. Juviler provides an insider's insight into the fate of freedom, human rights and interethnic relations in these post-communist states. In addition to being

Professor of Political Science at Barnard College, Columbia University, Dr. Juviler is Codirector, Columbia University Human Rights Center.

The Renowned Art Historians and Art Lovers,

JUDSON AND ELINOR LEVIN,

Will Show Slides and Explicate the Work of the Proto-Impressionist Frederic Bazille (1841-1870), who Helped Lay the Groundwork for the Later Flourishing of the Impressionist School in France and Throughout the World. As Jud will Explain, Bazille was as much a Realist as an Impressionist, but His Play of Light and Shadow and the Resulting Chiaroscuro Effects Were Reflected in Much of the Work of the Later Impressionists. Frederic Bazille, Not Yet Well Known in America, Was Given Significant Exposure in the Recent Impressionist Show at the Metropolitan. Jud, a Retired Lawyer, and Elinor, his Charming Wife, Travelled Throughout France, Staying at Bed&Breakfasts in Remote Locations, Gathering Background on the Impressionists, Their Work and Their Period, by Interviewing Curators,

Family Members and Others Who Were Affected by the Impressionists. Frederic Bazille is One of Jud and Eli's Favorite Subjects. Bazille was a Medical Student who Quickly Shifted to an Art Career. He was Not Much Exhibited in His Lifetime but was Very Close to the Other Famous Names of the Period. 6'6" Tall, Frederic Bazille was Killed at the Age of 29 in the Franco-Prussian War, for Which He Had Early Volunteered.

The Famous Litterateur, Pedagogue and Writer,

PERICLES (PERRY) ANASTOS,

Will Read and Explicate the Prize-Winning and Published Poetry of Your Host's Sister, BARBARA JANE SEAMAN FREESTONE. Mr. Anastos Has Translated Some of Ms. Freestone's Poetry into French and Demotic Greek, Which He Will Also Read and Discuss. Ms. Freestone, After Much Pathos in Her Early Married Life, Raised with her Husband Three Children, All of Whom Became Engineers. One, a Girl, Became Pennsylvania Engineer of the Year in 1996. One of the Sons Became an Officer on a Nuclear

Submarine. Ms. Freestone is now Retired from Employment and is Devoting Herself to Her Poetry. She Recently Won a Prize for the Poem "The Magic of Winter" Published in the Se (sic) La Vie Writer's Journal. More Significantly, Another Poem Was Recently Published in the AAUW Collection, "The Light and Depth of Mirrors." Mr. Anastos and his Translations Will Help Illuminate the Work of This New Voice.

The Beautiful and Brilliant Writer, Poet, Actress and Model,

STEPHANIE SELLARS,

Will declaim her ORIGINAL POETRY in French and English. Stephanie graduated PHI BETA KAPPA in French and English from Gettysburg College. Her poetry has been published in "Re: Verse!" and her poetry and fiction can be VIEWED ON THE WEB AT FREEWILLIAMSBURG.COM. Stephanie recently read her original French verse at the COLUMBIA U. MAISON FRANCAISE and acted in "Les Liaisons Dangereux" with STUDIO DRAMATIQUE. She has offered original

PERFORMANCE ART at the AVIGNON FESTIVAL in France. She makes her living as an ESL teacher and as an ARTIST'S AND PHOTOGRAPHER'S MODEL (as you will see later) and has recently completed a one-act play based on her modeling experiences and also the relationship between MAN RAY AND LEE MILLER. Stephanie also recently completed and is preparing for publication her MAJOR FIRST NOVEL (in French and English), partly AUTOBIOGRAPHICAL, entitled "DANDELION MOON."

The Rising Young Adventurer, Filmmaker, Writer and Ecdysiast,

JANE ALICIA ROSE,

Will describe her recent trip to AFRICA, in the company of our former presenter, Jenny Mundy-Castle, and Ben, Jane's beau. Jane will Discuss MEMORABLE INDIVIDUALS She Met, Vanishing WILDLIFE and Changes in VILLAGE LIFE. Jane has TRAVELED ALL OVER THE WORLD in search of ADVENTURE AND MATERIAL for Her Writings, Including Excursions to India, Nepal, New Zealand,

Europe and Israel. She has FRIENDS ALL OVER THE WORLD. Jane attributes Some of HER ADVENTUROUS NATURE to Her Mother, Who Put Jane on a Horse When She Was 12 and Said "Jump." Jane Has JUMPED Many STALLIONS BAREBACK. She has Also BOXED with the COLUMBIA U. BOXING CLUB. Jane Graduated From COLUMBIA UNIVERSITY'S GENERAL STUDIES PROGRAM in 2001. She has Worked as an ARTIST'S AND PHOTOGRAPHERS'S FIGURE MODEL (Initially for Your Host). She Now MAKES FILMS with a GUERILLA FILM GROUP in the BOHEMIAN COMMUNITY of Williamsburg, Brooklyn. Your Host STARRED in One of Them. Jane now ALSO PERFORMS as an EXOTIC DANCER at The GALAPAGOS CLUB in Williamsburg. She Has Written for SEVERAL PUBLISHED SEX GUIDES to NYC. Jane has Also MOVED FURNITURE for a LIVING. She Plans to SKYDIVE With YOUR HOST this Spring or Summer. Originally from the HIGH COUNTRY of NORTHERN NEW HAMPSHIRE, Jane now Makes Her Home in Williamsburg.

The Illustrious Poet, Prose Writer and Journalist,

PENELOPE KARAGEORGE,

a DIE-HARD NEW YORKER ("I love the wicked city, its people, art museums, theatre, diversity.") also considers herself a "LEMNIAN," spending summers in her STONE HOUSE in LICHNA, once her grandmother's. ("No TV, just the hum of CICADAS."). She has made SHORT FILMS, and is writing a FEATURE FILM SCRIPT, <u>Drinking the Sun</u>, set on the Greek island of LEMNOS. Born in Newburgh, New York, Penelope began her journalistic career as a <u>Newsweek</u> magazine reporter, INTERVIEWING CELEBRITIES as diverse as Jane FONDA and Salvador DALI, and was publicity director of <u>People.</u> A graduate of Simmons College with a master's degree from CUNY, she is the author of TWO NOVELS, a mystery, <u>Murder at Tomorrow</u> (Walker Publishing) and <u>Stolen Moments</u> (Pinnacle Books), published in England as <u>Winners</u>, and in Germany as <u>New York, New York</u>. A PRIZE-WINNING POET, Pella Publishing published her first collection, <u>Red Lipstick and the Wine-Dark Sea.</u> Penelope's short story, <u>Day Trippers</u>, will be published in the literary journal, <u>The Charioteer</u>, in November;

four poems will appear in an upcoming mutli-cultural anthology, <u>Heal</u>, to be published in January; and SHE WILL BE GIVING A READING at the New York MidManhattan Public Library, Midtown, on Nov. 15 at 6:30 p.m. with poet Constantine Contogenis as part of the MidManhattan Library's Hellenic series. Penelope is writing a COVER STORY for <u>Odyssey</u> magazine on <u>The Greeks of New York</u>. Penelope returned in August from the prestigious SPOLETO WRITERS' WORKSHOP in Italy, where (as Penelope humbly reports) one critic compared her work to DOROTHY PARKER's. Her talk and/or slides will delight us today with depictions of her FURTHER ADVENTURES in Spoleto, Assisi, Siena, Orvieto and elsewhere in Tuscany and Umbria.

The Renowned Vocalist, Animal Rights Activist and Humanitarian,

ANONYMOUS,

Graces ELEUTHERIA Today. The REDOUBTABLE and CELEBRATED Ms. A is a Smashingly Reviewed CABARET and RELIGIOUS SINGER in Such Posh Clubs as JUDY'S (next to the

Hotel Algonquin) and other Hot Spots in Manhattan and Elsewhere. Ms. A is also a FORMIDABLE ANIMAL RIGHTS ACTIVIST and has been the Group Leader in Eliminating the HIDEOUS DRAIZE TEST (Used on the Exposed Eyes of Rabbits) from the Labs of SEVERAL MAJOR COSMETICS GIANTS. Ms. A's Game Plan is to See the TOTAL ELIMINATION of the DRAIZE TEST in HER LIFETIME. Ms. A is also an ARDENT and NEAR-ABSOLUTE VEGETARIAN, which Ties in with her Subject Today. Some years ago, Ms. A worked as a SEXUAL SURROGATE in a Large SEX CLINIC under MEDICAL SUPERVISION. Ms. A brought her COMPASSION and KNOWLEDGE to the Aid of many SEXUALLY DYSFUNCTIONAL MEN of All Ages, Restoring Most of Them to FULL FUNCTION, Sometimes BY PSYCHOLOGICAL MEANS and Sometimes BY MORE DIRECT INTERACTION. In Telling Us about This Very Important Work Today, Ms. A will also Explain that CHANGES IN DIET would have PREVENTED Many of These Men's DIFFICULTIES (Such as Prostate Trouble) FROM ARISING. Also of Great Interest are the PSYCHOLOGICAL and SHYNESS

DYSFUNCTIONS of the MUCH YOUNGER MEN, and How Ms. A COPED with this.

The above will give you some idea of the range of topics considered by the presenters. The last one above, ANONYMOUS, was especially interesting. Unfortunately, she is now working in a sensitive job with children and had to withdraw permission for me to use her name. This is not a complete listing of topics and presenters. Eleutheria has gone on for more than 15 years and there have been more than fifty presenters (with occasional repeats by the same presenters, each speaking on a different topic). I have thoroughly enjoyed putting on all the Eleutheria Shows and I want to thank everyone who has helped me do so, either financially or by presenting.

Holding to Tradition
1968-2009

I don't hold much with tradition. I like to think of myself as an irreverent iconoclast, a la Dr. Albert Ellis. But there is one set of traditions that I do try to keep. That is the Winter Solstice celebration, co-opted by the major faiths as Christmas, Chanukah, Divali, etc For a while, I tried to celebrate Saturnalia, the ancient Roman pagan winter solstice festival, but now I just say I celebrate the Solstice. Saturnalia is of interest because it was a precursor to Christmas. There were Saturnalia trees and gifts were given. In certain periods, profligacy was the rule. Most interesting of all, for this one day, the masters waited on the slaves.

But what does my celebration consist of? Since December, 1968, when I was age 32, I have hosted a large Dutch treat Christmas Eve dinner at a classic old style Italian restaurant in Greenwich Village, New York City. I haven't missed a single year. The number of us present has ranged from two to 12. This year, 2009, there were six of us, four women and two men, including me. I regret that most of my men friends of earlier years are now dead or incapacitated. But we carry on. This was the 42nd successive annual observance.

Starting in 1968, we met for dinner at "The Grand Ticino," a venerable Italian restaurant on Thompson Street. In its early days, the walls were painted forest green, you could get a plate of spaghetti and meatballs for a couple of dollars, and it was a hangout for older Village intellectuals. More recently, the place was purchased by a group of Albanian Muslims, from Tirana, who painted the walls white and who did continue to run the place in the old classical Italian style. However, they did eventually take all the money out of the business and it closed in 2000. We met in The Grand Ticino for 33 years, less three years when Christmas Eve fell on a Sunday and the place was closed. What had I done when Ticino was closed? We had to find another place, and we did, Minetta Tavern on Minetta Lane and Macdougal Street, another venerable old Italian restaurant with a good cellar. When Ticino closed for good, I just moved our base of operations to The Minetta Tavern. The *zabaglione* here is even better than at Ticino. Later on, as I add this, the Minetta tavern closed and reopened as a too expensive French restaurant, so we have had to look elsewhere. We've tried a couple of other nice places.

What is zabaglione, you ask? It's the high point of the evening every year, for me. Zabaglione is a frothy very light pudding made from eggs, milk, sugar and herbs and heavily laced with Marsala wine. Once you taste it, you'll be a devotee for life. It costs $7. a shot and is sometimes prepared at your table. Delicioso!

The Italian dinner is always followed by a visit to the Episcopal Church of the Ascension, at Fifth Avenue and West 10th Street. The long religious observance is prefaced with a half hour carol service of preludial music. We go only for the carol service; most or all of us do not stay for the religious service itself

The choir is currently directed by Dennis Keene, an accomplished and much recorded musician, with his group, this choir, known as The Voices of Ascension.. The program of carols, selected by Mr. Keene, is noteworthy. There are Old English, Latin, Old French, Old Church Slavonic, and Old German carols, sung in the original languages. The program is esoteric enough for even my most jaded dinner companion.

Last year, in 2002, Mr. Keene made the program into a more modern carol service, with more popular carols, mostly in English. I didn't like it, and, in January 2003, complained to him in an e-mail. Sure enough, he responded, said there had been other complaints, and that he would restore the older program. And he did.

Psychiatric Explorations

1957-2010

Opening another topic in my memoir, I will here consider my experiences with psychoanalysis, psychology and psychiatry. My experiences have not been good. Two breakdowns and three hospitalizations ensued resulted from my entry into a depth nondirective Freudian psychoanalysis, and one of the hospitalizations was a year on the violent ward of a local state mental hospital. It all started early in my Swarthmore College years, when I felt I needed some sort of counseling. My grades were poor (C + average) and I was having no success with the girls. However, as I knew myself to then be sane, if neurotic, I decided not to risk becoming unbalanced in therapy BEFORE I RECEIVED MY B.A. DEGREE. I had read enough to know the possibility of becoming unbalanced in therapy existed, and, as it turned out, that's just what happened, a couple of years later. Besides, I was only a 16-year-old kid. So I waited.

So, back in New York City after graduation, and working as a copyboy on the now defunct *New York World Telegram and the Sun*, I embarked on a program of psychotherapy with one Dr. Nathan Stockhamer, a follower of Dr. Harry Stack Sullivan. Nathan, a Navy veteran, was gentle with me, but nothing happened. After a year, I felt I was going nowhere, so I contacted one of the orthodox Freudian psychoanalytic groups in the city, seeking something deeper. Too deep, as it turned out. This organization sent me for a consultation with a Dr. Felicia Lydia Landau. Going to see that woman was the greatest mistake of my life.

The interview lasted an hour. In the course of it, Dr. Landau commented that I seemed to be "over-intellectualized," which I took then, and still do, as some kind of put-down. I replied, innocently enough, "What else is there?" I mean, at that time, I already had some life experience, and had done and seen a good number of great things, including enjoying some sex, but I still felt that the highest calling was the life of the mind, at least if you were equipped for it. And here was this woman, telling me I was NOT equipped for it. Anyway, Landau next said, "You're in for a surprise," to which I said nothing. In retrospect, what I SHOULD have said is that, "I DON'T LIKE SURPRISES, MYSTERIES OR EPIPHANIES," but I was too inexperienced to come up with the sane answer then. Landau also told me, "Things will get worse before they get better," and "Your analysis will take 20, 30 years, even more." All right, worse, but how much worse? If she was contemplating a year for me on the violent ward, I should have been told so more specifically. If properly warned, I might have stepped back. And as to the 30 years, I just didn't believe it. Was I STUPID or something?

Anyway, the upshot of the Landau interview was that I agreed to enter a depth orthodox Freudian psychoanalysis, PERHAPS an existential psychoanalysis (I was never told this), four 45-minute sessions a week, with one Dr. Irving Sternschein (last name means "starlight" in German – what a misnomer!), an ex-military psychiatrist (rank of Major, never saw combat) who had also worked in reform schools. Tough guy. Wrong for me, as it turned out! This was, I think, late 1959.

I should mention that, at the start, I found an insurance plan that would pay for most of the analysis, at least for the first year and a half.

I didn't like Sternschein from the start, but my life outside in New York City was going nowhere, so I decided to pursue the analysis. I never got a good look at him, the room was always dark. But he was overweight and had a deep voice, which quivered and quavered with emotion. In fact, he seemed physically to tremble at times. I said to myself, "I don't want to end up that emotional." Such a state might be good for landing at Tarawa with the troops, but I felt it wouldn't help me in my life. In fact, if I had to land at Tarawa, I'd rather go in like a butcher in an ice locker.

One more thing. By this time, I had a better job as Science Editor of The Columbia University Press. My Editor-in-Chief there, Bill Bridgwater, who thought I had a good mind and encouraged me in every way, commented that I had a Germanic intellect. This might bear on my opinion of Sternschein's trembling and quavering. It might also bear on my negative opinion of an existential psychoanalysis. Bill Bridgwater's observation might have come from his Roman Catholic background. R.C.'s like to tremble, too. But I don't!

So I pressed on with Sternschein and the 30-year psychoanalysis. It became clear right away that his main drive was to attack me at every turn. The man was obsessed with DOMINATING me. And I wasn't going to be DOMINATED! I thought my intelligence and judgment were as good as his, or better, and I wasn't going to SUBMIT to him. So, UNRESOLVED OEDIPAL COMPLEX? NO TRANSFERENCE? I don't understand all the jargon, but I then understood enough of it that I began gradually to realize the process wouldn't work for me. But I persevered, for lack of any better alternative to improve my life. If only I had been able to see the catastrophe that lay ahead.

So Sternschein and I pressed on. I talked on. I emptied my mind (which is NOT a good thing to do, let me warn you). Sternschein would make no, one or two comments during a session. Never more. Generally, his statements were negative, like, "You are a parasite on society" or "You're dependent on money." I began to focus all my efforts on the relationship with Sternschein, dropping an unsatisfactory girl friend and leaving a job (my family was still alive at this point and helping me). I broke more and more outside ties. Sometimes the analyst's statements were more cryptic, such as, "You want to get to the bottom of things." More bad advice. More about that later.

Finally, August (1960), the month of analysts' vacations, rolled around. I believe I had started the analysis in December 1959, so about eight months had passed. I was completely focused on Sternschein and the analysis (though I had not permitted him to dominate me). The analysis was the center of my universe. My entire personality butted up against the analyst's personality, with no other support. When that support was removed at the beginning of August (his vacation), I flipped. I had a psychotic break in the second or third week of the month. I know the exact moment I snapped. I could tangibly feel, or sense, the moment of the snap. I had drunk half a bottle of red wine and was listening to an LP of an Anglican boy choir.

As my neighbor, a philosophy student in the next building, said, "John, you're SPOOKED." That was putting it gently. I began to have all kinds of bizarre thoughts and feelings, many of a religious nature. Now, I don't believe in God and consider myself (then and now) an Atheist, so these impressions were very hard to bear. Furthermore, I was disoriented, and heard things that weren't there. Bright lights fazed me. I didn't go entirely to pieces right away, but the process was started. On the evening of the red wine, I immediately knew my life, as I knew it and wanted it to be, was finished. I looked around that same night for the means to kill myself but found none. No surefire method available. But I was no longer the person I wanted to be. I was someone else, someone I didn't like. I knew my life as I knew it was effectively over. I thought then that ex-mental patients are pariahs. I still think that, to some extent. Did you ever try to get a job, when that fact was known? I was determined to try and avoid a hospitalization, so eventually I took to the streets. But I'm getting ahead of myself! What happened when Sternschein returned from vacation in September?

Of course, I tried to get other help in that month of August. Landau wouldn't see me. She referred me to a children's psychiatrist, the only man available, whose name I have forgotten, who advised me, since everything was in flux for me, to "be formal." The trouble was, my judgment was so impaired, I couldn't distinguish "formal" from "informal."

So, on the appointed day in early September, I stormed into Sternschein's office, refused to lie down on the analytic couch, sat in a chair, and demanded of him that he "Do something!" I couldn't bear any more of this nondirective nonsense. It had driven me nuts. All Sternschein replied, however, was, "I can put you in a mental hospital." I immediately got up from the chair, left the office without a word, and hit the streets.

Perhaps Sternschein could have suggested tranquilizers, or had an earnest, supportive conversation with me. After all, probably none of this would have happened if he'd agreed to my request for a covering psychiatrist (during that fateful August). But no. All Sternschein could suggest at the beginning of September was the mental hospital, which I was determined to resist. I know that if I'd gone in then, before I deteriorated completely, they would have let me out in six weeks or less. I would have avoided a year or more in all those places and perhaps many years on the street. But if I had gone in then, Sternschein would then have had control over me, or so I thought. And I didn't want to be turned into a time serving drone.

I wasn't homeless right away. Friends and my father kept me going for a couple of months, and then one of my college roommates, now Dr. Barry Silvers, seeing my plight and wanting to help, suggested I come down to Philadelphia and take a furnished room near his place, near the Wistar Anatomy Institute at The University of Pennsylvania, where he studied and worked. Well, I stored all my stuff (subsequently lost) and Barry drove me to Philly.

But I was too far gone. Things went from bad to worse. I began walking the freezing cold winter streets, couldn't hold a job, and was driving Barry batty. Finally, he committed me to Pennsylvania State Hospital for the Insane, where I spent a couple of weeks until my father came down and got me out. This was, I think, in February of 1962. So far nothing REALLY terrible had happened to me. So I lived with in my father's apartment for a while. I was childlike but able to manage if supervised. That is, I could manage, if I didn't have to go to work, pay the rent, go to the bank, and so on. But this was the end of my luck. In May 1962, while on a business trip to London, my father had a stroke and died suddenly. I was on my own, in my miserable condition.

I had one married sister, then in New Jersey, who refused to take me in. This was just as well. She had similar problems of her own. Runs in the family, I guess. And I couldn't stand my brother-in-law.

So, at the end of May, I gave up my father's apartment (I couldn't afford it) and moved into the nearby shabby genteel George Washington Hotel, for $35./week. They also had a decent kitchen and I would order steaks from room service, which would come with those rounded stainless steel covers . How could I afford this? I had inherited a little over $10,000. from my father (a fair sum of money in those days), which, as it turns out, kept me going for part of the next year. You'd think I was doing very well, but my mind was in a jumble. I was troubled by bizarre thoughts, hallucinations, poor judgment, and, often, the inability to find my way around the city and back to the hotel in my distracted state. In that event, I would spend the night in an abandoned building somewhere, and, in the morning with a slightly clearer head, find my way back to the G.W. I will comment that the best place to sleep in an abandoned building is the bathtub.

I had several brushes with the police, but they usually let me go. The NYPD is accustomed to harmless wandering nuts in New York City. At one point in that year, hallucinations and all, I got myself together enough to take a plane to Mexico City, where I also wandered the streets, and then to take the bus to Acapulco, and then the bus to L.A., where I stayed for a couple of months. I tried to get work as a steel rigger in L.A., but they weren't hiring weirdos. I remember that I stayed in the Sahara Motel in Hollywood for a few weeks, where the staff didn't know what to make of me. Finally, the bizarre thoughts and hallucinations got to be too much for me, and I boarded a transcontinental bus to go home to Manhattan.

Why don't I discuss more the nature of the bizarre thoughts and hallucinations? It's painful to do so, even now, 47 years later. But I gave you some earlier.

Here's another. On some days, ordinary things in my everyday world would suddenly blaze with light. This could be mildly interesting for 20 minutes, tedious if it continued for an hour or two, and painful and exhausting if it went on longer. This could have been the Existentialist Heidegger's *lichtung,* "the light in the clearing in the forest," or merely a psychotic aberration, or maybe something of both, depending on which modality you choose. But more important, you cannot hold an ordinary job or attend to your affairs while this sort of thing is periodically affecting you.

So, I was back in NYC, as unbalanced as ever, and the money was running low. Actually, there was a bit left, but I was so distracted and disoriented, I couldn't regularly find my way to the bank to get it. I was also losing weight from not eating regularly. Things were tough.

This brings us up to October of 1963. I was desperate. I hadn't been fully in control of myself since August of 1960. I couldn't work and support myself. The inherited money was running out and I couldn't always get to it. I had lost a LOT of weight. My thoughts were disordered and filled with hallucinations. My judgment was poor. I had exhausted the patience of the very few people I could call friends.

Finally, in October 1963, I snapped completely. One morning, I left the George Washington Hotel, very distraught and angry, and somewhere on the curb near 5th Avenue and 23rd Street, I pulled out a razor and began to slash my wrist. All this occurred in broad daylight with people looking on. A cop was summoned, who asked me if I wanted to go to the hospital. I said yes, and was taken off to Bellevue (where else?) in an ambulance.

Bellevue is merely a collection point for mental patients, from where the patients are diagnosed and routed to various state and private psychiatric hospitals for longer-term care. I was at Bellevue for about two weeks. Since I was unable to properly look after myself, it was a relief to be somewhere where I was cared for. This thought, however, was tempered by the idea that my life, my career life, was now over and I could never amount to anything, because of the stigma that attaches to mental patients and ex-mental patients. Oh sure, I knew that with proper rehabilitation, I could still become a doctor or lawyer or some such, but it would always be with the sufferance and condescension of my peers. I thought that, effectively, I was finished. In a way, I was right.

Then there was the thought that I had picked up in my family while growing up, that once you went into a mental hospital, you never got out. This was to some extent true, until the 1950s and the advent of the new psychotropic drugs, which (partially) emptied the mental hospitals. I was dimly aware of this fact at the time I was taken in.

Anyway, to get back to my experiences at Bellevue, I was duly interviewed by psychiatrists and consoled by nurses, battalions of them, who would come to the ward in the evenings in large numbers to chat us up and play cards with us. They even brought toast with butter and jelly. This was inordinately delicious. I should add that my taste buds were affected by my condition, and most foods tasted preternaturally delicious. I don't know if the battalions of nurses were part of the cure or the diagnosis process, or what, but we were very fond of them. I began to regain some of the weight I had lost. After the "processing" at Bellevue (three weeks), I was sent off to Manhattan State Hospital (as it was then called), to the violent ward. This section is about psychology and psychiatry. I cover my mundane experiences in the state hospital elsewhere. Here I'll only talk a little about the exit interviews, conducted before a panel of psychologists/psychiatrists. They wanted to see if you had rehabilitated enough to function on your own outside the protected environment. I believe I had three exit interviews before they finally released me. It's just as well. I was still hallucinating badly in the first two interviews. But, as you progressed in your recovery, you recognized your hallucinations for what they were, and could ignore them. But it took 15 years for them to abate completely, although I was in minimal control of myself for most of those 15 years. Anyway, Manhattan State, in 1963, even set up jobs for us. We were coached into caseworker jobs with the New York City Department of Social Services. I learned a few things from this job, but mostly it was a time-serving position. The level of expertise was very low. I held the job for about a year, while I slowly strengthened my psyche.

The next thing to happen, in 1966, was my obtaining a dream job as Science Writer in the Public Relations Department of The American Institute of Physics, then on East 45th Street near the United Nations. This gig has been discussed elsewhere. But it was a real opportunity. I also had an interesting girl friend, a fine roommate, and a good apartment. The girl, Rachel, got pregnant, I had to arrange a safe illicit abortion (to kill my child), then we went to Europe (the first time for both of us). It was all too much for me. I lost my mind again. I had not been taking tranquilizers since 1964, thinking I was cured. Big mistake. After passing through this second breakdown, on my own I embarked on a regimen of 250 mg. of Chlorpromazine (Thorazine), continued for the rest of my life, at least until the present (44 years). 250 mg. is more than the hospital had prescribed, but I didn't want to take any chances. It worked. I've stayed sane since 1967. Maybe the Thorazine makes me less emotional and deprives me of a richer fantasy and creative life, but I don't give a damn. I want to be able to think straight and hold a job. All of this would be impossible without the Thorazine.

Anyway, I had avoided shrinks since 1963, wanting nothing more to do with them. But after the second breakdown, I realized I needed their help to effectively manage my life. I found that the best thing for me was group therapy. It helps you adapt to social situations. One-on-one therapy makes me introspective, which is not particularly good for me. I find I do best when I strive to be objective. Hallucinations are not objective. I sometimes said to myself at this time, "I want a rich outer life, not a rich inner life." I didn't want to be locked away somewhere, like poor Van Gogh in Arles, wallowing in my visions (and even perhaps making some kind of art out of them). I wanted a normal life, and I've had it for the past 20 years, at least, as I write this in late 2010.

Anyway, the course of the second hospitalization was more straightforward. I was picked up by the police, half naked, in a park in Brooklyn. I can't remember the name of the hospital in Brooklyn where I was diagnosed and processed, but after three weeks I was sent out to Kings Park Hospital on Long Island. I was only there for six weeks before I was released (I hadn't tried to kill myself this time, that makes a difference). But I was hallucinating intensely again. I knew most of the hallucinations for what they were, and was able to discount them. But it was still a struggle.

My ex-lover Rachel visited me in the hospital every other day. It was a long trip from Manhattan to Kings Park, and Rachel came faithfully for all six weeks that I was locked up (But, in the meantime, Rachel had taken another lover. The affair was over, but we remained friends,). Other friends came regularly to visit me, as well. This was a big difference from my previous hospitalizations, when I'd been isolated and alone. I'm sure it made a helpful impression on the management. Perhaps they realized that, because I had so many friends, I'd be better able to manage on the outside. Anyway, they quickly decided to let me leave.

They let me out too soon. I couldn't, right away, find a stable job and place to live. I began to live on the street again, but not so much in alleys. I lived in flop houses where a bed was $1.00 and a little cubicle with chicken wire netting over the top was $1.25. The flop I stayed in was clean and had showers. Soon, I managed to find work with MANPOWER, INC., as a day laborer. I would shape up every morning for a few hours' work, heavy, medium or light. Heavy was too hard, like moving foundry equipment. I couldn't do it. But I could do medium and light. Anyway, I got along in this way until I found a permanent job as a clerk (then manager) in a bookstore and a furnished room, about a year later (1968).

But again, that's enough personal history about mundane things. This section is about psychiatry and psychology. I am now going to tell you about the shrink who helped me most of all, at a total cost of about $6.00. That man was/is Dr. Albert Ellis, who, as I write this, recently passed away at age 93. He had physical limitations toward the end but his mind was as sharp as ever.

Sometime in 1968 or thereabouts, I wandered into one of Dr. Ellis' Friday night Workshops, where, for the then fee of $2 (now $10), you could get up on the dais with Al (Dr. Ellis) and he would figure out what was wrong with you (according to his cognitive behaviorist brand of psychotherapy) and give you a few ideas to work with. I had hit bottom, but three sessions on the stage with Al were enough to enable me to get ahold of myself and start fixing my life. His system is now called REBT (Rational Emotive Behavioral Therapy). It is loosely based on ancient Epicurean and Stoic philosophy. It's VERY GOOD for crisis intervention, though not too great in dealing with sophisticated cultural subtleties. But Ellis helped me get a grip on myself for $6.00 whereas I had spent many thousands on other shrinks to no avail.

Anyway, two of the ideas that most helped me, were, "If you're not in severe physical pain, no matter what your other circumstances, you're O.K." and "Nothing anybody says to you can hurt you unless you let it do so." These statements gave me a much greater measure of self-control.

A psychologist friend here in the cooperative recently showed me a book which summarized more of Ellis' ideas. The book is, *Abnormal Psychology and Modern Life,* Butcher et al. The book says, I quote, "Ellis (1970) believes that one or more of the core irrational beliefs below are at the root of most psychological maladjustment.

(a) One should be loved by everyone for everything one does.

(b) Certain acts are awful or wicked, and people who perform them should be severely punished.

(c) It is horrible when things are not the way we would like them to be.

(d) Human misery is produced by external causes, or outside persons, or events rather than by the view that one takes of these conditions.

(e) If something may be dangerous or fearsome, one should be terribly upset about it.

(f) It is better to avoid life problems if possible rather than to face them.

(g) One needs something stronger or more powerful than oneself to rely on.

(h) One should be thoroughly competent, intelligent and achieving in all respects.

(i) Because something once affected one's life, it will indefinitely affect it.

(j) One must have certain and perfect self-control.

(k) Happiness can be achieved by inertia and inaction.

(l) We have virtually no control over our emotions and cannot help having certain feelings."

One incident that I want to relate happened in about 1967, at about the time I found Dr. Ellis. One rough day, when I was particularly bedeviled by religious (and other) hallucinations, I staggered into the Russian Mission to the United Nations, then at East 68th Street and Park Avenue. I was thinking I wanted help in controlling and expunging my religious thoughts. What better place to go for this than to the Atheist Communists? I knew about Pavlov and conditioned reflex therapy (also offered in variants in the U.S., I believe), and I thought maybe the Russians could help. I even thought maybe I should go to Russia. (Like Raskolnikov in Dostoyevsky's *Crime and Punishment,* who kept saying, "I am going to America," just before he threatened to shoot himself).

Well, the Russians were very gentle, recognizing my condition, sat me down in a chair, and talked to me for a little while. I then decided that I didn't want to go to Russia, thanked them, and went my way, back on the street. A small adventure.

So, thanks in part to Ellis, I was able to get a job in a bookshop. Within a year, I was Night Manager. I stayed there six years, while I slowly healed and the hallucinations (which I could recognize and discount or ignore) slowly abated.

During this time, I entered group therapy with Dr. Harold Brody, a psychologist and navy veteran, who I will always remember as being very proud of his rectus abdominus muscles. He ran up the stairs to his 11th floor office every day. I don't remember much else about him. His group helped socialize me and helped me in interacting with other people. I was there five or six years, until I got a job as an associate editor on a computer magazine in 1974. NOW I thought I was rehabilitated, but I later realized I still had a long way to go.

I did well at the first computer magazine, a small operation with a three-person office, the boss, a secretary and me. But it did not last. The magazine folded after I had been there a year or a year and a half. I did get to go on a business trip to New Orleans, where I was treated to dinner at Antoine's. But I had to go back and be Night Manager at another bookstore for a couple of years. THEN I landed a fairly good job with a New Jersey computer magazine (1980). I had to buy an old car to get there and back every day. Keeping that car running eventually bankrupted me, but that's another story.

So, with my better paying magazine job, more possibilities were opening and I thought I would try psychotherapy again. Someone referred me to Ms. Diane Gregory, a psychotherapist who was a Nurse and had a Master's Degree in Psychology, or possibly Psychiatric Nursing. She followed no particular school, but considered herself to be "eclectic." She was an observing (more or less) Episcopalian, which annoyed me, in my Atheism. She and her banker husband and their two kids had a town house in Brooklyn Heights, where I occasionally went for sessions, when Diane was not in her Manhattan office. She had a comfortable life, and I think she felt I should strive for something similar.

For example, as I was about 50 or 55 then, she thought I should settle down with some 35-year-old woman and raise a family. I wasn't interested. I wanted a lot of conquests and no entanglements. Diane said I could never get that, which disenchanted me with her. I stayed with Diane for 18 years, and accomplished a few things, but mostly just maintained the status quo. One big thing I did do was to begin, in 1989, photographing female nudes in my home studio. This has occupied a large part of my spare time since then. For example, I now have a web site, http://jseamanclassicnudes.Artspan.com, where I display my work and try to make a few sales. I've had a few local shows, including two recent ones at Riverside Church, of all places, won a few prizes, and my bio appeared in the 57th Edition of Marquis' "Who's Who in America," publication date, December 2002. I didn't get in the next year's edition, however, possibly because I didn't buy the book.

We now (as of January 26, 2008), come to the next chapter in my 50-year saga with psychology, psychiatry and psychoanalysis. I sometimes think it has been a huge waste of time and money, not to mention the suffering entailed by it. But I was hooked on it and could not get along without it. The net progress has been minimal, although some of my friends say otherwise, that I have made great progress. But I don't see it. Anyway, I broke off therapy in 2009, partly because I could not find a therapist who followed Dr. Ellis.

Beginning in October 1998, I was in group therapy with Dr. Janet S. Resnick, a "neo-Freudian." Yes, I was back with a variety of Freudianism, despite all the damage the Freudians did to me. Why not more cognitive therapy, which is the regimen that rescued me? Because I think cognitive therapy (a la Dr. Albert Ellis) is excellent for damage control, but misses a lot, especially in the areas of sensibility and culture. Of course, a lot of culture depends on the subjective, with which I cannot cope. Dr. Ellis ignores the unconscious, and maybe that's a good thing, but in the long run, a lot of our deepest and most creative thoughts MAY come from the unconscious. I haven't worked all of this out in my own mind yet, and probably never will, but I know the unconscious can drive me out of control.

But I eventually became bored in group therapy with Dr. Ellis.

So I struggled along with Dr. Resnick's group. I looked forward to those sessions. The others in the group are very sharp professionals. But, unfortunately, Dr. Resnick's group disbanded in 2005.

I moved on. In February, 2006, Janet recommended me to a group led by Hilde Grey, LCSW. Hilde doesn't have a Ph.D, but she's a very sophisticated woman. I feel I'm working with someone who can understand my cultural and intellectual interests. Hilde lived in India for a while. And I don't hold her psychoanalytic training against her. Also, the other three (all women) in her group are also very accomplished. I have to strive to keep up with them. But I feel, finally, that I'm really achieving something.

But, then, a little later, after three years, I had to give up on Hilde Grey's group. The lay Freudian analyst and her other group members were probing too deeply. I could tangibly feel my character armor uneasily shifting around. I feared, rightly I think, for my sanity. I have now learned to stay away from disciples of Freud. Too subjective. Too much emphasis on the Unconscious for me.

My Friend Diane

Diane Gregory was my psychotherapist from about 1979 to about 1997 or 1998. You can read more about her in the Section entitled "Psychiatric Explorations." Diane kept me stable for 18 or 19 years, but I didn't make a great deal of progress, working with her. That had to wait for my latest psychologist, Hilde Grey, LCSW. I have included, in two Memoir Sections, letters I wrote to Diane during my tenure with her. I realize that, in these letters, I gripe a lot. Also, the tone is very unliterary. But I was urged to include them by my good friend who has helped me edit all this, the writer, poet and journalist, Penelope Karageorge

.Dear Diane:

By now you should have the check for $815., all I owed you. Please cash it promptly. And I'd be happier thinking you spent it on something enjoyable, not just paying bills!

A few comments:

When I started messing with psychoanalysis, etc., 40 years ago, I had a passable girlfriend and a good position with lots of possibilities. Life was easy. It's never been as good since. Sometimes it's been terrible, as you know. And life has always been at least 10 times as hard for me, with nothing of particular value coming out of it.

Irving Sternschein broke down my defenses, regressed me to an atavistic state, while at the same time trying to dominate me. Of course, I resisted all this. But when your defenses are down, you have to take a lot of shit, both in your external life situation and in what goes on in your head.

I've never been able to get my head back where I want it. Sternschein did a lot of permanent damage. All of you shrinks deal in illusion and fantasy. The only thing of any value is hard science and thinking like a machine. I made a dent in society thinking like a machine. Now, society doesn't care if I live or die.

Anything to do with religion, the transcendental, the spiritual, the aesthetic or the affective is illusion and fantasy. Good old Dr. Ellis would agree with that. You and your friends and colleagues make fun of him but his position is more philosophically sound than yours. And he helped me get ahold of myself for

$2. What have I gotten for the $50,000 I have invested in the rest of you but a lot of suffering?

As to women, you encourage me to sleep with "dogs." Never. My damnable esthetic sense, my self-respect and my intense fear that I might later find them beautiful (thereby losing my grip on one aspect of reality) prevents it. Even in a whorehouse they don't expect you to sleep with "dogs." Most of the women there are young and passable, unless an old friend of the madam happens to be working because she is broke and the madam takes pity on her. I had a lot of fun in the brothels and am sorry it's not possible to go now. A better investment than psychology. And in the expensive resorts the courtesans are extremely beautiful, intelligent and talented.

The whole psychotherapy, etc., enterprise is based largely on cultural values, not hard reality. I've always felt that psychotherapists were trying to sell me a "bill of goods" that had nothing to do with the real hard objective truth.

My intention now is to get completely out of debt (now under $2,000.). Maybe then I'll return to psychotherapy.

You're an honest, well-meaning woman with a lot of mother wit. I got more from that aspect of your personality than from the psychoanalytic theory. As I said in the phone message, statistically psychotherapy is about like roulette. One fourth get a lot better, one fourth get a little better, one fourth get a little worse, and one fourth get a lot worse. Aside from the drugs, of course, but they don't validate the theory. Actually, it's worse than gambling, because by using my wits, I've managed to stay somewhat ahead lifetime in the casinos. Maybe you should stick to poetry.

Yes, I was a wreck in 1979, but I would have gotten somewhat better anyway, just from learning from experience. And I'd been better at various times before.

Most important in my decisions now is the fact that I haven't been laid by anybody but a whore in 23 years and I haven't been laid even by a whore in 10 years.

In paying you off, I didn't have enough left over to completely pay off the radiology people. I paid then two thirds, and I'm hoping they'll now let me get the second test (upper GI series). I now have more than a little steady stomach discomfort.

I have lots of interesting things going on in my life, many "projects," most of which are probably futile, but I'm compelled to do them just to keep my damned "creative" equilibrium in balance. But it is very damning to watch all these young girls naked and not to be able to touch them.

I'm continuing to read philosophy. It's a lot more rewarding than the psychoanalytic literature. Maybe one day, I'll write you a more philosophical letter. I plan to write on such topics when I retire in 505 days.

I reopened the letter to add a couple of more germane comments. I have always resented these attempts to cure me by changing my value system. Philosophically, that's "begging the question." Who's to say my value system is worse than the therapist's? I grew up in middle-class America and went to Swarthmore where I picked up a lot of conscience. Therapy should be helping the patient do what he wants to do, not what the therapist thinks he should do!

Finally, I heard from Robin Rice, who said my work was "strong, and reflected a clear sense of purpose" but did not fit in with his/her surreal and ethereal interests.

Best wishes to you. The sessions have been very enjoyable but, I feel, not terribly productive. I wish you well

April 17, 1997
Dear Diane:

No, I haven't forgotten you! I apologize again for the tone of my last letter. The harsh tone was partly dictated by my current circumstances, but this tone also did reflect the side of my personality that I am trying to cultivate. It doesn't do any good to be loving and "spiritual," one has to be tough. If the world is going to be "tough" with me, I can be tough with it. And a lot of the things I said in the letter, harsh tone or not, are in large part true.

I don't want to come back just now, even for one visit, because you'll "mellow me out" and my thinking will be affected. When I'm seeing you, I live in sort of a perplexed, illuminated fog and get nothing done, puzzling over all these questions, some of which really mean nothing, about the quirks in my psyche.

And of course, I'm under a lot of physical stress now. I may have wrecked my health working so hard and living under so much stress over lack of money, etc. The expensive medicine for my stomach may not be working. What does this mean? More expensive tests? More expensive medicine? In part because of this, I don't want to spend the $80. a week on you just now.

You commented on my penchant for writing angry letters to terminate relationships. I realize that I've done this with you, Ralph Bentley, Maurice Sylvester, and others who helped me when I was "pathetically weak." I'm ashamed of having been so pathetically weak, and one way I can cancel it out is by attacking those who "stooped to help me." And of course, I always had to pay a small or large price to you all in condescension, patronization, humiliation, or, in your case, to deal with your anti-intellectual smugness.

Which brings up another point. I've read a little Freud which says he could not deal with and psychoanalysis would not help people who were abstract and objectified, psychoanalysis helps "cultural" intellectuals but not mathematical or scientific people. And Mahler never wrote a note after Freud got ahold of him. Freud can only deal with the "psychosocial-cultural-sexual mess," not with people who (try to be) free of it. I like being "alienated" from the "culture."

The Time Travel Colloquium was a great success. Rivka Kfia, my speaker, presented a lot of highly technical stuff, and recent evidence showing that it will indeed be possible. Then we had a "philosophical/theological" discussion with a rabbi and an Arab philosopher. Rivka commented that I asked a lot of good "theological" questions. Damn my head. Altho I hate to say I believe in omens, the fact that the Arab philosopher was an albino pleased me and I took it as a sign my strange presentations would have or were having an impact somewhere.

I'll see you sometime in the not-too-distant future, if you still wish to see me. But first I have to get my finances in order and get my head where I want it.

Best wishes,

John Seaman

April 23, 1997
Dear Diane:

Here's one more letter. It will probably be the last one for a while.

I've been very busy since January. I've been writing a lot of letters, copies of a couple of which I enclose. I'm still hoping to get a letter from you, with your statements of where you and I stand. You know I would treasure it and carry it around with me until the end, my only "Bible", like the Rorschach report I've carried around for 40 years. For all our time together, I have nothing tangible from you. It's all been so evanescent. And you did promise to send me a letter, and then went back on your word (or changed your intention, if you prefer).

I have my little successes, my friends think I'm a "God" (ridiculous), but I can't take any satisfaction in anything, because to this day I remain a humiliated, broken, crushed man.

I use the word "man" advisedly. You never gave me any real help with the problem of my lack of (much of) a beard. All you said was you didn't find hairy men attractive. The problem may not have mattered much objectively, to women, but it seriously affected my self-confidence. I was almost convinced I was sterile until Rachel got pregnant. I couldn't play the role of a macho man, looking as I did. And, when I was young, although I did all right with Swarthmore women, New York women (that I wanted) wouldn't come near me. Maybe the lack of a beard did have something to do with it. My proofer friend Kristin, not especially attractive but runnerup to Miss California because she danced and rode bareback so well, used to tell me how big my shoulder muscles were (and pat them). But her fiancé couldn't stand me. Anyway, you never told me I had great biceps, etc. And, of course, neither did my mother.

I can speak to large groups, Gunnar and other very experienced people said now poised and sophisticated I was in the Colloquium, but I can't talk to women (that I want). Perry, on the other hand, hides in the corner in large groups but can still (at 75) sweep young girls off their feet. I've seen him do it. Reich.

About the letters, when I was under 24, I never would have spoken with priests or corresponded with them. I thought they knew zero about reality. I still think that, but I feel something about them. I wish I could get rid of it. I want to know what they know so I can fight this damnable religious, spiritual impulse in me.

Of course, if I were to give in to all this religious, spiritual, transcendent, aesthetic, affective streak in me, the results might be marvelous. But it wouldn't MEAN anything. It would be more of "swinging thru the trees in the monkey colony". Abstract reason is all. Sex is OK but should be trivial, like a glass of water. Of course, if you don't get the glass of water, it becomes very important. You objected to this, but reproduction and sex are more important than the survival of the individual. The mother wolf dies defending her cubs, etc.

If God exists, he is mind, and can be ignored. I've abstracted God to such an extent that He no longer bothers me (MUCH).

You've said I'm not a genius. That means I'm so stupid I have to take things on authority. I hate that. I hate all received wisdom. Freud lamented in the Jones bio that he knew no math or physics, but he never tried seriously to remedy this. He should have. His work would have been less foolish. I at least try. Of course, the solution for me is to be an artist, but artists, serious ones at least, are half mad. Art was a great mystery to me when I was young, I only discovered the solution at 24, that they're partly insane, and so I wouldn't go near the art therapy in Manhattan State, although I was interested. I didn't want to expand my awareness and understanding of distorted perception. Instead I went to the woodworking shop, where I couldn't work for fear of cutting off my trembling, shaking, energized, emotional arm. I can even see that the trembling might have been a great feeling for some people, but not for a rationalist.

I've thought about my last letter, where I called you a smug anti-intellectual. I could say that's not true, that you're eclectic, you have everything in balance and harmony, but I can't accept that. The only thing that really changes anything in the long run is mind. The rest of it is "swinging thru the trees". "Peck order", etc.

Of course, I also object to your idolatry of the brokers, bankers, accountants and lawyers that infest Brooklyn Heights, people that manipulate other people's money to make a living, instead of doing honest work.

Of course, since I am dumb (except with a potential for the ways of feeling and the rest of it, etc., etc.), I should go your way, but I probably never will. I've stuck to my guns for 40 years and probably will to the end. I know what I'm missing, but I don't attach much theoretical value to it and I have to keep my shreds of honor and self-respect. But I do need that "drink of water".

I've had no work for 11 days, don't know why, I'm taking it up with agency management next week. Maybe I did something wrong, like ordering food at the printer's expense. I'm OK, tho, I'm drawing unemployment and my small pension.

Best wishes,

John Seaman

July 2, 1997

Dear Diane:

Just a few notes as follow-up to our recent session. It's quite clear to me that the world of psychological well-being you offer is based on illusion, fantasy and the transcendental, none of which I will have any truck with. Yes, I feel the power of these things, but I'll have none of it. They're regressive, atavistic and antisocial, nothing but hormones talking. My world is a hard, barren world of sticks and stones, but it's the truth. As to the other stuff, I can only repeat the quote from Bertrand Russell, "Even if it works, if it's wrong, don't do it!"

As to seeing a Priest, I would never go hat in hand to one, on his turf. They are dangerous fools. I thought in my early days priests were inconsequential nonentities and could be safely ignored, but now I fear them. How I have come down in the world from my lofty abstract plane. Look at the harm done in the name of religion historically, most of which is now hushed up. When I can meet a Priest on a level playing field, like at my Colloquia, however, it's O.K. I only wrote to the Buddhist Priest because he said you can be a Buddhist and an Atheist at the same time. I don't believe it, but I wanted to see if he could back up the assertion. He never replied to my letter. I just sent him a postcard reminder.

Also, being a Cynic, as I insist I am, doesn't mean you're cruel. Those who see clearly what's wrong with the World are in the best position to change and improve it. It's a pity analytic (not psychoanalytic) philosophers don't teach a little good psychology. But I do have B. Russell and A. Ellis.

I saw the world your kind of psychology offered me 40 years ago, at the beginning of my troubles, and I would have none of it. If I have to choose between being Happy and being Right, I'll choose being Right, even if it gives me only a kind of Socratic Negation. My problem is still my Philosophy, as the Rorschach said 38 years ago. I'm not going to worship endorphins running. I still feel this and will never change.

Truth is NOT Beauty and Beauty is NOT Truth and that's NOT all you need to know. Likewise, Love doesn't mean anything to me. I only know consideration, care and my kind of decency. Love seems to me to be a Fit of Trembling.

Yes, I do suffer more than a little thinking this way but I've reached the conclusion that there's nothing to be done about it, except maybe join Ellis' Group, so I don't get (outwardly) too wacky psychologically.

I'd love to see your letter to me. If you had a computer, it would be easier for you to write it.

Thanx for Everything!

John Seaman

More Diane

March 8, 1998

Dear Diane:

I'd hoped to ask you your opinion of the Gallery Deal, but I didn't get to it when we met last month. I'm not likely to get in anywhere else until I have a recognized name and more credentials, and I'm not getting any younger. Subculture Gallery might be a start. There are some things to be said for it. It has lots of traffic and press and it would give me a lot of time on the walls. Oh yes, all the local Communists frequent the place. But $1,800. is a lot of money. Your opinion?

Yes, I did find our relationship becoming static. Nothing new was happening. I'm sure you're aware that you espouse resignation and acceptance. And your (seeming) contentment did trouble me. You appear not to want anything very much. Too much rich inner life! No get up and go! Not what I want. And if it's only my misimpression, your giving that misimpression is as detrimental to me as if you really thought that way.

No, I do not want some passable 35-year-old to be my wife. I'd be bored with her in a year, as W. Reich says. I most emphatically do not want a frumpy little wife, an obscure niche in Society, and a rich inner life. Better to be a little notorious!

Also, most definitely, I have not discovered my REAL SELF, as you said. I've only discovered that there's nothing there, except a deep, irrational abyss. The existentialists teach that this is so and all we can do is accept it and have compassion for one another. For my part, I've discovered that there are a few shreds of reality left, along with everything else, which you can work with if you're stubborn enough to hang on to them and ignore the rest of it, the irrational, transcendental, etc., etc. You know the rest.

As for compassion, all you can do is help people help themselves. Loving them, making them more helpless, does no good for them or yourself.

All you can do is try to erect some kind of ramshackle, provisional structure on the edge of the precipice and hope it will hold together. That's not what I hoped for at all. My character is probably weaker now than it was in 1957, when I started all this. For what it's worth, the Buddhists also teach that there's no real self, only an ever-changing flux, made up of feeling, perception, disposition, consciousness, and body. (I just looked it up in one of those Marxist intellectual *Beginner* comic books I once told you about.)

Pursuit of the real self is the pursuit of a chimera. And not worth the price either (I don't mean the money—I mean the suffering.)

Yes, I do trust my own thinking now more than anybody else's, at least as far as my own character and welfare are concerned. On balance, I never got much but a lot of trouble from trusting anyone else. There's an old Yankee adage in my family that I told to Madison to try to help her in her troubles: "Never trust anybody farther than you can throw them." And, incidentally, why are so many of my friends (clinically) crazy or half-crazy these days?

I do continue to think that it's a correct characterization that what I owe you is that you undid SOME of the damage that was done to me by the others. But I don't think the result, photographing nudes, is an acceptable life. It's probably mildly weak and depraved, even though accepted by (the elite of) Society. I'm good at it, I enjoy the esthetics of it (I'm forced to admit) and it's a sexual outlet. But I'd much rather be a mathematical physicist or an analytic philosopher. I could respect myself then. But I don't have the brains for it, as you said. But I will continue to try when I retire. Most (not all) philosophers and hard scientists don't think much of artists.

As to achieving my goals, I haven't slept with a woman, any kind of woman, for 11 years, and I'm very, very bitter about that. Not your fault. But please don't suggest that I sleep with, or worse, MARRY frumpy 40-year-olds, "dogs," as I call them. I still have a few shreds of pride.

I heard an interesting woman, Caroline Mace, on public television the other day. I came in in the middle, so I couldn't tell if she was a psychologist, religious teacher, New Age teacher, or what. But she had THE LINE down pat. She said one should be vulnerable and open to change. "Being vulnerable" never got me anything, and, as to change, I've always had my Agenda. I still have it, even though I've realized precious little of it. But I still think it's a good agenda and I'll walk my perimeter to the end, trying to realize it, if I must. I'll consider change only when I've realized most of my Agenda. I'm Kybernos, the Greek steersman in the back of the boat (from which the word "Cybernetics" comes). But Caroline Mace knew the whole thing, she even said you mustn't mind "when your dishes don't seem to be in their proper places."

I couldn't send the $80. this week but I'll send it very soon. Thanks for all your efforts.

>Best wishes,
>John Seaman

September 21, 1998
Dear Diane,

Another missive. Another epistolary gem. Bear with me.

I was at an elegant Lincoln Center Patrons' Reception on Thursday with my good friend, ex-Party member Blanche Breslow, when I commented that, for years, I've said "I'll be glad when it's all over," when anything BAD happened. I could have added that I've said this since my unsuccessful attempt at doing myself in (I lacked the strength, the means and the training to do it properly) for which I have a collection of stitch marks as a memento mori.

Anyway, that's all old hat and behind me. What's new, as I commented to my friends, is that I now also say, "I'll be glad when it's all over," when anything

GOOD happens. I'm sick of being jerked around. I want everything level.

Somebody responded, "Everything level? That's Death!" My correct response occurred to me later, "No, that's Eternity!"

I'm learning a lot about Eternity in David Albert's class. Mostly it deals with Relativity. The sequence of time, though real in some sense, is only apparent in another sense. We are not made of Matter, We are only events (kinks?) in Space Time. Within the last five years, it has become generally apparent to the top physicists that some forms of Time Travel will be technically possible in the Distant Future. And the 15 people in his class are mostly better educated and sharper than I am. Blacks, Indians, three women, all sorts of people. It's wonderful. A very advanced course. I'm very grateful to David Albert for letting me sit in on it, for nothing.

. I was a little shocked on Saturday when Rivka Kfia, on a date, told me David Albert belongs to an Orthodox Synagogue. I'm awed at the intellectual tradition of these (Orthodox) people. David told me Shana's at Oxford now on the female equivalent of a Rhodes. Wow! But I'm still convinced the only solid point of departure for all this is atheistic scientific materialism.

Another story. I suspect that you know something about what I am going to mention, because of the art work in your living room in Brooklyn. Out of erotic and intellectual curiosity, I purchased a video on Tantric sex (I believe Tantric thought originated in decadent late Hinduism and late Buddhism). I was moved and touched by the carefully and thoughtfully made video. But what especially struck me, if you leave the Sex out of it, is how the description of the Tantric full-body orgasm phenomena equated with what I experienced at the height of my difficulties. Warmth, tingling, energy, vibrations, trembling, ecstasy, etc. And a great sense of Oneness with Everything, with the Universe.

This last, at the time, I hated because I felt it was an invasion of my privacy, my autonomy and my independence. Also I had no explanation for it then but God (now I have other explanations, of course). And finally, the Oneness made me think my existence would go on forever, which was abhorrent, I only wanted oblivion, not reincarnation and Eternity on religious terms. Those psychiatrists had said, in the beginning, that I would have a "surprise" (like this?) and I was not at all prepared for it. A little more respect for my autonomy would have been appreciated. I'll never forgive them.

Enough for now. All this will also be included in the Memoir, slightly reworded.

Best of Everything,

John Seaman

September 1, 1999

Dear Diane:

I wanted to communicate some recent developments to you, perhaps to get your comments and opinion.

Joan Bennett recently gave me $800. to help me with my debts, and Rae Karel left me a legacy of $1,500. to thank me for the good times I had shown her. She, 79, especially liked the Eleutheria Salons and the Bodypainting Beach Parties.

Most of the money is already gone. I'm spending the last of Rae's money on something tangible, a Pentium II clone computer which will give me Internet access in my studio instead of on the communal computer in the Co-op Workshop, and the final $500. (and more) on a 4-day trip to Las Vegas, where I intend to gamble away (or win with) a stake of perhaps $300. (Ralph may stake me), enjoy the surreal glittering environment, and, most important, go twice to the legal, government-inspected brothels in the desert.

The Governor of Nevada insists his girls always use condoms. It will be somewhat dangerous for me but I have to do something. My prostate may go at any time and I haven't had a woman (attractive or otherwise) in 12 years. The die is cast, the money is not refundable, and I've already paid.

There's some other possible money coming in, but I can't count on it. On January 1, 2001, Social Security will allow me to make enough money to start paying off my bills.

As I've said before about Sex, if you're getting it regular it's trivial, like drinking a glass of water, but if you're not getting it, it becomes very important, a major thing. Alexandra Kollontai. Gunnar says in South America they speak of a man's "Necessity," so all the women have this in mind there.

Apropos of this, I want to say that among the reasons I left you were that we were futilely going over the same old ground, I was unhappy with your resignation, even defeatism, and quietism (and the religion), and because I don't want to get into a quasi-Buddhistic state of not wanting anything.

My new shrink is not as bright (Ph.D. notwithstanding), sophisticated or experienced as you but for that reason she thinks I can still accomplish my goals and she encourages me to try to do so. Her group is full of capable people even though they'd rather talk about interpersonal relations (all the time) than Philosophy, which disappoints me a little.

I'm also making serious inquiries about skydiving. It's reasonably safe—a lot safer than hang gliding, which I consider reckless. Only one chute in several thousand fails, so they say, so I say. The first jump costs $200.-$250. and is a tandem jump strapped to an instructor. They might let me make my first jump solo with a static line, if you know what that is. With this, they don't have to worry about you forgetting to pull the ripcord. And it's cheaper, $100.-$150.

Why am I doing this? I'm not getting any younger, I'll be dead in 10 or 20 years, and I want to prove I'm not afraid of anything, including Death. I'll live my last 10 or 20 better knowing that. Not my idea, the skydiving sponsors promote it that way for older persons. Seems a good idea. Also, I want a big color photo of me in flight to add to the Gallery in my Studio, next to the Bodypainting Beach Party pic with Trina (who I propositioned unsuccessfully in an epistolary way, do you remember?).

Of course, I'm afraid I'll get up there and lose my nerve, but maybe not. I'll make them promise on the ground to push me out of the airplane. It would be humiliating not to be able to go through with it, so I'm a little afraid to go ahead. Any advice? The second jump would be easy for me, I know, I've done dangerous things like hanging from a vertical ladder 130 feet up or sailplaning (no motor, with a pilot. I took Eileen as a Birthday Treat.)

Rivka Kfia posed for our sketch group last night, for her first time, not for the money but for the experience and as a favor to me. You recall, she just took a double doctorate in physics and philosophy from Columbia and then got an NIH grant to work in the New York Presbyterian Schizophrenia Lab, on her own theories. She's educating herself in neurophysiology and making a lot of money to pay off her $30,000. Columbia U. bill. Beautiful sexy body, along with everything else. She's also classically trained in ballet, music and art (performs in all). And her parents brought her up in Komsomol in D.C. which she threw over and reverted to Orthodox Judaism. One mistake. She impresses me - I can't compare my attainments with hers.

The above (earlier) caveats notwithstanding, I have the highest respect for you and still enjoy meeting with you now and then. I will always cherish the memory of my many times with you.

I've paid off all of my bills to you except that $40. Lucy Yates still owes you. I think she's out of the country and I can't reach her. If she doesn't show up in a month or two, I'll pay you that last $40.

Love,
John Seaman

Letters to Janet

Following Diane Gregory, with whom I undertook psychotherapy from 1979 to 1997, I moved on to the group psychotherapy sessions of psychologist Dr. Janet S. Resnick. I attended these group sessions from Fall 1998 through Spring 2005, when the group disbanded. Janet tells me she will probably start a new group in the Fall of 2005, and I hope to be in it. I have become much more productive and am taking many more initiatives in my life, since joining Janet's group.

January 7, 2003

Dear Janet Resnick:

Here are a few suggested topics, with a little background and analysis, for our meeting on Thursday, January 15, at 5:00 p.m.

FINDING A (BETTER) JOB: Very hard at 66. My editorial, writing credentials are all 15 years old; there is no more legal proofreading (not just because of my nudes); since Enron, the temp work is too sensitive for outsiders; computers can do most of it now; and legal secretaries do the rest. Retailing? I occasionally see signs in boutique storefronts, but I don't think I'm elegant enough (at least to the general herd) and I'm not sure I really want to do it. Maybe when I get my teeth fixed. Barnes & Noble and Borders have turned me down. I'm going to try B&N again. But I think they give a lie detector test and a urine drug test, neither of which I will submit to in principle.

GETTING SOME SEX: Flo? Eva? Penelope? Emma? Megan? Ashley? There are others, as well, but I just don't seem to be able to make the grade!

MAYBE I SHOULD GIVE UP ON PSYCHIATRY, PSYCHOLOGY, ALTOGETHER: And just read Philosophy. Freud once said it is impossible to psychoanalyze intellectuals. Perhaps that applies to me. After all, I've been at it for 46 years with only very bad or no results.

MAYBE I DO HAVE TO LIVE MARGINALLY, MINIMALLY, TO SURVIVE AND KEEP MY SANITY: Some of my ideas are pretty far out and I have to exercise great control to keep them in check.

FREUDIAN CANT: To listen to the other group members talk about their interpersonal relations, their marriages, weddings, babies, pregnancies, parents, etc., ad nauseam is really intolerable to me. I feel I am listening to a lot of ideological Freudian cant. It's the way they do it, with your encouragement. People should get beyond all of that. Only Carol does it with any art, in a stimulating and provocative manner. She's the only one who brings any intelligence to it. The Freudian modality can be useful if it's done well, but if it's not, it's deplorable. Usually it is not done well. I know, after 45 years of psychology.

More on babies. This is partly, but not, entirely, sour grapes, but I will say there are too many babies. Give the poor old world ecosystem a rest. I shudder to think of the Hispanic mothers with 12 children and the huge Orthodox families in Crown Heights. Zero Population Growth. There are many more worthwhile things people can do than incessantly breeding like animals. We have minds to use And babies are not the "GREATEST FULFILLMENT" for a thinking being. Not for me, anyway. Childbearing should be discouraged.

And it seems to me the group members go over the same ground over and over again. I'd rather go to a book discussion or lecture.

I would much prefer to discuss the art professor's comments about my art ("reminds him of

Matisse's style") and how I can work on it. Also, his comment that I draw conceptually, from the concepts I have in my head, rather than what I see, was right on the mark.

HIGH SCHOOL BUDDY TURNS UP AFTER 51 YEARS: Richard Cocks saw my name and address in the Oceanside High School Reunion literature, and wrote and gave me his e-mail address. I promptly (December 25) barraged him with an animated electronic Christmas card and 8 attachments about my life: web site address, salons, model ads, colloquia, old beach party invitations, the Cap d'Agde story, resumes, etc. It must have been too much because he never replied. Or I shocked his wife. He lives in Ohio, worked as an engineer, has 5 kids and a battalion of grandchildren, so what can I expect?

YOU CONTINUE TO CUT ME OFF: My relationship with Denise could have been explored much further. Why do I care for this selfish, self-centered complainer? Similar experiences? But you cut me off and pumped up David again for his boring line on things.

THERE'S A LOT MORE I COULD SAY IN GROUP (cf. SOME OF THE ABOVE) BUT I CAN'T

DO IT UNLESS THERE'S A CHANGE IN APPROACH:

I'M GETTING STALE FROM LACK OF INTELLECTUAL ACTIVITY IN THIS COURIER JOB:

I DON'T WRITE ANY MORE:

SIR EDMUND HILLARY AND THE SHERPAS: There's a lecture at The Explorers Club on Monday, January 13, comes with a cocktail hour, in which a woman photographer will discuss Sir Edmund's work with the Sherpas and his understanding of them as a people. Consider the PSYCHOLOGY of the Sherpas. Are high mountains really "SPIRITUAL, HOLY PLACES?" Or are they not? There aren't any such places, are there? Tough Buddhism; their courage; their relationship with the Red Chinese megalithic power just over the border; their vegetarianism (this last concerns me a little. I've told you how impressed I am with my highly principled, Roman Catholic, Vegan friend who worked as a surrogate in a sex clinic with dysfunctional men because she thought it was a socially useful thing to do). Anyway, I've been interested in vegetarianism but I'd never want to give up on regular French and Chinese cuisine. Perhaps in a thousand years we can worry about this. Or when we can replicate meat without killing animals. Right now there are much more important things to do But factory farms are terrible. Did you see the new book, "Dominion," on this topic? But I don't suppose these topics are FREUDIAN enough for Group discussion. But they concern me a little.

MY SEXUAL INFERIORITY COMPLEX: Lack of any beard at all until age 35. (Now I shave once a day). I thought I was sterile when in high school and college because of the lack of a beard. I didn't dare try to be a sperm donor when I was 18 and we were asked to do it because I thought it would be confirmed I was sterile and I didn't want to know that just yet. Later, when I did try to be a donor, at age 54, it was too late. And, anyway, I had made Rachel Chouxfleur pregnant in 1967, if she didn't lie to me. At the donor clinic in 1993 I found out I was not sterile, just undersexed. Sperm count of 40 million per cc instead of 60 million per cc which would have been normal for my age then. And they also rejected me because of my long stay in a mental hospital. (They overlook short stays.) I've thought of trying again since I got in *Who's Who in America*" ?? But oh yes, that's right, there are too many babies.

FLO SAID BOTH HOWARD HENSEL AND I WERE "INNOCENT." Maybe so. But I've seen some strange mental states like having the exact same thoughts as someone else and saying exactly the same things as your partner at the same time, which experiences I want nothing to do with. I like my privacy. My Rorschach (1959) said I didn't experience other people directly enough to function properly. Very true. Fine. But I still don't want other people's thoughts in my head. INTELLECTUALLY, I KNOW the other people's thoughts weren't in my head, but EMOTIONALLY, it seemed that way. If that's what real intimacy consists of, and not just the sexual act, I don't want it. I don't want any weird sensations, thrilling music, smells, lights, preternatural orgasms. No preternatural sex. I'm perfectly content with clinical sex in a brothel. I want to preserve my rationality, sanity. This might be a topic for group discussion, but I don't think any of the others know anything about it. What is the nature of LOVE? I don't believe in it. Only in WILL And CARE. *Sorge* in German. Heidegger.

I WOULD BE HAPPIER IF YOU WOULD GIVE ME YOUR E-MAIL ADDRESS: I COULD REALLY KEEP YOU UP TO DATE WITH

DIATRIBES LIKE THIS. BUT NONE OF MY NEEDS ARE BEING MET BY THE GROUP.

ARTISTS (AND PHOTOGRAPHERS) ARE INADEQUATE AND SECOND BEST: Clearly, I am INADEQUATE. I can't meet my sexual or financial needs very well. And I must be VERY WELL CHARACTER ARMORED to cope with this fact. We've been over some of this. Freud said artists were inadequate, and only get women by pandering their fantasies. Plato said artists were less than philosophers, because they only deal with POOR IMAGES of reality. Most artists would not make very good mathematicians (the highest calling) (But David is not a very good example, in my opinion). When I was young, before puberty, I wondered how artists came up with some of the wonderful ideas they have. Was it a GREATER TRUTH? It was a GREAT MYSTERY to me. Then I encountered sex, and psychosis. I discovered the TRUTH was that artists were HALF CRAZY. NO GREAT MYSTERY AFTER ALL But, unfortunately, due to my maternal grandmother who played the piano and died in a neurological institute, and my hysterical mother, I have ARTISTIC TALENT, which I must LIVE WITH and USE. It's IMPERATIVE TO DO THIS

OR I WOULD GO CRAZY AGAIN. I do it in the MOST DIRECT, SEXUAL, WAY POSSIBLE, by photographing young female nudes. It pleases me that my chosen mode of art is a little perverse. I get back at "ART" that way.

I'll close here. This is already too much. But I could go on in this vein almost indefinitely I could even "empty my mind" and get back to the VOID, NADA, NOTHINGNESS. But perhaps some of this would be valid material for group discussion. What do YOU think?

Dear Janet:

I don't know whether I should attack all the Swarthmore Hawks on the Web. What they say certainly goes against Friends traditions. I personally was hoping for a quick victory but it doesn't look now like we're going to get that.

I was mentioned again in the Swarthmore Class Notes. They even gave my web site a plug.

Joan paid for $320 of my $360 New York Philharmonic 2003-04 Subscriptions. Up until now, she's only paid medical expenses, but she's so impressed with my working out in the cold as a messenger, she decided to do this for me. I'm very grateful.

To get to a serious matter, when I had my mental break, one of the worst things about it was the surprising realization that reality might not be unitary, fixed and unchanging. That there might be more than one aspect to reality, or worse, that there might be multiple realities. All this would be extraordinary, but there would be no point to it. There would really be no point to any human endeavor. To put it another way, if miracles can happen, what's the point of any kind of human effort?

I found the Eric Partridge book, *Origins,* at a street vendor and bought it for $5. I was unable to find this out-of-print book on the Web. I was so pleased. It was a cherished book I had lost (twice) when I lost everything.

RELIGION IS FOR PEOPLE WITH WEAK MINDS. SEX IS FOR HIGHLY SEXED PEOPLE WITH WEAK MINDS. ART IS FOR PEOPLE WITH WEAK MINDS. YOU KNOW WHERE I STAND ON PROCREATION. All this lets me out of the above. My philosophy has taught me a measure of acceptance and resignation. I can live without sex if I have to. After my mental break, I realized (perforce) that I was ESTHETIC and CREATIVE. But this is a poor consolation for not having a POWERFUL INTELLECT.

I once had a chance to break into the writing big time. In c.1985, *The New York Times* gave me an assignment to write a Sunday Magazine article (at my suggestion) on "Artificial Intelligence in the USSR." but I couldn't write the article to their requirements (several tries). I received the air fare and a $250 kill fee. But I couldn't place the article anywhere else, either. Failure.

I finally got a lawyer's opinion about the medical malpractice suit for my sister's death. The lawyer said we had a case, but there's nothing in it for me. All proceeds from the suit go directly to Barbara's Estate, and I don't believe I'm mentioned in her Will, if she even had one. So much for that. I told this to the relatives and told them I would still help in the suit, if only to punish negligent people who kill POETS.

I saw part of a Channel 13 documentary on the ALGONQUIN ROUNDTABLE. I would have liked to have been in on something like that, or perhaps the 1960s PARTISAN REVIEW editorial meetings. I never particularly wanted to be a PROFESSIONAL, after checking out some of the possibilities. I did consider being an ARTIST, until I realized many of them were half crazy.

My protégé, KATHLEEN CONNOLLY, who taught me some Japanese and was my protégé and foil for a while, said she thought my mind was at least as good as hers. But she mastered Japanese, became a lawyer, and graduated SUMMA CUM LAUDE from HARVARD (20 out of a 1,000 in her Class). Can we attribute that to her early Dominican Academy training? Maybe a Catholic education is good for something!

There is a particular Naturist Video I want to buy. I wish to discuss this with you.

As to my teeth, I went for an examination to the Northeast Dental Plan dentist recommended by a friend of Penelope. He says he can fix me up with a bridge covering the 2 missing front teeth for $2500. This is still too much. I contacted Medicaid and they sent me a lot of information which I couldn't figure out. I gave it to my accountant, Jim Welch, CPA, who for $50, will find out whether I can get any Medicaid or not. I was highly annoyed by all those immigrants at NY Presbyterian getting expensive Medicaid work done on their teeth, while I couldn't get any of it. Tentatively, I was able to learn that, given my income, Medicaid will pay any dental expenses in a given month exceeding $930. If I can get Columbia Dental to bill me the $4,000 for the full upper left bridge in one month's bill, I might do well. Jim Welch will check it out. Meanwhile, none of these dentists will fill any of the cavities in my remaining savable teeth until I do the bridge work. Why?

This Agenda is a little DISJOINTED. I apologize for that.

John Seaman

December, 2003
Dear Janet:

I am writing to try to summarize my feelings at the end of the year. I thought it might be helpful to do so.

But first, there is the financial matter we must square away. Your Secretary billed me $180. for three group sessions in October and three group sessions in November, with December still to be added. I believe this is incorrect. My records show that I am paid up through the end of October, and that I now owe you $180, for three group sessions in November and three more in December. Please check your records and see if you can correct this. I was getting ready to send you another $90. this week, for November, but I am going to hold up until this is cleared up. It's very disconcerting to this patient.

Next, I want to thank you for allowing me to bring some of the tools I learned from Dr. Albert Ellis, the Epicureans and the Stoics, into our group. I've learned to "flip the switch," but I'm afraid most of the others are too emotional to get the hang of it. I believe Dr. Ellis says you can only get upset if you LET somebody else upset you. An individual is in control of whether he or she lets himself get upset. This has almost always worked for me.

Of course, the practical, "nuts & bolts" thinking that lets me do this, also reduces my emotionality AND sensibility. Sometimes I feel like an ABSOLUTE KLUTZ in group. But I'm not prepared to dispense with the only system that has made it possible for me to lead a relatively normal life. The methodology limits my sensibility, but not my practical performance.

Finally, my life as a whole is O.K. except for some (minor?) physical health problems. I have an appointment with a dermatologist on December 22nd and with a urologist on January 8th. I am engaged in a course of physical therapy for my foot and leg.

> So far, so good!
> All good wishes,
> John Seaman

December, 2004

Dear Janet:

Thinking upon the 9/22 group session, I was distressed by David's and Ellis' discomfiture. Is it wrong (over-intellectualized) that I use a little philosophy to avoid getting in such messes? Ellis laughs at Cognitive Psychology (Albert Ellis). I also employ Stoicism and Epicureanism, and maybe even a little Freud (I am very selective about this last), and all these philosophies help me. And I was annoyed, perhaps ignorantly, at Ellis' enthusiasm over his nephew's "Bris." Mutilation of the infant. But perhaps I shouldn't say this.

Also, there's Existentialism. I don't agree with it. But I've been in touch with the Existentialist "Void," where Nothing makes any sense, where Reality doesn't exist, and where the Laws of Cause and Effect do not hold. But I don't agree with them that this is significant. I think it's an aberration, a mistake. A Grand Illusion.

Reality comes back (more or less, for me) and it seems like all the Nada never happened. Maybe, not quite like "never." There is residual damage. I have to use more philosophy, German idealism in this case, to hold Reality in place. Being defines Existence, Existence doesn't define Being. I project my interpretation and extensive knowledge of Reality upon my weak, faulty Perceptions and hold everything in place. This goes against the Existentialists.

Dr. Irving Sternschein, the Existentialist (?) Orthodox Freudian Non-Directive Psychoanalyst, put me in touch with great "religious" and other visions, experiences, emotions, body feelings, and hallucinations, none of which I wanted anything to do with. My mind couldn't accept any of it. I am an Atheist. There's no intellectual reason for believing in God. I didn't want any part of the "visions," etc. But it took me at least 20 or 30 years to get over all of this, as Dr. Felicia Lydia Landau, the consulting psychiatrist who sent me to Dr. Irving Sternschein, had predicted.

I was more or less dysfunctional for 20 years, at least. And none of the dysfunctionality accorded with my Intellect.

When I went into Dr. Sternschein's analysis, I wanted success with women (I had had little since getting to New York, after College. I looked juvenile.) and an improved ability to do my Differential Equations and Advanced Calculus. I wanted Power, not Love, I guess. I still do. Dr. Sternschein showed me something else. It was "interesting and "passionate," but I wanted no part of it. It was alien to my thinking, tradition, upbringing, Germanic intellect, and previous experience. Maybe I was wrong to reject it, but I still don't think so. And NOW, I can't do higher math at all. I am damaged goods.

I was reading Dr. Wilhelm Reich's "Character Analysis" the other day. On Schizophrenia, he says the patient is opened up to "Cosmic Energy," while the normal patient is only opened up to "Orgone, or orgasmic energy." Reich says the schizophrenic cannot deal with these cosmic feelings, because he has a weak organism or functionality. Only a few people are strong enough, functional enough, to handle this "Cosmic Energy," and these people become "great religious teachers" or "poets" (quoting). Well, that's interesting, but I am weak, and I never wanted to become a great religious teacher (that's anathema to me) or a Poet. But I think it shows what Dr. Sternschein had in mind for me.

All of it seems to be Nonsense to me. Besides, Sternschein et al. forgot about the fact that I had to earn a living. All these "visions," and this type of analysis, might be O.K. for very rich people, but not for me. I couldn't cope with them and didn't want them. Indeed, I didn't enjoy living in flophouses (and alleys) for years.

I guess, Janet, you know all this about me already, but I just wanted to order my thoughts on these topics and get it down on paper.

>Thank you for your attention.
>John S.

My Life in Photography and Art

Some of the material which follows has been included elsewhere. I will try to not be too redundant. I don't remember any art instruction, or art play, in Mrs. Hobson's kindergarten class in Cranston, RI, at age 4 (1940), which I otherwise mightily enjoyed. But I might have forgotten the art, if there was any then. I suppose you could say my first definite exposure to Art was Princess Rosebud's finger painting class in the Indian Village at Jones Beach State Park, at age 6 or thereabouts (1942?). I haven't forgotten that happening so I suppose it made some impression.

I can't recall any other exposure to art, or art practice, until the age of 11, in the 8th grade at Baldwin High School, where I was asked to take an Art course. I didn't do very well, in my opinion, but I did learn perspective. At about the same time, maybe age 12 (1948), my mother enrolled me in Leah Hoffman's art classes near our home on Long Island. My mother was the Special Education teacher in the Merrick, LI, elementary school; Leah Hoffman was the art instructor there.

Leah conducted her private art classes on a screened-in porch behind her house. Leah was a very unusual woman. You might even say she was eccentric. She ALWAYS dressed in green, from head to toe, and she drove a green Studebaker with the propeller on the front (how many of my readers remember those?). Leah was a mature woman, but she dyed her hair bright red. She had divorced her husband, but she let him stay in the house as long as he paid rent.

Well, Leah's classes were remarkable! I drew VERY WELL. No figure drawing at that age, except bunnies and such. But I drew wonderful bunnies and sailing ships and such. Her suggestions for colors were extraordinary. My mother framed one of the sailing ships and put it up over the sofa in our living room.

In fact, I drew TOO WELL. I began to think (a little crazy, already, at age 12) that Leah's class was a little UNCANNY. I suspected that she, in some unspoken occult way, was guiding my hand (from a distance). The woman mesmerized me, but I think in a good way. Incidentally, Leah also ran some of the leagues at the Baldwin, LI, bowling alley, in the town where my family then lived, and, thanks to Leah, I duly became a fill-in in the leagues for absent league members. I also learned to set pins manually (now, all bowling alleys have automatic pinsetters, so manual pin setting is a lost art). I was rather proud of myself, learning to do this and working with tough older kids. It wasn't easy. You had to learn the grips to quickly set the pins, four at a time, and then climb up to perch above the pins as the bowling ball came down the alley. I really earned the few dollars I made doing this.

But I digress. Back to art. In high school, I first encountered the names and work of the most famous of the great international artists. Then, or perhaps a little later, the creative process became a great mystery to me. How could they have such imaginative conceits and wonderful fantasies? Only much later did I partially solve this problem. I discovered that many, or most, of the great creative artists were in some ways a little crazy, and actually SAW things as they represented them. It wasn't always imagination or fantasy.

You dispute this? I will give some examples. El Greco, Rouault, Van Gogh and Gauguin have all been retrospectively diagnosed as psychotic, usually schizophrenic. (Of course, the psychiatrists don't often know what they're talking about, either.) Well, when I was schizophrenic, I saw, in my "visions" or "hallucinations," equivalencies to El Greco's shimmering, elongated, phantasmagorical figures,

Rouault's heavy dark outlines of objects and people ("The Old King"), Van Gogh's bright lights in the sky ("Starry Night") and Gauguin's women with halos. All these visions are from memory. I wasn't yet that familiar with the artwork in question when I was schizophrenic.

I believe most of the hundreds of thousands of schizophrenics "see" visions like this, but only a very few have the hubris to try to turn what they see into art. "Outsider Art" indeed! And I suppose that I still think delusions like that should be suppressed and forgotten about, not trumpeted into fine art, to disconcert other people. But, alas, for some reason, I still love those artists and their work. Life is complex. The abovementioned artists seem to have turned their isolation into communicativeness. Insanity, creativity, art and genius are all related, said the Greek philosophers, so it's not just my idea.

My interest in art faded a bit in Oceanside Senior High School, where I completed the 10th, 11th and 12th grades. I was being eased into a science and math curriculum, with which I went along, thinking nothing else was of equal importance. I still think that, to some extent. So I had no further art instruction (or even art history instruction) in high school.

I believe my family shared my view that great art was too mysterious to understand. There was no art work in our home, other than a couple of old nature photographs and scenes, until my mother framed and put up my art work from Leah Hoffman's class. I was never taken to an art museum as a child. In fact, I never went to an art museum until I was a student at Swarthmore College.

I had no art instruction at Swarthmore, either, but nonetheless Swarthmore opened many new horizons in art and art history for me. The great artists, past and present, were treated with awe by the faculty and other students, and Freudian and Reichian notions of creativity were rife on the campus. It was all still a great mystery to me, one which I thought that I would never understand. I only came to understand it a little when I looked deeper into my psyche. Descending into madness brought a measure of enlightenment, at least in this area.

Not to be forgotten is the connection of art with sex. The figure is of great importance in art. I sometimes think that the young female figure is the most beautiful thing that exists. But how do you separate appreciation of beauty from lust? Or don't you?

After Swarthmore, I didn't do anything further in the areas of art and art history until 1974, when I began to take anatomy and drawing classes at the Art Students League here in NYC on West 57th Street. I didn't begin art classes until I had found a way to satisfy my lust for women. The same week that I started going to my NYC brothel, I signed up for art classes. I wanted to keep my lust separate, at least to some extent, from my esthetic appreciation of the model. You may think this is a fine distinction, but the way my mind works, I had to do it. And it worked. I learned to draw (passably). In 1987, I became a Member of The Art Students League, and in 1997, a Life Member. To become a Life Member, you must be voted in. I was rather proud that I had achieved this distinction.

There was more to my drawing and painting career, a little later. In 1989, my friend, the older artist Carl Ashby, whom I had met in 1963 when briefly renting an apartment at 18 Cornelia Street in Greenwich Village, agreed to let me be his Monitor in his Summer classes at The Parsons School of Design, a division of The New School, also in the Village.

For those of you who are not familiar with the term, a Monitor is a sort of Assistant Instructor. He or she sets up the easels, gets supplies, deals with and poses the model, answers student questions, runs the class while the instructor is giving individual instruction, and cleans up and puts everything away when class is finished. There's no remuneration, except that you get to attend the class free, which could be a saving of several hundred dollars. It's a great opportunity to work closely with a talented instructor. I loved doing this, and I did it every Summer with Carl from 1989 through 1995, when Carl was eased out of his position because he was more than 80 years old. I learned a great deal from the experience of working as Carl Ashby's monitor. Carl and I remained great friends until his death in 2004 at age 90. I have a photograph of Carl on my wall, along with a collage and a sketch that he did. Carl helped me a lot in my life drawing and painting work.

As I mentioned, my old friend Ralph Bentley bought me the Minolta 370x camera that enabled me to start my work photographing young female classical nudes. I put up notices at nearby Columbia University and Barnard College, and also in the City's art, drama and dance schools (sample notice earlier in this Memoir) and there were a lot of responses. I did my first photograph for a Holiday card in, I believe, 1989, and the first complete model shoot was also in 1989. My first photo model was "Alison," about whom I remember very little, except that she had a nice young body.

The photo shoots were done in my small living Studio. At the time, Carol Link, a management consultant, lived across the hall here in the cooperative, and she showed me how to hang neutral drops from a 2" x 4" plank stretched across and between the tops of a couple of my bookcases, and held in place by C-clamps. I purchased what I needed from the lumberyard and the hardware store, and I eventually bought drops in neutral beige, bright red and black from the textile outlet. It was necessary for the model and me to move the furniture, some of it heavy, so that the bed could be the model stand, before each shoot. Oh yes, I purchased bed sheets in black and dark red to complete my setup. And I was in business.

The question has been asked, "Where did I get ideas for poses?" Some of the inspiration was in the back of my mind, from work I'd seen elsewhere. For example, I paid homage to such famous photographers as Man Ray, Edward Weston, Bettina Rheims, Lee Friedlander, Lucien Clergue and David Hamilton, by using their poses as points of departure for my own imagination.

Artists such as Amadeo Modigliani and Gustave Courbet also gave me inspiration. I also got ideas from my models, some of whom had long experience with other photographers. Even the neophyte models often had clever notions on how to pose themselves.

I must confess that it was thrilling for me to have so many of these beautiful young college women come into my Studio and disrobe in front of me. Their young bodies were so sexually stimulating to me. But there's nothing wrong in having the erotic inform classical art photography. For example, the great photographer Edward Weston has been one of my icons. Speaking of Weston, the author Jorge Lewinski writes in *The Naked and the Nude,* a Museum of Modern Art publication, that Weston's work "was almost the first time that a photographer had been able to show in his photographs not only his admiration for the beauty of a woman's body but also his desire for her...."

With Weston, I believe the erotic, without too many gimmicks, has a place in classic art photography. I have tried to express this with balance and sensibility. I feel I've made considerable progress, but I know I still have a lot to experience and learn.

I want to relate some of my interesting experiences with some of the best of the models, of whom there have been a hundred or more, so far (2008 as I write this). Chris, a Religion student from Columbia U., was one of the first to impress me. She posed several times for my camera, and I have put an excellent collage (dating from 1989) of Chris' best images up on my foyer wall. Once she came to me after a Summer vacation, heavily tanned, but she'd been wearing a bikini on the beach. Ordinarily I don't like tan lines and think they are a distraction from the figure. But Chris' case was special. The dark tan outlined and highlighted her whiter breasts and genitals in a marvelously erotic way. These photographs are remarkable. I could hardly contain myself, photographing her.

Then there was Jennifer, another model I employed early on. Jennifer was 31 years old at the time she posed for me, a little older than most of my subjects (I asked in my ad for ages 18-28). Jennifer knew I was inexperienced, and taught me a great many new poses. She was a dancer, and I went to a couple of her performances. In the middle of a performance, she would spot me in the audience, and wave to me from the stage, right in the middle of her routine. Jennifer was a good sport!

Two best friends, Trina and Simone posed for me in c.1995. Trina came to me first. I made a wonderful image of Trina inspired by Manet's *Olympia*. Trina was very beautiful, but she said to me, "I'll bring you my friend, Simone, who is even more beautiful than I am." And Trina did, and Simone was even more beautiful than Trina had said. I made my signature photo, *Psyche,* based on Greek mythology, with Simone as the model, and also photographed the two of them together, as Greek Maenads. I was very successful working with both of them.

Trina also accompanied me on an early bodypainting expedition, and painted me at the time. You can see what she created on me in the "Lighthouse Beach..." section of this Memoir, which is a reproduction of an article which I wrote for publication in a naturist magazine.

Unfortunately, I lost contact with both Trina and Simone, when I wrote them both (at the same time) expressing an interest in a closer relationship. They were both shocked and never spoke to me again. That was one of the two or three times that I had, very properly and with great restraint, made advances to a model. I would never make an advance to a model while she was posing. The models are much too vulnerable at that time. But Trina and Simone were both so beautiful, and I thought I could be a closer friend to both of them. But I was disappointed in this. And if you think it's reprehensible to make an advance to a model, I give you the example of Picasso, who seduced or married several of his models.

Also among my favorite models was Sara, a dancer and a very good one, last with the Jody Oberfelder Dance Company, where I have watched her perform, to the applause of the claque I brought with me. Sara had a solo writeup, with a picture, in *The New York Times*. Sara had an indistinct scar on her abdomen, I don't know from what surgery, which was not visible to the naked eye, but which the camera lens could pick up. No matter, it just added to the image's interest.

Sara had been in "yoga rehab" at one time, I don't know for what infraction or lapse. She was cured and went on to become a yoga instructor. She always came to pose, bringing her yoga mat. Incidentally, I am very suspicious of yoga, it has religious associations, and besides that, yoga never helped India's civilization much, India is still largely a very poor and backward country. But Sara Joel has seemed to benefit from the yoga practice.

Megan was a voluptuous young English model with whom I was able to get some very fine images. One of them shows Megan, nude, sitting in front of my personal computer and monitor. The title of the work is "Choices," that is, "Which is more important, the girl or the computer?" This is a question for many people of our era, sitting in their office cubicles with their computers. Also noteworthy about Megan was that she was heavily tattooed, pretty much all over, in bright colors. Her photos are unique in my collection.

Megan, being English, was a little conservative. I believe she was shocked by some of the wall hangings in my Studio, particularly the map of legal Nevada brothels, and the bodypainting nude beach picture of Trina and me.

Ada was one of my most interesting models. She was from the USSR, from which she and her mother were able to escape in the 1980s. Ada's father, a deceased ethnic Russian, had been a Professor of Mathematics at a leading Leningrad university. Ada's mother, a Muslim from Uzbekistan, was also a mathematics scholar. Ada responded to my ad in the Student Employee Office at New York University, where she was attempting to earn an undergraduate degree in Mathematics.

Ada was petite, with a perfectly formed small figure. She was very easy to work with, and posed for me, for sketch and photo, seven or eight times. She had never posed before, but she was very brave about it, and, the first time, she stripped right down, to my exceeding delight. I have an early collage of her color photos on my foyer wall. Initially, she had masses of long black hair in Oriental ringlets, which overpowered her small face and figure, but I encouraged her to cut it, and she then got a short boyish haircut, which made her look very smart.

Ada and I were very close. We might have had a relationship, we got as far as kissing, but I discovered she had hepatitis, I couldn't find out what kind, and I was afraid of sexual transmission of the disease, so I backed off. We continued to be friends, and I helped her mother with some job applications.

In the end, however, there was trouble. Ada acquired a "tough" as a boyfriend, perhaps a fiancé, who called me up and demanded all Ada's pictures back, or he would do me violence. I don't know of Ada's complicity in this. I was prepared for this development, however, as I always obtained signed notarized absolute releases from my photography models, giving me perpetual total control of any images I created. I took Ada's release to my local police precinct, Manhattan's 26th, and the detective called the tough up and told him he had no rights to the pictures, that I was protected, and that he should desist at once. That worked.

Of course, the boyfriend denied the threats, and I never heard from him again. His papers probably weren't in order, anyway, and he had a lot to lose. The police can be very effective, sometimes. Ada did call later to apologize, but that was the end of our relationship. As far as I know, she gave up her academic studies and probably got married.

Next in my "harem" of models is Stephanie. Stephanie was very bright, a Phi Beta Kappa graduate of Gettysburg College (PA), and a poet and writer, in French and English. She also came from a wealthy family, and had a Trust Fund. One grandfather was a very important executive at Johnson & Johnson, on the Board, I think, and regularly replenished the Trust Fund. Stephanie had written a novel, in both English and

French, but was unable to find a publisher. I told her to publish it privately, with Grandfather's money, but Stephanie would have none of this. I have a manuscript copy of her MS and I think it's pretty good. I don't know why she couldn't sell it.

Stephanie had never modeled before she answered my ad and came to me. After modeling for my camera several times, Stephanie began posing for the Tuesday evening life sketch group I have organized and run for five years for the Morningside Gardens Cooperative, where I live. Out of this experience, Stephanie wrote a fine play, entitled, *Twenty Minutes of Immortality,* the title referring to the twenty minutes a life model poses without a break. The play was successfully produced Off Broadway by Yankee Rep, on West 23rd Street. In it, Stephanie appears as a studio life model before a fictive class of art students.

There's also a lot in the play about the life in Paris of Man Ray, the expatriate American artist and photographer, and Lee Miller, his lover and protégé, who also became a photographer of note. Stephanie had never heard of Man Ray and Lee Miller until she met me, so I was very proud of my connection to the play. I wrote the publicity for the play and succeeded in getting the play a few announcements. The play ran for several weeks, and I brought claques (not that Stephanie needed a claque) of about ten people on two occasions.

Stephanie was petite and thin, but I was fascinated by her figure, particularly her most intimate parts, which were ample and fleshy. When she told me she was sleeping with three men seriatim, all in the same time period, I asked to be taken aboard, into the group, but she turned me down. I was very angry, after all I'd done for her, and I broke off with her right away. If she was that promiscuous, one more partner wouldn't have made a difference. I never saw her again, except perhaps a couple of times on the subway, when she glared at me. I regret the ending, but I still have many great classic nude photographs of Stephanie, which continue to delight me, to remember her by.

Jane Alicia Rose, the next model of whom I shall speak, has become a special friend. But not romantically. We are simply very good friends. Jane Rose first came to me in 1999, when an undergraduate in the Columbia University General Studies program. This is a program for adults who are older than typical undergraduates. Jane was about 24 in 1999. She hailed from Northern New Hampshire, where her mother,

Brenda, had turned Jane into an accomplished rider at a very early age. Jane, at 12, could jump stallions bareback. It's not easy to ride a stallion, particularly bareback.

And Northern New Hampshire is really frontier country, a good place for a strong young woman to grow up. Jane graduated from GS a year or two later, in 2002 or 2003. I was at her graduation, which was also the GS graduation of her best friend, Jenny Mundy-Castle, about whom more later. I believe the reason for the late graduation was an early unsuccessful marriage, but I'm not sure about this, and Jane never discusses it with me.

Jane knew what I wanted and was a very good model. Her pictures, in 11" x 14" B&W format, are among the few that I have sold, for several hundred dollars each. Her images are very popular with my clients.

Jane has retired from modeling now, but is trying to work in burlesque, not for the money but for the fun of it. She writes for various NYC sex guides. And, last I heard, she was moving furniture for a (good) living. She IS strong!

Earlier, when she was short of funds, Jane did various kinds of work for me for $10/hour, including painting furniture, clerical work, and party hosting. Now that she's more independent, I've had to find others to help me out. But that's fine! Jane still helps me find people among her younger friends.

A couple of years ago, I asked Jane to serve as one of my Executors (along with the aforementioned Jenny Mundy-Castle, and Jim Welch, my accountant). Jane was happy to accept. And, with the proceeds of my Estate, if anything is left after terminal medical expenses, Jane (collaborating with Jenny) will write and publish (privately, if necessary), a photo-essay of my classic nude photography, and will write a partly biographical sketch of what it was like to work with me, from the viewpoint of a model.

I got the idea for this project from seeing a similar photo essay on the illustrious Edward Weston, written by one of HIS models. Jane and I have already checked out printers and distributors. Of course, I'm leaving remuneration for Jane and Jenny, above the cost of producing the book, but I know that's not why they're doing it.

Also, Jane has very interesting parents. Her father is a New Hampshire doctor and her mother, Brenda Jones, divorced, is a schoolteacher in an Athabascan Indian village North of the Arctic Circle in Alaska. The only way to get to the village is by bush plane. Brenda just remarried, to an environmental engineer based in Fairbanks, but, as far as I know, she still teaches in the Athabascan village. Now, 2008, Jane tells me Brenda is getting divorced again and is planning to leave Alaska. Oh yes, I've met Brenda, and she loves the nude photos I've created of her daughter. Jane's father, the medical doctor, is a little more conservative, but he did pick up the check for ten of us at Columbia U. Faculty House, at Jane's graduation dinner.

I will now describe my experiences working as an actor in the films/videos that Jane makes with her Williamsburg-based guerilla film group. Jane wants a career in filmmaking. She already has one. And I had one hell of a good time making a couple of short films with her.

Jane gets some of her material from the writings of H. P. Lovecraft, an early 20th century writer of macabre and fantastic tales. Yet these tales seem very true to life, even if they involve contacts with infernal or extraterrestrial beings.

I had played in one short film of Jane's, only a few minutes long, the plot and title of which I now have forgotten. Then she asked me to act in a more ambitious project, a realization of the Lovecraft story, "The Testament of Randolph Carter." In this tale, an eccentric, half mad scientist, played by me (type cast?), descends through a hole in the ground to the infernal regions, where he does battle with unknown "things" (creatures). The scientist loses in the struggle and is destroyed. All of this is related in a later Chapter of this Memoir, entitled "Making Movies with Jane."

There's lots more to say about Jane, but this is my biography, not hers, so I will now turn to Jane's best friend, Jenny Mundy-Castle. Jenny and I were not as close as Jane and I, but Jenny and I had a great deal of respect for each other. I believe Jenny took her General Studies B.A. with Honors, or possibly High Honors. She only posed for me once or twice, but she was very competent at this.

Jenny was an extraordinary writer, and read from her works to great acclaim at one of my recent Eleutheria Salons (Jane also read creditably from her own works at that time.). After graduation, Jenny became a NYC Teaching Fellow in the City program that paid the costs of a Master's Degree program if the recipient agreed to teach for two years in NYC's (Inner City) schools. Jenny very bravely taught for two years in Bushwick, a very difficult area in NYC. Inner City schools are not easy places in which to work. But Jenny was successful.

Jenny had planned to be an educational consultant and teacher in Accra, Ghana, after completing the Master's program, but she fell in love and decided to return to her home in Santa Fe, NM, with her new lover, a U.S. Park Ranger. After a year or two in Santa Fe, they decided to get married, and then both take well-paid teaching assignments in Dubai, in the United Arab Emirates. This should be quite an adventure. But as I write this, they're not yet married and have not yet left for the Middle East.

Jenny comes from a family of old Africa hands. Her father, a college professor, was the first person "to introduce LSD to Africa." Jenny's mother, Victoria, separated from her father, has lived in Nigeria for many years, knows and takes part in the village life there, and often wears African dress. Victoria cooked a memorable Nigerian dinner for a group of us, friends of Jenny and Jane, in Williamsburg recently and it was quite an experience.

Jenny does not hide the fact that she is, or was, bisexual. I once commented at a party in her home in Williamsburg, Brooklyn, that one of her shy woman friends there "was a bit of a wallflower," and Jenny nearly bit my head off.

Anyway, knowing Jenny has been quite educational. Jenny married a park ranger in June, 2006. Jane obtained free buddy passes from a friend who worked for JetBlue and I was able to fly to the wonderful wedding at a chalet in the John Muir Woods near Oakland, CA. Nigerian dancers and drummers performed at the reception.

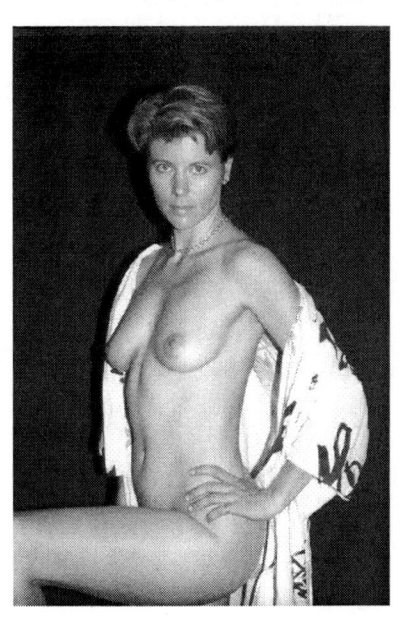

Meg, a physics student at Columbia U.

Then there was Meg, a beautiful married woman from Bermuda living without her husband in NYC while she studied for a B.S. in Physics at Columbia U. Her rich husband remained in Bermuda, I don't know why, I wouldn't have wanted to be away from Meg for long. Meg was very proud of the fact that she was descended from a signer of the (American) Declaration of Independence. Meg had a long, lithe body, with a beautiful, well formed poitrine, and was very cooperative in taking poses in photo work and in the sketch group.

However, NYC was too much for Meg. On 9/11/2001, the day of the World Trade Center disaster, she was scheduled to pose for the Tuesday MG sketch group. Despite the disaster, we went ahead with plans to meet, partly because the Mayor said we should try to continue with our regular activities. Meg never showed up. I was never able to contact her again, either by telephone or E-mail. I can only conclude she must have immediately fled back to the (relative) security of Bermuda. Alas, it was a loss for us to lose Meg. But I have some classic erotic photo images of her to remember her by.

Next in my photo model gallery is Emma. When Emma first answered my ad, she was a Junior at Columbia College, Columbia U. She was already an experienced dancer and nude photo model. Ideal qualifications. Emma would often assume extreme erotic poses, such as putting her feet and hands behind and underneath her on the floor and arching her back, which projected her genitals up and forward. Very provocative!

I never learned much about Emma, except that she eventually graduated from Columbia and later on acquired a new boyfriend and lover, "Brad" from Virginia. After a while, Brad took exception to my photography, and made Emma stop working for me/us. This was a great disappointment. Emma was a very beautiful young woman. One cosmopolitan friend had referred to Emma as a *mignon*.

Emma, *mignon*

The penultimate model that I will introduce you to at this time is the "sensational" 3D animator, book artist, printmaker, sculptress, painter, installation artist, writer, poet and "Holy Madwoman," Yana. Born in Baku, Azerbaijan, Yana lived to the age of 12 in Israel, and then, with her family, emigrated to the United States. She now lives in Clinton Hill, Brooklyn, where she currently is pursuing her MFA in 3D animation at Pratt University She also has worked as a studio life model for a number of artists, including me. One of her hobbies is scuba diving, and she helps her father make his illuminated underwater art installations (e.g., Buddha heads) at a depth of 100 feet.

Yana began as a painter, earned her BFA in printmaking (lithography, woodcut, intaglio, silkscreen and digital), developed a passion for book arts (having studied with Antonio Frasconi) and now extends the idea of combining her visual and narrative art in computer animated form. Yana also makes macabre clay dolls, somewhat after the style of Hans Bellmer. She has exhibited her dolls at the famous Dollhaus Museum in Williamsburg, and also at the CGBG Gallery in Manhattan. Her style is between naturalistic, expressionist, surreal and dadaist (Max Ernst, Francis

Bacon, Francisco De Goya, Frida Kahlo) and all her work deals with human psychology in addition to a variety of conceptual issues.

All the above two paragraphs are modified from a blurb in my Fall 2004 Eleutheria Salon flyer, where Yana was a presenter. She's so very talented and deep that I thought you should read it. In her writings, she mentions her experience with psychosis, but I've never asked her to amplify that. Right now, her public manner is extremely professional, restrained and correct. I have observed only that she might be a little lacking in spontaneity, and might have to exert considerable control on herself, as I also do. She's certainly not at all restrained in her creative work, which is quite remarkable. Incidentally, I learned later on that she's a very good friend of Jane Rose.

I picked up Yana in late 2003 at a show at the aforementioned Dollhaus Museum. I gave her my card and my model ad and she got back to me. Yana said she wanted to try life modeling for me (she hadn't modeled before) because, as an artist, she wanted the experience of working on the other side of the easel, on the model stand. She's since become a very good friend. She has worked many times in our Morningside Gardens life sketch group, and often shaves her pudenda, which I like (and this would be good for photography). I haven't photographed her yet because, although she is very pretty, her figure is not quite the type I want for my classic nude photography. But I do suspect that Yana will soon go on to become quite famous.

Yana recently said she couldn't afford to model any longer for our sketch group at our current pay rate, because it takes her three hours and $4 in subway fares to make the trip, back and forth, to and from Clinton Hill. She says she will come back to us if I raise the rates or make the sessions longer (more pay hours), and I can understand that. She is now helping me find other model candidates.

The last model I will discuss at this time in this "model review" is Barbara, a charming beauty from Philadelphia, who periodically comes up from Philadelphia to visit her relatives in NYC. She makes her living in the restaurant business (and by selling her own art quite successfully), and just left a good job at Le Bec Fin, a fine Philadelphia restaurant. She also works catering gigs on the side.

Her own career as an artist does quite well. She does monotypes of horses and subway scenes, among other subjects. Barbara has lived and studied in Florence (Firenze) for several years. She has sold her pieces for a thousand or more dollars each.

Barbara saw my ad somewhere, and I interviewed her and took her on. She has posed twice in a special situation, small Studio groups in my apartment, where I invite three or four close friends and serve refreshments, including good baklava, good cognac and grappa, for a small life sketch group.. It's all very *intime* and friendly. We have a great time and there is a lot of philosophical and art conversation. It's really a special time for me, and for the others, including the model. Barbara likes it and thinks my Studio is "cozy." Barbara has also posed for our regular MG Workshop life sketch group, but she prefers the Studio Salons. I don't blame her.

Barbara's figure is quite remarkable. Her breasts are fine and large enough, but they're not differentiated like separate organs, as they are in many women. Her breasts blend in, in a very attractive way, with the rest of her figure. She's "streamlined." Anyway, I offered Barbara a 5-day weekend, staying at my place, with a Friday photo session, a Sunday Studio Salon, and a regular Workshop sketch group on Tuesday. I also offered to take her to Columbia U. Faculty House, the Philharmonic, and the recently reconstructed Museum of Modern Art. She accepted, but refused my offer to stay at my place, which was a great disappointment for me. She'll stay with her relatives in Brooklyn. Too bad. I had high hopes for the Weekend.

I also asked Barbara to shave her pudenda for me, for the photo shoot. It makes for better, more erotic pictures. Why? The external female genitalia are beautiful. But pubic hair is not beautiful. But Barbara refused to do this for me, at least so far. Another disappointment! Oh well, maybe something will develop over the Weekend anyway.

That's the end of my review of some of my most outstanding models. This has just been a selection of the most interesting individuals out of the more than 100 girls/women who have posed for me. It's been very satisfying working with them. It is a privilege not many people get. I'm very happy that I decided to embark on my photographic career, exclusively photographing young female classic nudes, in 1989. I've had 16 years of pleasure, as I write this. Of course, most of it has been somewhat sublimated, but that's O.K. with me.

Here are a few words on how I work with my many photo models. Most come to me, having seen my model notice (printed elsewhere in this document) at Columbia U. or Barnard College, or in an art school, acting school or dance academy (or in a busy laundromat, for that matter). I always carry notices and thumbtacks with me and seize every opportunity to widen my esthetic reach.

After the initial phone call or e-mail response, I invite the neophyte (others are experienced) to my Studio for an interview. If they're timid, I tell them to bring a friend. When they arrive, a Bach Orchestral Suite might be playing and I offer them coffee and pastry (good baklava, if I have any on hand). This usually breaks the ice. I show the neophyte my work, and add a few words about my naturism and skydiving, just to see if this puts them off. It occasionally does, but I'd rather not work with anyone who is not open to new experiences.

Then I show some examples of the work of the Masters that I emulate, Edward Weston, Man Ray, Lee Friedlander, Bettina Rheims, Lucien Clergue and David Hamilton, for example. In an actual shoot, we may use the Masters' poses as points of departure for our own work. All this usually gives the new model a fair idea of what is expected, so she can make her decision. If she says yes, we set up a date for a 3-hour session, in which I will shoot three or four rolls of 36-image film. This includes color prints, B&W prints, B&W transparencies in the new Scala format, and possibly a roll of color slides, although I don't show color slides much any more. The B&W slides are so well accepted.

And now, what happens in the actual session? The neophyte arrives, I greet her warmly, offer her coffee and pastry again, and then give her a pretty kimono to wear between pose sequences. The model goes into my changing room (it's the bathroom), and emerges, in the kimono, expectant and a little fearful. I ask the model to open the kimono a little in the front, not showing too much, and I take a few photos, perhaps with her standing before the easel, to ease her in gradually. Then, 10 minutes later, when she's become a little more comfortable, I ask her to reveal everything, which she usually does. It's as simple as that, and it usually works.

I explained the furniture moving and drop hanging necessary to set up the Studio for a shoot earlier on. As I said then, I worry more that a model will injure herself moving the furniture than that she will complain

I'm behaving inappropriately. But so far, no accidents. Minor difficulties have included menstrual bleeding on the sheets and tampon strings that pop out into the field of view, but we've been able to deal with such matters. Actually, I believe it's a biological fact that women are randier during their period, so perhaps they pose a little more eagerly then, and we get better results. Some of the best models (also in our life sketch group) are the ones who feel the most empowered. More power to them, if they like to act in my scenario.

I could discuss at length the limited number of props that I use to help the models look their best, but perhaps you'd do better now just to look at my Web site, http://jseamanclassicnudes.Artspan.com and figure it out for yourself. I'll just say I have a few tricks in my repertoire that help me do my work better.

After every shoot, I have two sets of commercial prints, two each of 4" x 6" and of 3" by 5" made, at considerable expense, and I give one complete set to the model. Occasionally, a model will object that a pose is too erotic or explicit, but I can usually deal with this. I explain that "erotic" is the name of the game.

Next, when I get the funds together, I engage a young darkroom helper (I've had several, over the years) to assist me in making large 11" x 14" B&W prints from the best of the B&W negatives, as we see the images in the small commercial prints. I should explain that my Morningside Gardens Cooperative has a well-equipped darkroom, which I am able to use as a dues-paying member of the MG Camera Club. I give a couple of the large prints to the model, and offer to make her more, for a consideration, which might be cash or perhaps more modeling, free this time. I think this is generous, since I've been able to sell some of the 11" x 14" prints for $200 each or more, and the darkroom helper and I can make only about 20 acceptable large prints in an 8-hour darkroom day.

That's a brief look at how the large images come to exist. The next step is to show them, to bring them before the public eye. You've already been directed to my Web site, from which I've had a good response in the four years it's been up. I also regularly show my slides at my biannual Eleutheria (means "Liberty" in Demotic Greek) Salons, given right here in my Studio to audiences of 20 or 30, tightly packed in. There's more about my 15 years' experience with Eleutheria in a special Section of this Memoir.

I've also had shows with the Morningside Gardens Camera Club, Morningside Retirement & Health Services (the old folks love to look at the young nudes), and Riverside Church (Riverside Emerging Artists League, R.E.A.L., hosted by my good friend and fellow tenant/cooperator, Dr. Joaquin Flores). I gave an informal show at my 50th Swarthmore College Reunion, in June 2006, which was well received. Like the models, I feel empowered when I get a Show.

As already discussed, Jane Rose and Penelope Karageorge are preparing a photo-essay and brief bio, including something on how it was to know me and work with me. If we can find a publisher, it may appear while I am still alive. Otherwise it will be privately printed with the cost paid by the proceeds of my Estate, which will chiefly consist of the funds from the sale of my home, my cooperative apartment.

That about covers my experiences in photography and art up until the present, March 2005, age 68. If you read this before I'm dead, I would appreciate any inputs you might have.

John Seaman Publicity

From the Model Stand

Not since Edna St. Vincent Millay bathed nude in the Washington Square Fountain in 1906, has a young American woman author attempted anything as daring, until now, as does the playwright, poet, novelist, actress and life model Stephanie Sellars in her new short play, *Twenty Minutes of Immortality,* to be presented at the Gotham City Improv Theater, 158 West 23rd Street, New York City, (212) 367-8222, appearing Thursdays, November 16 and 30, December 7 and 14, 8:00 p.m., under the auspices of Yankee Repertory. Admission will be free, with a suggested donation.

Directed by Kevin Mahoney, Ms. Sellars' new play will intersperse poetic soliloquies on life, art and modeling, given "from the model stand" in a fictive class by an *au naturel* life model, played by Ms. Sellars, herself, in a role she knows well from her work as an artist's and photographer's model, with vignettes from the lives of other male and female models. (The "twenty minutes" of the play's title refers to the period of time that a life model usually poses on the model stand, between five-minute breaks.) But most especially, *Twenty Minutes* includes sequences from the 1920s Paris relationship between the celebrated American photographer, artist and constructivist Man Ray, and his protégé and lover, Lee Miller, who later became a famous photographer in her own right.

The Man Ray/Lee Miller scenes are very important in the unfolding of the play and also in Ms. Sellars' own thought and development. How can a young "ingénue" break into the creative world? The play shows how a talented, beautiful and adventurous young American WASP socialite could in the 1920s begin an entire creative career by going to Paris specifically determined to link up her fortunes with those of the already famous American expatriate artist Man Ray (his pseudonym, Man Ray's origins were Russian-Jewish). Their tumultuous relationship is the heart of the play. We see how Lee Miller forges herself into a remarkable artist herself, out of the maelstrom of avant-garde Paris of the 1920s.

Mr. Mahoney, the Director, has directed plays in New York, Atlanta and Los Angeles. Although most of his experience has been in classical and modern classical work, he welcomes the opportunity to work with Ms. Sellars in her "untraditional" play. *Twenty Minutes* is part of Yankee Rep's "New Artists/New

Works" series, which aims to develop the voice of new writers through a thorough examination of the collaborative creative process by writer, directors and actors. *Twenty Minutes* is on a double bill and will be presented on the four Thursday evenings after another short play, S*pace Lift*.

Ms. Sellars' other credits are already extensive. She has written poetry in English and French, much of which has already been published, particularly in *Re: Verse!* and on the "Freewilliamsburg.com" website. Ms. Sellars recently read her original French verse at the Columbia University Maison Francaise. She acted in *Les Liaisons Dangereuses* with Studio Dramatique here in New York City and she has offered original performance art at the Avignon Festival in France. She makes her living as an ESL teacher and, as already mentioned, an artist's and photographer's model.

Ms. Sellars also recently completed and is preparing for publication her major first novel (the novel has passages in both French and English), partly autobiographical, entitled *Dandelion Moon.*

Ms. Sellars hails now from Massachusetts and is a Phi Beta Kappa graduate in French and English from Gettysburg College. She lived for a considerable period of time in Brooklyn, then making her home in the Williamsburg district. She now lives on Cape Cod but she is often on the New York scene.

Pix of Stephanie Sellars as a Life Model upon request.

Making Movies with Jane

Jane Alicia Rose was one of my photography and sketch models for several years. She was very good at it. I have sold more images of Jane than of anybody else. I wrote a biographical sketch of Jane in this Memoir, in the section entitled, "My Life in Photography and Art."

Jane has stopped modeling a year or two ago and is now trying her hand at appearing in the Burlesque at the Galapagos Club in Williamsburg, Brooklyn. I have also made her into one of my Executors and charged her with the task of compiling a photo-essay of my work, with accompanying biographical notes on what it was like to work with me.

I will now describe my experiences working as an actor in the films/videos that Jane makes with her Williamsburg-based guerilla film group. Jane wants a career in film. Indeed, she already has one. And I had one hell of a good time making a couple of short films with her.

Jane gets some of her material from the writings of H. P. Lovecraft, an early 20th century writer of macabre and fantastic tales. Yet these tales seem very true to life, even if they involve contacts with infernal or extraterrestrial beings.

I had played in one short film of Jane's, only a few minutes long, the plot and title of which I now have forgotten. Then she asked me to act in a more ambitious project, a realization of the Lovecraft story, "The Testament of Randolph Carter." In this tale, a n eccentric, half mad scientist, played by me (type cast?), descends through a hole in the ground to the infernal regions, where he does battle with unknown "things" (creatures). The scientist loses in the struggle and is destroyed. All of this is relayed to us by the scientist's assistant, who remains above ground, connected to the scientist by an improvised speaking apparatus and a pseudo-video connection. The assistant was the only other character in the film, though there were extensive voiceovers.

For the scenario, I had to memorize five short paragraphs of dialogue, dress in appropriate tweedy costume, and descend into a pit in the ground. All this was accomplished in a raging thunder and rainstorm in a huge vacant lot on the Williamsburg, Brooklyn, waterfront. Jane had particularly waited for the storm to do the filming. Necessary background. We could easily have been hit by lightning, in our exposed position on the flat plain. But we were lucky that night.

There were six or seven of us, in all, in the film crew, including cameramen, lighting helpers, and prop people. We set up an improvised tent to shelter from the rainstorm (and the lightning?) between film sequences, but we all got very wet. Luckily, Jane had brought lots of (cheap) beer. Red Stripe, I think it was. There was also plenty of hot coffee. I should add that Jane had obtained all sorts of "interesting" props, obtained from various junk shops around town and also from an army/navy "junk" shop in Nevada, adjacent to an atomic testing range, where she had recently vacationed. The props included all sorts of spaghetti- or intestine-like tubing, and a collection of fake eyes, all of which showed up in the fake video the eccentric scientist (played by me) purported to transmit from his journey in hell. There were other interesting props, as well, the exact nature of which I now cannot remember.

Anyway, the session was a real Gotterdammerung, and I wanted to tell you a little about it. The filming was a tremendous lot of fun. Much later, Jane gave me a VHS video of the film, about 15 minutes long. I show it from time to time at my various Eleutheria Salons and other entertainments.

Notes on Family

Here I include some brief stories about myself and my relatives, from the notes I compiled for my nephew, George A. Freestone. These will serve as a brief guide and supplement to the balance of the Memoir, where I will treat these same topics at length.

Notes for John Robert Seaman

As a 12-year-old, I raised hundreds (thousands) of golden hamsters. I did a psychological research project with them, then took a competitive exam, and was a 1952 winner of the Westinghouse Science Talent Search. As part of the prize, I went to Washington, DC and personally met and chatted with President Harry Truman (I was age 15). (Later in my career, I was at banquets for President Johnson and then for President Bush the elder. I also ran cross country with Michael Dukakis when we were both students at Swarthmore College.) I led the Swarthmore College Outing Club all over the Northeast and Southeast mountain ranges, in all seasons. I wrote and edited all science articles for various Columbia Encyclopedias and Supplements. I was the Chief Science Editor at The Columbia University Press at a very early age (23-24).

Later, I wrote laymen's versions of Physical Review and Physical Review Letters articles for The American Institute of Physics (AIP). I edited and wrote for The Association for Computing Machinery (ACM). I wrote and traveled all over the world (many trips to Western Europe, two trips to the USSR, one trip to Japan) for *The Data Communications User*, *Electronic Products* and *Computer Decisions* magazines. I wrote and edited one book, *Data Communications: A Manager's View*.

About 1986, changed careers, became an art photographer (classical and contemporary nudes) and artist. See my web site, http://jseamanclassicnudes.Artspan.com . I am a Life Member, Art Students' League of NY. My bio is included in the 57th Edition of Marquis' *Who's Who in America,* publication date, December 2002, primarily for my photography and art work. I worked 3rd shift as a legal proofreader to support daytime art & photo activities. I am an active Naturist (Nudist). I go to Cap d'Agde in Southern France (65,000 naturists at one time in high season) as often as I can. I have written published work about Cap d'Agde and other naturist resorts. For many years, I have organized and led Summer bodypainting (harmless water-based theatrical bodypaints) expeditions to the local free (naturist) beaches, for members of my liberal Morningside Gardens cooperative (and outsiders). I skydived on my 64th Birthday.

Notes for Robert Gurdineer Seaman (my father)

RGS was a boxer at Cornell. He was a quiet man. Enjoyed business trips all over the country with the family in the family 1936 Chevrolet, and later, air trips alone to business meetings in Europe. RGS died on a business trip to London.

Notes for Robert Gurdineer & Bertha May (Family)

BMLS had rheumatic fever and polio as a child, and never completely got over this. She worked full time as a teacher and also ran the home, but she could not climb stairs and always worked on the ground floor. In 1957, her heart mitral valve began to fail. The open heart valve operations were very new then, and the doctors told Bertha that if the operation worked, she'd be as strong as a horse, but there was a 50% chance she'd die on the table (experimental surgery). Bertha did not have the nerve for this, and died a year later, without the surgery. The operation is now (2003) routine.

But first, about my Father. He wasn't exactly introverted, he was the strong, silent type. He and my Mother fought all the time, both drank and smoked a lot (and therefore died young). I believe my Father consorted with prostitutes. My Mother was always yelling about "Gert," who I think once called the house looking for "Robert." I was afraid of my Father. I always thought it was Jungian synchronicity that my first Lover was named "Gert." Robert was only 5'8" but he was very strong. He only hit me once, while I was growing up, but I always feared that. Robert Gurdineer Seaman was definitely not epicene or retiring (or mild and introverted). He just wanted nothing to do with kids.

My mother was always ambitious, if not for herself, then for ME. I was her little "thing." "star," yes, but also "thing." She got that from her very successful Father, Elmer J. Lewis, about whom you've read. I was very dependent on her emotionally until I went away to College. Once I got away from her, I just wanted to distance myself from her possessiveness. I wouldn't go home on College vacations. Instead, I'd lead groups of 30 college kids (unchaperoned) off into the Wilderness

By then, I couldn't bear my mother's possessiveness. And I let her die alone. I must expiate that sometime.

Notes for Robert E. Seaman (my paternal grandfather)

Robert E. Seaman was a printer by trade, I believe. I think he retired early. He died at age 86 in 1965. He was healthy and would have lived even longer but his eyes were "ripening" for cataract operations, and, temporarily, he could not see well. He was hit by a truck while walking across Route 9W in Nyack. He lived for a day or two, but the doctors said it was a mercy he died, as they would have has to amputate both his legs. Robert E. was not an educated man, I doubt he had the imagination and mental resources to cope with the loss of his legs. Robert E. outlived his only offspring, Robert Gurdineer Seaman, who died a natural death in 1962.

Notes for Robert E. & Carrie Gurdineer (paternal grandmother)

I know very little about Carrie, other than that I believe she died in about 1945, when I was 9 years old. Both RES and CGS wintered in Jacksonville, FL, in later years.

Notes for Elmer J. Lewis (my maternal grandfather)

He had worked his way up to a high post in the Treasury Dep't (Customs). He was second in charge of the Customs House on Bowling Green Park at the Battery. In 1936, he bought three 1936 Chevrolets for his three married daughters, Bertha Seaman, Florence Dawson and Hazel Grotz. He worked his way up from driving a tram on 125th Street.

Elmer J. Lewis was a customs agent in Montreal during Prohibition. He, taking his teenage daughters with him, along with other Treasury agents, would drive open "roadsters" across the tracks at either end of a railroad trestle crossing the St. Lawrence River, stopping a train filled with "hooch" on the trestle. Then Elmer, his daughters and the other agents would walk out on the trestle, pry open the boxcars with crowbars, and they then would break all the bottles of hooch on the rails and throw them into the river.

Elmer J. Lewis visited Hawaii sometime before World War II. I don't know if it was a business or pleasure trip. I know he had a rousing good time there. There was a collage of photographs in the family when I was a child showing Elmer in Hawaii in a top hat, surrounded by liquor bottles, palm trees and half-naked hula girls. I wish I still had that.

Notes for Amasa Lewis (my great grandfather, Elmer's father)

Amasa Lewis, my-Great-Grandfather, ran away from Petersburg, a little farming village at the conjunction of NY, VT and MA, where Elmer grew up and Bertha and the other daughters went Summers, in 1862 at the age of 13 to be a drummer boy in the Union Army. But drummer boys needed parental permission, and the woman who raised Amasa, Sybil Lamphere, wouldn't let him go, and sent someone to the Quartermaster's Office in nearby Troy, NY to get him back. The Quartermaster got on the telegraph, they found him in a distant camp, and sent him home on the train right away. Good thing. We might not be here if Sybil Lamphere had not done this. The Union Army was well-organized and equipped, way back then, 142 years ago. This story may be apocryphal, but I think it's true. Amasa died in 1935, at the age of 85.

As a 5-year-old, Amasa was abandoned near Petersburg by his father, Leonard Lewis, a wagonmaster going West to Chicago, because "he was in the way." He would have frozen to death, but he was picked up and taken in by a blind woman, Sybil Lamphere, who raised him to maturity. Amasa had a very happy home and worshipped Sybil and read the Bible to her every night. He could quote the Bible "like a Minister," from all this reading to Sybil.

Earlier Genealogy

I don't know how much reliance I should put on what follows, but it is interesting. A Quaker Swarthmore College schoolmate, Esther Darlington, instructed me that "Seaman" is an old Quaker name, dating back at least to the time of George Fox (17th century C.E.), the Founder of The Religious Society of Friends (popularly known as "Quakers," because they are "moved," (by the Holy Spirit?) at their meetings for worship, and tremble, or quake. (I will add that I was once at a Quaker meeting for worship, and a well set up young man was giving testimony about his redemptive work in the prisons and mental hospitals, and he began to tremble violently, and the pew began to shake, and then the whole building began to shake (or so it appeared to me). I have no ready explanation, except that perhaps it was a sympathetic hallucination.)

Before Quaker times, the name (earlier, "Seeman," from the Teutonic languages) is said to have come through the Vikings, or Norse marauders, who ravaged England is the first millennium, and then settled in the Danelaw, a part of England where English law did not hold. Instead, the Norsemen answered to Danish law, hence "Danelaw." It should be said that the Norsemen were more technologically advanced than the English, and brought many improvements, even if they were marauders. I take a little vicarious pleasure in my bold ancestors. This may have helped me go through with my skydiving.

I must add that by far, most of the Quaker men in the book section Esther photocopied for me were named, John, or Robert, or even John Robert. I am John Robert Seaman, as you know. This is a remarkable coincidence. My parents had probably never heard of the Quakers, before I discovered them at Swarthmore College, which the Quakers founded.

Some of the remarkable persons in Esther's marvelous book about the Seaman were Knight Crusader Sir John Seaman, with a coat of arms and all that; Dr. Robert Seaman, Professor of Theology at Cambridge in Elizabethan times; and Captain John Seaman, who brought Governor Winthrop, the first Royal Governor of Massachusetts, and a fleet of nine ships filled with settlers, over from England in the 1630s. Captain John Seaman then settled in Hicksville, Long Island, New York, the first of the clan to settle there.

Of course, I realize that, with the dilution of the generations, I don't have a tenth of a percent of the genes of these people, but the facts are still entertaining.

My Departed Sister Barbara

The marvelous poet Barbara Jane Seaman Freestone, my only sibling, died in January 2003, at the age of 71, of an unnecessary hospital infection. I had never been particularly close to her, but I greatly regretted her passing, especially because I had lately come to appreciate her creative work as a simple, honest, yet subtle poet.

Barbara was born on March 5, 1931, the first child of our parents, Robert Gurdineer Seaman and Bertha May Lewis Seaman. There are data on my family in the earlier Memoir Section, "Notes on Family," but I did not treat my sister there. Barbara was born in Providence, RI, and was the only child until I came along, five years later. I don't know much about Barbara's childhood, except that she was a very pretty child (I've seen the family photographs) and that she passed her menarche at age 9.

Barbara played with me only occasionally when I was a small child, I suppose because the age gap was too great, and also because I preferred to play alone. I do remember being put in a tub with her, both of us nude, by our parents, when I was six years old. This was very unusual for my parents, who were usually very prudish.

The next striking memory of my sister occurred when I was seven, and she was 12, quite the pretty little sexually attractive girl. Two of her male admirers (admirers from a distance, I'm sure) came to the house to see her and brought a beautiful balsa wood airplane for me (to impress Barbara). The plane was beautiful, quite complex, ribbed with balsa wood and covered with colored tissue paper. I loved it, but it was delicate, and soon broke under my rough handling. That was in 1942 or 1943. I believe I was more impressed than Barbara was.

Next thing, Barbara was in Baldwin (Long Island) High School, where she graduated, third in her class (top girl, class of about 200) in 1948. Her high school swain had been Frank Clark, a handsome, sensitive writer, and the older brother of my friend Fred Clark. Frank was a great catch except he had a heart condition. I'm certain the physical relationship didn't go to far, but in any case, I'm sure my family discouraged it, because of Frank's heart condition. Our parents encouraged Barbara to go out with another classmate, George Dudley Freestone, a rather stolid, unimaginative character I did not like. But Barbara, after college, married George.

In September, 1948, Barbara went away for her Freshman year at Duke University in Durham, North Carolina. She earned all "A"s, but could not handle the boys. And of course my parents were determined to keep her a virgin, before marriage. I remember many frantic phone calls to our house between Barbara and my father about what to do about the boys. My father would be screaming into the phone and Barbara would scream back. It was all too much for Barbara AND my parents. They couldn't allow her to develop normal sexual relationships. So they brought her back to New York after her Freshman year and enrolled her at Barnard College, part of Columbia University in Manhattan.

Barbara at first lived at home on Long Island and commuted to the City, and later she took a dormitory room at Barnard. Her college career at Barnard was undistinguished, she earned "B"s and "C"s at this tougher, Ivy League school. She graduated in 1952, with a degree in English Literature, I believe.

Barbara returned to the family home on Long Island, taught elementary school for a year, and then married George Dudley Freestone, the hirsute, unimaginative engineer that my parents felt secure with. The marriage was stormy. There were more frantic phone calls to my Father. But there were also three children. Anyway, marriage to George was very hard on Barbara. She began to have recurring nervous breakdowns and was repeatedly hospitalized (more than me, and she never quite got beyond it, as perhaps I did).

But she stuck with George, perhaps for want of a better alternative. The family lived first in Cleveland, OH; then in Berkeley Heights, NJ; and finally settled in Camp Hill, PA, a suburb of Harrisburg. When she was more or less recovered from mental illness, Barbara worked as a shop assistant at Bolton's Department Store. She also became active in the Harrisburg Chapter of The American Association of University Women (A.A.U.W.), a rather stuffy group, I think, but the participation gave Barbara great pleasure.

Later on in life, Barbara began to write simple, honest, unaffected poetry, some of which my literary friends have said was quite good. After her death, her son, George A. Freestone, put together a tasteful, illustrated, computer-generated portfolio of her work, of which I have a copy. If I ever have any money, I'll have her work published privately, and I will also put up a

Web site just for her. Perhaps there will be enough to do this if my cooperative apartment is revalued substantially higher, which development seems to be in the wind. I will include one of Barbara's special poems at the end of this Section.

Barbara was quite overweight late in life, and contracted Type 2 diabetes, from which she was able to recover, with a substantial amount of self-discipline. But the weight ruined her knees. In 2000, she had a knee replacement, which seemed to go O.K.

A year later, though, there were complications. The doctors (in the dumb little Catholic hospital in Camp Hill) said the cadaver tendon which had been used in Barbara's original knee replacement had become infected and would have to be replaced. Barbara was told this would be a simple procedure and that she would be in the hospital for two weeks, at most. But it didn't work out that way.

The doctors in this unsanitary hospital (I tried to get the Family to move her somewhere else, but nobody would listen to me.) replaced the tendon three more times, and each time it became infected again. This all took several months. Then they said they would have to fuse, or permanently straighten, Barbara's knee. By this time Barbara was greatly depressed, and then comatose. The knee was fused, but Barbara quickly developed lung congestion, an infection acquired after six months in the hospital. She was quickly gone.

Her doctor, the Irish Dr. Lanergan, enraged me by e-mailing everybody that Barbara's death was "God's Will." It was not. It was human incompetence, particularly Dr. Lanergan's.

I will close this brief section about my Sister by including one of her wonderful poems, as an Epitaph:

The Edge of Morning

Collected Poems of

Barbara Freestone

January 2003

Version 4-20 April 2003

Frills and Femininity After Fifty

I was always a straightforward woman,

Not mannish, but conservative.

A skirt and sweater suited me,

I never wore spike heels.

Now that I am older,

A sprinkling of frills appeals to me.

I like flowered towels for drying,

A pretty hat is often on my head.

It's not a complete changeover,

I still own a "basic black dress."

It's just a new feeling,

Of trying to be feminine.

What the feeling is, I believe,

Is an attempt to experience everything.

Before the door closes,

On me.

REST IN PEACE, BARBARA!

This chapter first appeared as a published article in a leading naturist magazine.

PICKNICKING AT LIGHTHOUSE BEACH

New York State's Best Tended Naturist Beach

By John Seaman

Now in my 60th year (as this was written), I first encountered nude beaches on a visit to Mykonos, an island in the Greek Cyclades, in 1989. I was amazed and delighted and have been an avid naturist ever since. I go to Paradise Beach on Mykonos for a few weeks every summer, but I have also tried to get into naturism nearer home.

But, just what is naturism? Is it simply the practice of public nudity, or is it something more? According to the International Naturist Federation (Agde, 1974), Naturism is "a lifestyle in harmony with nature, expressed through social nudity, and characterized by self-respect of people with different opinions and of the environment."

In 1992, I heard there was an interesting nude beach adjacent to Field 5 of Robert Moses State Park on Long Island, about 35 miles from my home in New York City. At that time I only had access to public transportation, so I took a bus from Manhattan to Robert

Moses Field 3 (the nearest stop to the nude beach). Unfortunately, this was not the best plan as I had to walk along the beach for about three miles to my destination.

Robert Moses is a New York State Park and does NOT allow full nudity, even though a 1993 court ruling permits women to appear topfree in public.

The situation is different on federal property, where the law permits nudity, although the National Seashore jurisdiction has the option of following local (in this case, State) law. We are fortunate that the Superintendent of the Fire Island National Seashore and Lighthouse Beach in particular works with all the local groups to ensure that the long tradition of nudity at Lighthouse Beach continues. This man is Jack Hauptman and he is much admired by New York naturists.

I found that Lighthouse Beach is a wonderful, very cosmopolitan place. All sorts of individuals and groups are welcome, including singles (including single women), straights, gays, couples, families, children of all ages, all races, etc. Fire Island National Seashore is under the care of the National Park Service, a division of the U.S. Department of the Interior. It is supervised by the U.S. Park Rangers whom I have not known to cause anyone any trouble.

The beach is named for an old lighthouse, formerly belonging to the U.S. Coast Guard, on the property. Kept in excellent condition, it is a Mecca for busloads of small children. The visits of the children caused a bit of a problem. It has been resolved by restricting the area immediately adjacent to the lighthouse; now, nude sunbathing is not permitted there. One wag commented that this was really too bad for the children, since visiting the nude beach might be considered part of a young person's education.

The change in policy has had the unfortunate effect of splitting the naturist area into two parts (you have to don clothing to pass from one to the other). This was the best compromise Jack Hauptman could work out among the varied groups that use the property.

Everyone on the beach, in my experience, is friendly and strangers are welcome. Nudity is not obligatory; those who are more comfortable keeping some or all of their clothes on during their initial visits can do so. "To see and be seen," as it says in the 19th-century Russian novels, is the order of the day. Nobody gawks and nobody is made to feel uncomfortable.

I struggled alone to Lighthouse Beach on public transportation three or four times, all the time learning more about it. I learned that is much easier to take the Long Island Railroad from Penn Station in Manhattan to Babylon (train fare perhaps $12 round trip) and then take a local taxi (about $15 fare one way for the first person, $1 for each additional person – you can arrange with the taxi to pick you up when you're ready to leave, hours later) to Field 5 of Robert Moses State Park, from where you can walk an easy ¾ of a mile to the marked area for nudism at Lighthouse Beach on federal property. There are no restrooms or food concessions on Lighthouse Beach, so you have to take care of these necessities at Field 5. Most people bring a picnic anyway.

After a year or two of this, I began to arrange expeditions for small groups of my friends to Lighthouse Beach, finding friends with cars to transport us. This is much easier and cheaper and makes the whole expedition much more fun. We bring a good picnic spread including roast chicken, potato salad, macaroni salad, green salad, SNAPPLE iced tea, and so on. The only limitations are your imagination and the necessity to carry it all ¾ of a mile from Field 5 of Robert Moses

State Park along the beach. A word of advice: don't bring heavy cans and bottles of beverages, and don't bring heavy fresh fruit. There's lots of lighter stuff in paper or plastic containers that you can bring. Wine is OK, but I never much liked drinking alcohol in the hot sun. Lighthouse Beach is enough of an inspiration and turn-on without it.

The Nude in Art

For my second expedition to Lighthouse Beach in 1995, on August 27th, I got the inspiration to arrange a bodypainting party. I called Jack Hauptman's office, and his people said it was perfectly O.K. – beach visitors do it all the time, and there would be other bodypainting groups on the beach.

I researched the technical aspects of the project. I called Joi Newman, the doyenne of U.S. bodypainting, now in San Jose, Ca. Newman

Trina, John, nude bodypainting at Lighthouse Beach

advised us to use a mix of paints including tempera, which she said was very inexpensive. She also advised us not to paint below the waist, which can sometimes arouse the ire of prudish local authorities. However, we saw other groups doing full body paintups, so we went ahead and did the same thing.

I was a little afraid to use the mix of tempera and other paints that had been suggested, so instead I decided to use theatrical body makeup, which I was more confident was safe and easy to remove. After much hunting around I discovered "The Makeup Shop," at 131 West 21st Street, New York, NY 10011, Tel. (212) 807-0447, which had just what I wanted. I spent under $32 for three containers of body makeup, in red, blue and yellow (all I could afford) and bought a few large, cheap (non-sable) brushes elsewhere (don't get the wax or grease body makeup – I don't think it's as easy to get off). It was enough, even though I feared we would not have enough materials for full body paintups of our group. Actually, we had plenty, and I have a lot left over for next year's expedition.

For the grand neophyte bodypainting expedition I had four volunteers. Trina is seen painting me in the picture that accompanies this article. She was a sensation on the beach. Trina's bodypainting patterns were the best of our group. She painted me in dynamic swirls, and she painted some of the others in bananas, strawberries, etc. Really great stuff, and she'd never done anything like this before. Anyway, we had a great time and plan to do it again in 1996.

If you want more formation about the beach or you want to help safeguard Lighthouse Beach's free ambiance for the future, write or call Ms. Sharon Curley, President, Friends of Lighthouse Beach, P.O. Box 571, Babylon, NY 11702, or call (516) 582-8830. Lighthouse Beach needs all the friends it can get.

You'll always be able to find one or two daring souls among your friends or in your office who will go along, and once the whole thing is a success, there's no stopping it. Everybody wants to get on the bandwagon. Bodypainting can be a primitive, spiritual, tribal exercise. I've felt myself to be a changed person, in a number of ways, since trying it. The experience has greatly improved my body image and also I find now that I'm motivated to take better care of my body and work out somewhat more. Try it!

TRINA, an artist and model from Oklahoma, after painting her design on writer John Seaman, on right.

A revision of this chapter also first appeared as a published article, in *Travel Naturally*.

THE NUDE GASTRONOME

by John Seaman

Have I mentioned my penchant for the nude lifestyle? At home in Manhattan, nothing is more relaxing to me than sitting back in my easy chair – naked – with a beer, and watching a ball game. I have also some experience in organizing nude bodypainting beach parties nearby in New Jersey and New York. So when I heard about Cap d'Agde – probably the largest naturist resort in the world – *and* in the South of France, I knew I had to go there. Now I'm not sure that nudity will lead to world peace and universal joy – some people are too inhibited, restricted, glum, morose, and just plain negative – for all of that to come to pass – but if one can just drop *a few* of his or her misgivings, she or he will have a great time. This chapter of mine will tell you about that little paradise, and you can judge for yourself. And, most important, the food is fantastic!

This is a Nude Metropolis with 40 nude restaurants, cafes, brasseries and bistros, pools, cinemas, malls just like in suburbia except nude, post office, bank and even butcher shops? A vision of the future? No, it exists today! It's a topsy-turvy world much to my liking. I revel in the lifestyle, and the fantastic food. Of course, if you're a well-traveled naturist you'll know right away that I could only be speaking of Cap d'Agde. In high summer, as many as 65,000 naturists at any one time gather here on the Mediterranean coast of France near the Spanish border to enjoy themselves.

Looking at the press literature before I went, I realized that although much has been written about the place, nobody has described the really excellent cuisine you get there at reasonable prices and with a wonderful ambiance. The restaurants are as good as those almost anywhere in France, all ethnic cuisines are available, and you have the added advantage of being able to dine in the nude. Prices are reasonable, too.

There's so much to see and do at Cap d'Agde. On arrival, I was a little overwhelmed. I had never been to a Nude Metropolis before. I was told I'd be staying in one of the seven or eight huge complexes, some of which have nearly a thousand apartments, that make up the place, a closed compound which does not admit the outside public unless one pays admission.

On my first trip to Cap d'Agde, I stayed in Heliopolis. This is a large circular structure with a mall, pool and kiddie carousel in the middle. The first thing I did was to take off my clothes and go down to Cafe 1664 on the edge of the mall. I chose a *demipression* (small draft beer). I could also have indulged in a creme (cafe creme, coffee with cream). Then I settled down to watch the passing scene, which I'll have a lot more to say about later. It was easy to strike up a conversation with fellow travelers. A little French helps, the mostly European visitors and the French staff in the mall shops really appreciated it that I knew a few words of French, but I got by in English. I soon picked up a few more pleasantries in French, anyway.

I heard an interesting story about the inception of Cap d'Agde, more than 20 years ago, told to me by Izzy Abrahami, the Dutch TV video producer and writer that I met and became friends with on my year 2000 tour. Izzy told me that on one occasion in the days before Cap d'Agde existed two Jewish businessmen (an architect and a fiduciary) were lunching with the then mayor of Agde, who complained to them that most of the tourists (in those days) were going straight through from central France south to Spain, without stopping to visit in the lovely Agde region in Languedoc-Roussillion. The two businessmen proposed opening a large nude resort, and the mayor agreed. The three then checked with the central French government, which agreed to the project on the terms that it be fenced in with a nominal admission charge, to keep the unwary from wandering in, and that outside financing be found. All this was done, and that's how Cap d'Agde came to be, according to Izzy, at least.

I should say a few words about the costs of the restaurant food (and the whole trip, for that matter). Reasonable two-week tour packages are available through the resident English-speaking naturist travel agents, starting at about $1,200 for accommodations (a nice room with a double bed and two bunk beds—same price no matter how many, 1 to 4, are using it—a little hard on singles). The rate may vary at other times in the season—I was last there in July.

I enjoyed the 5-hour TGV ride (*tres grande vitesse*—very great speed trains, over 100 miles per hour) from Paris to Agde. Although I enjoyed life in the compound, I was able to augment the already superlative pleasures of Cap d'Agde with a series of optional excursions outside the compound. There are dinners in the old town of Agde (clothed) at least once a week. I joined one to a muy tipico place along the river in the old town, where the meal was excellent and the locals at table near us regaled us with French folk songs, joined in by everybody. The dinner and transportation cost (about $20 each). The previous week, there had been a sukiyaki expedition which I missed.

There were also longer excursions at reasonable cost to the nearby medieval walled city of Carcassone, Camargue and the Provence countryside, Nimes and Avignon, the cathedral town of Bezier and lots of other places, nice when I had an itch to leave the compound.

But, to get to my main subject, how about the meals? First, I will say that there were a few budget gastronomes about, on a starvation budget, living on bread and cheese and supermarket wine. They confided that they lived very cheaply and perhaps lost some weight Some even camped out in the camping area and saved money that way.

Others prepare their own meals on the little electric stoves in the apartments. My staple bit of home cooking was "Steak Hache Jean," which means chopped steak sautéed in olive oil with sliced green peppers and white onions, in my own personal style, "Jean,". or "John" in French. Very tasty, washed down with the good French wine from any of the several good wine shops. I particularly liked a bottle of 1994 Merlot I bought for $6.50 in a shop in the Heliopolis Mall. I wonder what it would cost now.

A note about those small electric stoves: they take twice as long as a gas stove to cook anything. It took 25 minutes to cook up my Steak Hache Jean. Also, I had to be especially careful while cooking, frying or sautéing in the nude! Oil burns are painful! I wore an apron, if nothing else!

There was wine by the liter bottle for a dollar and change in the supermarkets. But I nearly ruined my stomach on my first trip to Cap d'Agde (starvation budget), possibly from drinking the supermarket wine, along with almost nothing but bread and cheese (but I had really wanted to see the spectacle of Cap d'Agde, and the glorious sight was easily worth the minor gastrointestinal distress).

About the local food: The locals claim the fruits and vegetables grown here under the Mediterranean sun are the best in the world. I can only add to that, that the peaches, bananas, grapes and apples

I bought while shopping nude in the Mall were totally without imperfection. Incidentally, some of the local population here still speak the old Languedoc language, or perhaps you would say dialect, of French. I'm told the Languedoc language is similar to Catalan. You hear it spoken as you watch the locals play an indigenous game, *petanque*, that seems to resemble the Italian bocce, with which I was familiar from visiting Little Italy here in New York City. I often watched the locals and some of the more adventurous visitors play *petanque* from my sidewalk table outside Cafe 1664, where I was comfortably seated with my *demipression* or cafe creme.

I enjoyed having $400. in my pocket to spend during my two-week stay, on the restaurants, cafes, brasseries, bistros, etc. I should add that on my Cap d'Agde visit where I did my research for this chapter, in High Summer 2000, the French were engaged in converting their monetary system from Francs to Euros. So, to avoid confusion, I have translated all prices into the Dollar equivalent at the time.

For example, a full meal at a Cap d'Agde restaurant cost $12-$25, at the time. One extravagant Indian meal cost me $35, but that was an exception. I didn't want to eat out every night, If I didn't want to cook my own from scratch, most of the restaurants offered selections (prepared entree portions) to take out. I consumed these on my little terrace with a bottle of good wine for considerably less.

Dining on my terrace was fun. Not only could I watch the passing scene, beautiful people returning from the beach, but I could also watch the local overhead bird show blitz, dozens of martins, small European swallows, swooping and diving and catching flying insects at dawn and twilight. It's quite an air show. And I say "beautiful people," by which I mean just about everybody with their clothes off.

I made one trip to Cap d'Agde flying as a courier. It's easy. I paid a registration fee (perhaps $75, good for a year) with a tourist-oriented courier service in Manhattan. I indicated approximately when and where I wanted to travel, and that was it. They called me with a week or two notice to assign me my flight, which cost me very little. The courier service I used at that time offered Paris or London for $250. or even less total round trip at certain times of year.

Of course, I should explain my courier assignment. I carried a 9" x 12" manila envelope which held the invoices for the freight in the bottom half of the plane, a regular passenger flight. Yes, regular passenger flights carry a lot of freight. I picked up my manila envelope at my point of departure airport and delivered it to the correct freight agent at my destination airport, at a special luggage carousel, near the regular carousels but behind a screen or fence. I then inquired if there were any invoices going back and where to pick them up.

Sometimes, there's nothing going back and the job is done. But sometimes there are indeed return invoices. The courier agency asked that I dress nicely, and I had to give up my luggage space and take only carry-on luggage. I do the latter all the time anyway, so it's no hardship for me. I took a rolling 22" bag for the overhead and a big camera bag for under the seat. The catch with couriers is that I could I could only go for one week (or sometimes two). But it's a great way to explore the world! The couriers fly to all major commercial centers around the world (but not the resorts).

If you're really interested in courier work, you can explore the technical couriers. Unlike the tourist-oriented couriers, technical couriers cost almost nothing (perhaps $25.) but they expect you to fly on three hours' notice. If I wanted to fly with a technical courier, I would have to keep my bag packed all the time. I would never know when I would get the call. A technical courier will call at 2 a.m., out of the blue, and expect me to be at the airport at 5 a.m. Tourist-oriented couriers broker the technical couriers' work and make something off the top. Clever entrepreneurship!

I got to Cap d'Agde from Paris on the aforementioned TGV, the train with *tres grande vitesse* (very great speed). It's a wonderful, comfortable, very fast train, which will go even faster when all the track roadbeds are rebuilt to accommodate it. One drawback of the TGV is that the train buffet food is expensive and not very good. The buffet's O.K. for a beer, though.

To get back to Cap d'Agde, in my opinion, nearly everybody looks better with clothes off than clothes on, and it's very hard for me to put my clothes and heavy shoes back on after two weeks totally unencumbered at Cap d'Agde. At that point it seems almost obscene to wear clothes, desecrating the beautiful human form. Watching from the terrace at Heliopolis, you see the family groups returning from the beach, you become aware of the closer naturist family bonding, or you can watch the children of all ages playing nude in the twilight under the trees. It's really a vision of the Metropolis of the Future.

Incidentally, this Metropolis of the Future has all kinds of sights. I was amused by the queue in front of the nude ATM (automatic teller machine) and by the nude cellular phone users, busily conducting their affairs without wearing the obligatory French businessman's double-breasted suit.

I had to be careful in the scorching Mediterranean sun, however. At certain times of day, I could only stand the direct sun for ten minutes or so. When I first arrived, I had to wear some clothes some of the time until I acquired a bit of a tan. I used lots of high number sun block, and I was all right. The strong sun and beneficent climate have other advantages, though. Small scrapes and cuts, which one is bound to get if one plays hard in the nude for any extended period of time, heal very quickly.

I have a theory as to one of the reasons that children seem to take so well to naturism. I know they play harder and seem happier than I have seen anywhere else. My theory is that children's clothes are styled differently than adult clothes, and serve to set the children off as a separate, inferior caste. Without the clothes, this problem doesn't arise. Everybody's equal, on the same footing, in a way. Another idea: children come to us "trailing clouds of glory," as William Wordsworth said, and certainly, where they came from, when in this state, I doubt if they were wearing clothes. My own early childhood experience was not quite so dramatic, but I do remember one or two immanent moments, such as the time in 1939 (I was 3), when my father carried me all the way up the steps to the top of Mont-Royal in Montreal, to get a portion of sherbet in a little silver dish.

When I was last at Cafe 1664 at Heliopolis, a *demipression* cost about $2.50, at the then rate of exchange. Your cafe creme at the bistro will cost about the same. A small cafe noir (black coffee) was about a dollar. A small glass of wine will range from 1 to 3 dollars. Yes, in France, wine is cheaper than coffee, generally. I would have a glass of water with my beverage and I could make it last for an hour or more. Cheap enough entertainment, what with the marvelous passing scene.

Occasionally, I bought a meat sandwich on a baguette (on long crispy French bread, very tasty) for 1 or 2 dollars. And, I enjoyed indulging in a soft ice cream in a cone (many flavors) for 1 or 2 dollars.

My first meal out was at "Chez Rene," which replaced the former "Les Delices Alsace" ("Alsatian Delights"), an Alsatian restaurant in the Heliopolis mall, which I had visited on my earlier excursions to Cap d'Agde. A lot of the Alsatian menu survives in Chez Rene. Ordering was not difficult. The help spoke French and German, and a little English. Incidentally, although I was nude, the waitresses were clothed. It's a French government hygiene rule that the help and the servers at places like Cap d'Agde must be clothed. Also, it's a general rule that, if you are dining nude in a restaurant or seated in some other facility, you must bring your own towel to sit on.

Anyway, at Chez Rene, I ordered the specialty of the day, Goulasch Boeuf (beef goulash), which was well spiced and excellent. It was spiked with black pepper, bay leaf and other spices that I could not identify. The meat was tender. The entree, a *demipression* of Kronenbourg Alsatian beer, and a cafe creme came to about $18, which I was able to put on my Visa card. Interesting to note, the French waiters and waitresses all carried little portable computer terminals, which by radio were able to verify your credit all the way back to the U.S.A., right at your table. I hadn't seen these at the time in New York City.

In case you do not know, Alsace and Lorraine are two partially German-speaking departments of France, known for their cuisine and beer. The French and the Germans have fought over these provinces for hundreds of years, which explains the use of the German language.

Nudity is obligatory on the beach and generally also the rule in the rest of the compound, except on the very occasional cold, rainy day, when lots of people will wear warm tops, no bottoms. Also, in the evening, in the cooler days of the season, some people wear clothes, but this is not universal. I'm told that during High Season, July and early August, the warmest part of the year, many people are clothes-free even in the evening. But all this reminds me of the essay by Michel de Montaigne, 16th century French writer, entitled, "Of the Custom of Wearing Clothes." Montaigne pondered whether our wearing of clothes was the result of a "natural law," or whether it was "invention." Seeing how these visitors were attired on these cooler evenings, I can only come down on the side of "invention."

The second restaurant I tried in the Heliopolis Commercial Center, or Mall, was "Ghymnos," which I am told means "Naked Male" in Greek, a pizzeria and more, with a wood-burning oven (*feu de bois*) for the pizzas and the meats. This is partly a place for families, particularly at lunch, when I found whole families, with children of all ages, dining nude, all seated on their towels.

On seating myself for the first time in Ghymnos, I was served a complimentary glass of Algerian kir. I looked at the various pan pizzas and grillades on the menu, and selected a pizza Napolitaine (Neapolitan), which had as toppings tomato, mozzarella, anchovies and small black olives. I had extracted the olive pits from my mouth as I ate, no problem, there were only seven or eight of them. The pizza with the charcoal flavor was delicious, although I thought it was a little pricey at about $7. A coke was $2.50. But the place was very enjoyable, very gemutlich, and at night there was a long line of people waiting to get in. This is the only one of the 50 or more restaurants in the compound I can say this of.

On another occasion, I had the ubiquitous spaghetti bolognaise at Ghymnos for about $6. Tasty, but a little low on meat. Spaghetti bolognaise (spaghetti with meat sauce) is the budget traveler's staple at Cap d'Agde and in Europe generally.

One of the more interesting aspects of the passing scene at Cap d'Agde, a little shocking to some people, was the body jewelry and body art. By this I mean body piercing. If one is not too squeamish, it's interesting to watch as one savors a *demipression* or cafe creme.

Generally, gold or silver rings are worn in the body piercings. Body piercing is not terribly common at Cap d'Agde, but there's enough of it so that it is a regular feature of the passing scene. Starting from the top, of course, I have seen pierced eyebrows. Pierced ears are a commonplace. Although, even this can be carried to extremes. Then there are pierced noses and cheeks. Usually, it's not the most beautiful women who have these artifacts. It seems to be something of a compensation for nature's injustices. I saw all of this before it was embraced by all-American kids. But I still believe that the unadorned human form is the most beautiful thing going, and any such attempt to improve on it is bound to fail.

But, proceeding downward, the next thing was pierced nipples, on both men and women. Generally, the people who have these features were a little older, 30s and up. I observed one 40ish couple, very proud of their matching nipple rings.

Of course, after one considers nipple rings, there's nowhere else to go but down. After pierced navels (the beginners are often pierced in this way), pierced vulvas are not uncommon (technically, most of the rings pierce the labia minora). I saw one still-attractive mature woman, elegantly coiffured, with numerous expensive-looking vulval rings and also a gold chain hanging from the rings.

Some may say these piercing practices are harmful physically and psychologically to men and women. However, I can think of other, more widely accepted practices, that I think cause more harm. High heels, for example. One fashion expert here in Manhattan, where I live, told me the purpose of high heels is to cause a woman's breasts to project out more, supposedly making them more prominent and more attractive to men. Of course, the result is a lot of broken arches and other unnecessary foot trouble. I say, if a woman wants to draw attention to her breasts, let her take off her clothes, go to a Naturist resort, and wear comfortable sandals.

But the feature that causes me the most sympathetic pain is the pierced penises, the ring going right through the glans penis, I think. It must be extremely painful to have this done. I hope it's done with an anesthetic. But, it does look sort of macho, and I'm told pierced men's love partners are very appreciative of the implement.

I was told that most of the pierced naturists were German. A Frenchwoman told me most French consider the practice decadent. I wasn't able to pick out any pierced Americans. But, decadent or not, the piercings are a startling sight to see.

Finally, there are the tattoos, ranging up to full-body treatment. Some of it was attractive to me, except that the obvious narcissism of the tattoo wearers was a little off-putting.

Of course, if all this piercing got me down, I could always go to the outdoor L'Akthios piscine (pool) at Port Nature (I can only guess at the meaning of the name—none of my sources could tell me) where the French teenagers hang out. There are lots of beautiful, unspoiled, unpierced, undecadent young nude 14- and 16-year-old French girls, amusing themselves in the pool and on the terrace. I don't know where the boys were, but it was just as well. I could enjoy the sight of the beautiful young women unhindered by any raucous young men.

I will say a word more about these poised young French teenagers. Some Americans are still awkward in dealing with nudity, but not the French. A pair of nude young French teenage girls, perhaps 13 or 14 years old, already with beautiful figures, caught sight of me watching them from just outside L'Akthios pool. Thereupon one of them did a nice pirouette, so I would have a better view. Such poise in one so young! Vive La France!

Earlier, in the malls, I had been astonished at the sight of what were apparently 10- or 11-year-old French girls with nearly full figures. One opinion I heard expressed was that this was partly due to the growth hormones fed to the cattle from which the fast-food hamburger beef is produced. I'm certain that this is the case in the United States, but I also heard the French Government does not allow the growth hormones to be fed to cattle in France. Perhaps it's just general better nutrition that causes these children to grow up so quickly. I hope they have time for some kind of childhood. But it is an arresting sight!

After trying the better Heliopolis restaurants and cafes, it was time for me to move out to other venues in Cap d'Agde. Next, I tried a couple of the beachfront cafes near Port Nature, another of the residential complexes. The two places I tried were named "Calypso" and "Mississippi." In either of these places, I could station myself with a cafe noir and perhaps a tasty gruyere omelette in the morning at about 10 a.m. and watch the procession of beautiful people heading for the beach. So many teenagers! I was reminded of another nude beach I once stumbled on at Perissa, on Santorini in the Greek Cycladic Islands. Perissa at that time was a nude beach intended exclusively for teenagers (maybe it still is), but I managed to get in. So many memories of naturism, brought back by the sands and scenes of Cap d'Agde!

Anyway, the omelettes are better at Calypso, really good French omelettes, but the demipressions, cafe cremes, and iced teas were cheaper at Mississippi. I had a great Salad Nicoise (with tuna and a lot of other stuff) at Calypso. But the food was not the main attraction at either of these places. People watching and the ensuing conversations were. One of the interesting people I met in a restaurant at Cap d'Agde was my friend Izzy Abrahami, the Dutch film maker who was traveling in a *ménage a trois* with two of his Dutch women friends.

Having covered some of the better eateries at Heliopolis and on the beachfront, it was time for me to move on to another of the Cap d'Agde complexes, this time the mall at the Port Ambonne Commercial Center. One of the most pleasant and reasonable places here is the "Rotisserie," near the Port Ambonne pool. I could watch the comings and goings at this piscine from my comfortable seat in the mall passageway just outside Rotisserie. This restaurant (a small place) offered a prix fixe dinner for under $9, plus a 25 cl. glass of good house white wine (*vin ordinaire*) for $1.

I chose a big pork chop , smothered in onions and accompanied by French-style scalloped potatoes (*pommes de terre boulanger*). Delicious. As a starter, I was given a large portion of smoked salmon with dark bread. I finished up with coffee ice cream with caramel sauce. A real (modest) banquet. And it all cost under $10, including the wine.

Also in the Port Ambonne mall, not far from Rotisserie and the pool, was "La Poissonnerie de Maxime," a slightly more stylish seafood restaurant. One night, I treated myself to a $15 prix fixe dinner here (Menu A), again keeping in mind that when on the coast of the Mediterranean, seafood is the best choice.

I took a table in the well-ventilated, well-lit mall corridor, so as to better watch the most interesting passing scene. Included in my complete dinner was an appetizer. Watching all the beautiful nude women pass by had encouraged me to build up my masculinity, so of course, I ordered the oysters (*huitres*). The oysters were not on the half shell, but in full shell, which had just been opened. The oysters couldn't have been fresher— they were alive five minutes before I ate them. I felt very macho after consuming them. Of course, who wouldn't feel macho, watching all these beautiful women parading around *au naturel*. I say this despite the prevalent conception that naturists are not much interested in sex.

La Poissonnerie was able to meet my request for a *meuniere* sauce (butter sauce) for my selected entree, the grilled salmon daily special, even though *meuniere* sauce was not on the menu. That night the well-prepared salmon came with three or four different vegetables, including a saffron potato, tomato farci, green beans, and another I could not identify.

I also had a demi-pitcher (50 cl.) of good local white wine, which was enough to wobble me. La Poissonnerie has every kind of seafood you can think of, the daily catch was brought right in, and the restaurant is very popular with the regulars here. My total bill for complete dinner, wine and coffee, including service, of course, was under $21. and well worth it to a jaded New Yorker. And of course, the passing parade was free.

One more social comment about the passing parade. Generally, naturism seems to me to be a godsend for the physically disadvantaged. They're more readily accepted in this environment, and they can forget about their limitations for a while. I watched one happy group of a cerebral palsy victim and three or four so-called "normal" people, including a couple of good-looking women, having a wonderful time in the Port Ambonne pool.

I think part of the reason for this is that most clothes are cut for the so-called "normal" person, and look awkward on anyone with a perceived limitation. In naturism, this problem doesn't exist.

Naturism, for me and perhaps for others, is an attempt to approach a mythical "original state of nature." In this "state," all of us are equal, even the young and those with "perceived" limitations.

For my year 2000 restaurant tour, I knew I had to try the highly touted newcomer, "La Grange Gourmande," also located in the Port Ambonne mall. I arranged a lavish dinner party for six, including some of my new friends. The first thing that strikes you on entering La Grange Gourmande is the wonderful ambiance, with soft lighting, beautiful large Mediterranean crockery pieces that could be considered works of art, and the abundant napery.

We started off with some of the wonderful white Languedoc (local) wine, and managed to consume several bottles before we were through. Among the appetizers that our group consumed, the most noteworthy was the *huitres gratinees au champagne,* or a plate of oysters in a cheese sauce soaked in good champagne. This cost about $7., and we all shared it.

Among our entrees, the most spectacular was the *poelee de gambas flambees a l'Armagnac,* or flaming shrimp served in an Armagnac sauce (Armagnac is a variant of cognac). This was our most expensive entree, costing about $13. I should add that restaurants in Europe do not generally shell, vein or decapitate the shrimp before serving, as is the practice in the United States. So we went ahead and struggled with mess and finally consumed about half a dozen large shrimp, or prawns, in that wonderful sauce.

For my part, I had the *escalope de saumon a l'oseille,* or escalloped salmon in a sorrel sauce. You probably already know that the French will successfully make sauces from many sources not ordinarily used in the States. Learned critics around the world debate whether French or Chinese sauces are the best in the world. For my part, I thoroughly enjoyed my *saumon a la oseille.* It cost about $11.

Finally, the highlight of our desserts was the *creme Catalan,* a variant on creme caramel reflecting the Catalan influence from nearby Spain. The entire meal for six, including abundant wine, came to under $21. per person. Where in the world other than Cap d'Agde could you enjoy a splendid banquet in the nude at such a modest price? Incidentally, although service is included in the billed price in France, I tipped an additional $20 because we had been so well treated and had had such a good time. The restaurant staff didn't even mind the popping flashbulbs.

Moving on to the very large residential and commercial complex called Port Nature, I started at the landward end (away from the beach) at "Tex-Mex," a cute restaurant with lots of festive decorations and comfortable outdoor and indoor tables. I didn't find the food to be sensational, but it was adequate for a fun place of this kind, best for drinking quantities of Mexican beer.

At Tex-Mex, I had the combination plate of two meat tacos, rice and refried beans, along with a few fresh veggies. The other fare is standard Tex-Mex, lots of enchiladas, etc. I ordered Corona, but was served Sol, another Mexican beer. With a bottle of beer and a *cafe con leche*, the whole bill came to about $16.

Particularly in the evening, you'll have a good time here. The place is adjacent to the Port Nature mall, where there is a string of bars and restaurants, with a lot of pretty girls. I think I even saw an Apache in one of these places (look up in your French argot dictionary for the meaning of a bar "Apache" in France).

For my next-to-last dinner, I visited "Rajasthan," a grandly appointed Indian restaurant at Port Soleil, at the edge of the Cap d'Agde compound, near where the boats dock (yes, Virginia, you can sail to Cap d'Agde if you want to. They have complete docking facilities.).

This was my big splurge. I certainly did not want to be encumbered with a lot of cash on the way home, as I was traveling light. So Rajasthan set me back $31. and change, but it was well worth it.

Rajasthan doesn't open until about 7:00 p.m. I was early, and went around to the back door to find the cook who told me (in a mix of French, English and Hindi) that they would open soon. That night, I really had two meals, because I started with a large Rajasthan salad (fresh and delicious, lots of shrimp and tuna, a meal in itself) and then went on to a lamb curry, cooked with tomatoes, onions, coriander and cashews, over basmati rice. I also had two Gymkhana Indian export beers. The whole thing was very filling and satisfying. Highly recommended.

Le Rajasthan has Tandoori, Vindaloo (hot and spicy) and regional Rajasthan dishes. I understand that the place is packed with naturists, day and night, in High

Season. I can see why. The food is good and abundant and the service is meticulous.

I've saved the best for last! Back in Port Nature again, this time at the seaward end, I found "Horizon," a very French brasserie/restaurant/glacier. (In France, a brasserie is a cafe that serves food and drink; a glacier serves ice cream specialties.) Horizon is designed and set up like some of the best brasseries in France, but with big sliding doors that open to the sea. One can dine nude indoors or out. I heard recorded Louis Armstrong emanating from the marvelous well-stocked bar. At night, there was sometimes live musical entertainment.

Horizon made me think a little of "Rick's Place," in the film *Casablanca,* except for the lack of gambling here. (Incidentally, there are casinos in the city of Agde, outside the naturist compound, if that's your pleasure.)

I had the daily special, sauteed lamb, which came with an original seafood salad, and a 25 cl. pitcher of rose wine, all for $13. and change, service included. It was all served by a very capable waiter wearing a bisexual symbol on his shirt. Horizon is a good deal, and it's just about the only place in the compound that is open all year.

I will add that there aren't many people of color at Cap d'Agde, but this worked to the advantage of the few that were here. I know mild black civil servants here in New York City who cultivate dreadlocks for the trip, and then go to places in Europe like Cap d'Agde where they are a sensation. Blacks are a novelty at Cap d'Agde! I saw one young African-American man, yes, in dreadlocks, followed around closely all the time by half a dozen nude French beauties, all in search of esoteric wisdom of whatever kind.

There's one topic I haven't covered - that's the nightclubs and discotheques, of which there are many. I'm saving this for the time when I go to Cap d'Agde with a female companion. You see, the clubs at Cap d'Agde are all for "nonconformist couples only." I believe the mores in them are quite relaxed. They don't open until 11:00 p.m., and I was so jet-lagged and depleted by the torrid Mediterranean sun that I couldn't stay up for them. But the clubs are just another aspect of Cap d'Agde. There's so much here! It would take several books to cover it all!

More on Nude Beaches and Bodypainting

My experiences on free, naturist and nude beaches are described in the two long earlier Memoir Sections on Lighthouse Beach and Cap d'Agde, both of which Sections were adapted from articles I wrote and published in Naturist magazines. In this brief Section, I will review how I got into Naturism, and mention three friends, now all passed away, who helped make a go of my free beach bodypainting expeditions. I will also include a number of photographs of our happy days on the free beaches.

John, bodypainted

Here I am, bodypainted by Morningside Gardens neighbor Edna , at Lighthouse Beach, on Fire Island, just off the South Shore of Long Island. See my Memoir Section on "Picknicking at Lighthouse Beach," which appeared in *Travel*

Naturally, a naturist magazine, filled with lovely pictures of nudes of all ages.

Mixed group of 5 naturists

In this photograph, we see, from left, an unknown young woman, me, two anonymous friends, and my French atheist artist friend Gil , also a Morningside Gardens resident, who passed away a couple of years ago. Gil especially loved my bodypainting beach parties.

Anonymous, shaven

This anonymous young lady, pictured bodypainted at Lighthouse Beach, got into the spirit of the

Trina, at Lighthouse Beach

thing by shaving off her pubic hair for the occasion. All the better for the photography!

Trina, bodypainting John

The above two pictures both show the beautiful Trina , one of my models of a few years ago, at

Lighthouse Beach. In the lower picture, Trina is seen giving me a full torso bodypaint job. I always admired Trina, both for her looks and for her talents.

Yousof, in his prime

Pictured above is Yousof Najibullah, my Afghani friend, who passed away a few years ago. At age 62, Yousof was moving furniture, had chest pains, went to the hospital, was kept for observation, and died of a heart attack the same night. Yousof loved my bodypainting beach parties, and had none of the usual Muslim squeamishness about nudity. He was a very good friend to me and to lots of others.

John, seminude, at Cap d'Agde   John, nude, at Cap d'Agde

The above two photographs show me *au naturel* at Cap d'Agde in Southern France, the naturist resort for 65,000 nudists in peak season, my favorite resort. In the top photo, I am wearing my New York Philharmonic tee shirt, a hat and nothing else. In the lower pic, I have doffed the tee shirt. I believe both photos were shot in beachfront Café Calypso at Cap d'Agde.

My bodypainting beach parties are very liberating for a lot of people. It's only sad that so many of my faithful principals have died off.

Skydiving for Seniors...

A New Way to Put Life and Death in Perspective

By John Seaman

Have you ever wanted to soar like an eagle, leaving troubles, turmoil and tribulations far below? Have you ever wished you could escape from

In flight, tandem jump

earthbound limitations? Well, it's not impossible. And I'm not talking religion. Consider this. Two days after my 64th birthday, in June 2000, I completed my first, and so far only, skydive. Afterwards, I felt I would not fear anything again and that I could conquer all obstacles. I have since learned that many senior citizens are skydivers, and that the practice is reasonably safe for seniors who are in fairly good health.

A skydive is not just a parachute jump. In a skydive, you jump at a high altitude, perhaps 13,500 feet, and allow yourself to fall freely for most of the descent. Only at about 5,000 feet, do you open the parachute. In a regular parachute jump, you open the chute as soon as you are clear of the aircraft.

I had been working as a proofreader for Citibank. My supervisor, one Craig, a rather powerfully built African-American, asked me to jump with him. I had to think about it. This was a rather daring concept. But, above all, there was the money. One first jump costs two or three hundred dollars, and I am always short of money. And, I had to work up the nerve to do it. So, at first, I declined Craig's invitation.

Then, one week in May 2000, I was lucky enough to earn over $600. This gave me what I needed. I immediately called "The Sky's the Limit" jump school at the Newton, NJ, Airport and made an appointment for a training jump. I should mention that, having been suicidal before, many years ago, as a troubled young man, I knew I could dig deep and tap into those desperate suicidal feelings, ever so briefly, to prepare myself for the dangers of the jump

On the appointed day, I took a Lakeland Bus from the Port Authority Bus Terminal to Newton. The ride took about an hour and a half. I was apprehensive, but not especially so. I was more afraid of being embarrassed by not being able to get myself out of the airplane door (not fear exactly, more like inertia), than by fear of the jump itself. I soon arrived and walked the half mile to the airport, and I was ready to go.

I suited up in a blue jump suit and cloth helmet, leaving my street clothes in a shed. I was given goggles to cover my eyeglasses, which I was able to wear during the jump. I'm myopic. I couldn't have seen anything otherwise.

Here on the East Coast, most first jumps, particularly high altitude skydiving jumps (13,500 feet), are made tandem. That is, you make your first jump strapped to an instructor. My friend and model (I am a photographer and artist), Jenny, made her first jump solo, from low altitude (5,000 feet), as a static line jump, in New Mexico, where the rules are different. Static line jumps are the way military parachutists usually jump. A hook in the airplane door opens your chute for you. You don't do it yourself.

Anyway, the jump school provided a videographer for an additional $85. This fellow jumped with me, falling at exactly the same speed, and recorded

Before the jump

my experience up close on a video tape. Simultaneously, he made 24 "still" (what a misnomer!) photographs. The jump was made, as I said, from 13,500 feet, and I and my instructor, Erik, fell in free fall down to about 5,000 feet, where Erik opened the parachute. We covered the free fall section in about 45 seconds, at a speed of 120 miles per hour. Air resistance prevents you from going any faster.

I was slightly apprehensive in the airplane before the jump, mostly because I feared I might not be able to go through with it. Once out the airplane door, however, I was absolutely fearless. As I later wrote for

Exiting the airplane at 13,500 feet

the March 2001 Swarthmore College Alumni Magazine, "I had no fear at all. I figured if this was the end, there was nothing I could do about it, so I might as well enjoy the ride. All problems and turmoil seemed earthbound and very far away. There was a great sense of freedom."

Stepping out of the airplane, strapped to my instructor, was relatively easy. At such high altitudes, the earth is very far away and not clearly visible. Stepping out of the airplane was somewhat like stepping into a warm steam bath (it was a hot day). At first, although you are in free fall at 120 miles per hour, there is no sensation of falling. You are so high up, there are no reference points to give you the sense of relative motion. The only object in my immediate vicinity was the videographer, falling at exactly the same speed, so he appeared stationary.

I should mention that shortly after we left the aircraft, Erik opened a small drogue, a tiny parachute which did not reduce our free fall descent speed but only stabilized us and prevented us from spinning around wildly in space. Also noteworthy is the fact that jumpers always carry a reserve parachute, which is rigged up with an altimeter to open automatically at an elevation of 2,500 feet, if the main chute has not opened by then. The reserve chute is a good safeguard, but the apparatus is far from foolproof. And sometimes the main parachute gets entangled in the reserve chute.

When the main parachute opened at 5,000 feet, I was relieved, but only mildly so. By that time, I was ready for ANY eventuality. The final 5,000 feet descent, with the chute open, took about 5 minutes. I landed on my stomach, which is not the desired conclusion, but I was unhurt, landing on the soft grass. The best practice is to land on your derriere, which is usually well padded (with your flesh). Within 20 minutes, I had donned my street clothes again, and picked up my video cassette (VHS). The cassette had been processed very quickly. It was very professionally done, with an accompaniment of Madonna and other rock musicians. I was told I could bring the video cassette back on a later visit, and, for $30., they would dub in Wagner or Bach or other music more to my liking, if I brought them an audio CD with the music I wanted.

So, the entire expense was about $265. plus the bus fare. I still want to do a solo high altitude jump but

In flight, tandem jump

the additional training (one more tandem jump with TWO instructors and several hours' ground school) will cost me $600.-700. I don't have it these days. Also, the arthritis in my knees is now (New Year's, 2004) much worse than it was in 2000. But I still am going to try.

There were people older than me making solo jumps the day I did my tandem jump. So it's still possible.

In this modern world, people are put in dangerous situations, in the military, in cataclysms, etc., without their consent. I feel much better for having faced danger of my own free will, rather than being ordered or forced to do it. It gives me an autonomy and independence that I might not otherwise have. There should be more ways for a person to test him or herself, rather than following the blind dictates of authority. My

"Thumbs Up," on making a safe landing

Quaker (Religious Society of Friends) education and training helped me here. When I was a young man, I tried to get work here in Manhattan as a steelrigger, working on high steel. I was not successful in getting the work. Much of that work goes to Native Americans, anyway. But there should be further discovery of ways for a young man to test himself and develop his character, rather than by being trained to kill people he doesn't know on someone else's command.

Back on Earth, I showed my video to friends in my apartment and also gave a video lecture, "Skydiving for Seniors – A New Way to Put Life and Death in Perspective," to the retirement group here in my cooperative. This made my reputation here. In my lecture, I said, "Surprisingly, skydiving is not especially strenuous and can be done by many seniors who are in fairly good health. And what an uplifting experience and what a new way to look at life!"

And what age is too old to skydive? I can't say! Former President George H. W. Bush, father of the current President, this June completed a tandem skydive, in his 80th year. I believe Bush plans further jumps. So age is no barrier.

Just how safe is skydiving, and in particular, tandem skydiving, compared to, say, airline travel? According to the statistics, skydiving is mildly dangerous. But statistics are not foolproof. They can also show skydiving as more or less dangerous than driving.

As for an expert opinion on this thesis, Dr. Joaquin Flores, psychology consultant, and mentor to students at Columbia University's Latino Alumni Mentor Program, offers the following:

"As we grow older, our free choices are increasingly restricted, as for example for physical and financial reasons. John Seaman has found a venue where a fairly healthy older person can make a free, life-affirming choice that involves an element of personal risk. Mastering the danger, a risk chosen gratuitously by the skydiver, can allow a sense of freedom and pleasure to the body and mind."

But the last word on this, for me, John Seaman, is, "You really feel you can do anything, once you've done this!"

Legal Overseas and Nevada Brothels

My whoring adventures, back in the days before AIDS, carried me all over the world. In this brief section, I will discuss the good times I have had and the people I have met while whoring in Nevada, Paris, London, Amsterdam and Hamburg. Nearly all of this was before 1987, when the AIDS epidemic began to get bad, and it became too dangerous to consort with these independent-minded ladies.

I'll start with Nevada. You may not know that Nevada, or parts of it, at least, is the only place in the United States where prostitution is still legal. And it's only legal in the rural part of the state, in counties with less than a population of, I believe, 120,000. Reno recently grew too big and prostitution was banned there. Las Vegas has banned legal prostitution for many years, although someone recently said, "All the women in Vegas are prostitutes," and the Governor vehemently denied it. There are now only about 30 legal whorehouses in Nevada, down from about the 100 that were open when I first went out there in about 1975. You can, however, rather easily get such services in Vegas, and good service, from the various escort agencies, although it's costly. I'll tell you more later about my adventures within Vegas city limits.

I first discovered (1976) Cherry Patch Ranch advertised in an illustrated ad in a free newspaper found in a mechanical street dispenser on a Vegas street on the Strip. It said the legal brothel could be reached in a free limousine from Vegas. The place was 70 miles out in the desert. I was busy at a meeting and a dinner all day, so I was picked up at my motel in Vegas by the courteous limo driver at about 9:00 p.m. I believe the Cherry Patch Ranch is still open all night and 24 hours a day, to accommodate the truckers and cowboys (and tourists) who frequent the place. There is also a small airstrip which is on the property of the place, so you can fly in, in your private plane for a bash. Anyway, the limo picked me up and drove me (fast) for about an hour, through the atomic waste sites and the various artillery testing grounds, to Cherry Patch. The limo driver said he would come back to pick me up at the appropriate time. I tipped the driver $20 and headed in.

I didn't like the low reddish lighting inside (difficult to see the figures and details of the figures of the girls) but otherwise the ambiance was great. I was greeted by one of the older hostesses and given a drink.

It was then time for the lineup, just like in that famous between the wars depiction of the presentation (lineup) at Suzie's bordello in Paris, a photo by Brassai (born Gustav Halasz in Hungary) which you can see in the excellent photo-essay, *The Naked and the Nude,* by Jorge Lewinski, a Museum of Modern Art publication. Incidentally, the 10 or 12 girls at the Cherry Patch were better looking (to my taste) than the girls in the Brassai photo. Thinner, anyway. In all my experience in the 1970s (and later), I only saw a lineup, or presentation, in one other brothel, that in the Palais d'Amour in Hamburg. And that wasn't a real lineup, it was more like a circulating cocktail party. More about that place later. Most of the other places I've been to in Europe and America had no more than two girls (and a madam and maybe a bouncer) and two bedrooms.

I can't remember now whether the girls at Cherry Patch in the lineup were totally nude (ganz nakt, as the Germans say) or simply in very skimpy lingerie. It was difficult to make your pick in the dim light, but I did well. I picked "Courtney," a young, attractive, petite Wasp, on my first visit. For the $100 or so that I paid, she was willing to do anything at all. I don't remember exactly what or how many different things we did, but I do remember that it was very pleasurable. In the 1970s, you didn't need to wear condoms at Cherry Patch, so you could intimately and carnally enjoy the real flesh. That's changed now, because of AIDS, and an edict from the Governor, who cares about "his girls."

I covered the protocols at a proper brothel in the first section of this Memoir, but I'll repeat some of the details here. After you select the girl, both of you go to a private room and you both take your clothes off. The girl then examines your genitals for disease, and washes them off with soap and water, in a small porcelain pan, which the customer holds. In most places, there are no time limits on your activities. Management wants you to go away happy.

On that 1975 trip, I made one more visit to Cherry Patch, where I picked a Hispanic girl, also petite, the way I like them, and whose given, or professional, name I forget. This time, because I had been with another of the Cherry Patch girls earlier in the week, I was asked to wear a condom, but I begged off, and the Madam said O.K., you don't have to, and I enjoyed the intimate flesh again. After our pleasure, the girl cleaned me up, and I went out to the salon, where I charged my pleasure to a credit card (it is legal, after all), and went out to meet my waiting limo driver. I got back to my motel about 2:00 a.m., which is not late in Las Vegas, which is open for business all night long.

Later, I read a little background material on the Nevada brothels. It seems the places advertise in various trendy newspapers throughout the country, and young women volunteer. In a ten-year career, a successful girl can put away half a million dollars away, and retire while she is still attractive. In one scenario, the "retired" girl then pays her way to a sophisticated, posh resort, where she will recline on a chaise lounge by the pool in a beehive hairdo, and be spotted by some rich adventurer, who, knowing nothing about her background, will carry her off and marry her into a life of luxury. She will make him very happy, except he may occasionally wonder how his wife ever became so knowledgeable about sexual pleasure.

Another interesting fact is that, at one recent time, you could invest in the Nevada brothels at The New York Stock Exchange. I believe, however, that the practice has now been stopped. Too bad!

Next, I will say something about the escort services in Vegas. They are not supposed to provide sexual services (illegal) but they do so and this practice is winked at by the law. I was staying at a good hotel on the Strip. I called one service that looked good in the phone book ad, and ordered two girls. Of course, I can only service one a day (I confess) but I wanted the second one around, just for fun. First, a man came to my room and checked out the situation, assuring the safety of the girls, and took my credit card charge for perhaps $160 (for the two). Then he left, and twenty minutes later the girls showed up. Unfortunately, the girls wanted an additional $100 each. I had not been warned about this by the security man. I could then only afford $100 more, so I said goodbye to the second girl and gave her $10 for cab fare. The girl I kept was a thin brunette and the girl I sent away was a slightly chubby blonde.

So, that night, for some reason, I opted for a blow job. It was very interesting, but the girl wouldn't swallow the cum, so I was slightly disappointed. However, I was so excited by all these clandestine, passionate activities that my ejaculation was very vigorous and shot up somewhere near the (low) ceiling, or at least, so it seemed. This was very unusual for me. I usually do not have a very forceful ejaculation. So I was very pleased and called it a good day!

My experience in Paris was unusual in that I did not make my contact in a brothel, or "house." Instead, I went to the Pigalle Metro Station, where I solicited (or was solicited by) an attractive young French prostitute, a Provencal girl named Mogali (a common Provencal given name, as I later learned). This excursion was partly a mistake, for reasons which I will shortly explain. But, oh, I had a good time with her! It's just that there were consequences.

I'm not sure about this, but I believe that within the last few years, the French authorities closed all the organized, supervised whorehouses. It is, however, still legal for a girl to sell her body, if she's operating alone, without a pimp. This policy is supposed to eliminate the criminal element. The prostitutes on the street are said to be supervised and licensed by the French health authorities, and are supposed to be fairly safe. However, they are NOT. I was very lucky. I made this contact in about 1977, in the days before the AIDS epidemic. I did not contract AIDS. However, I did contract the "crabs," or *le morpion,* as it is known in the French language. A few days later, my crotch began to itch like mad and I rushed to a dermatologist. He laughed at my discomfiture, told me I had the crabs, or pubic lice, and he gave me an ointment called Quell to get rid of it. I also had to wash all my bedclothes and body linen.

But the doctor's diagnosis was correct. The ointment got rids of the infestation in 48 hours and I was ready to go again. The moral of all this is to never go with a girl off the street. They are unhygienic and much more likely to be diseased. In a good house of love, the girls are inspected, trained in hygiene, and under medical supervision. I've never had any trouble in a good house, even as far into the AIDS era as 1987, which was the year that I quit my (illegal) whoring activities.

So much for Paris and the French. Now on to London, where many find prostitutes are found in little suites in the Leicester Square area. You can find little signs by the building doorways to guide you. Again, like in Paris, organized prostitution is illegal, but the women are allowed to conduct their "businesses" privately, "if they do not create a nuisance." Many of the women operate alone in small apartments, with an older woman in the front room who checks you out and serves tea (very English. I prefer beer on these occasions).

Anyway, at this time, in the 1970s, I preferred fellatio ("one-way sex," as an actress friend of mine in

Manhattan calls it, but so what, the girls are getting paid), which I could not then get from my backward social acquaintances in New York. Several of the ethnic English prostitutes would not do it either, but I was directed to a wonderful French whore, resident in Leicester Square, who gave me great satisfaction in this matter. I hunted her up on several later trips to London, as well.

Next, Amsterdam. The "red light" districts in Amsterdam are well advertised, filled with supervised "houses," and easy to find. However, there was a language problem. The girl I ended up with was of Brazilian origin, and spoke only Dutch and Portuguese. I speak smatterings of a dozen languages, but neither Dutch nor Portuguese. So we got along in my limited Spanish, which she could barely understand. But the whole sexual procedure is very fundamental, and we got along with "point and show." It was a successful excursion.

Finally, I will deal with my several experiences in the "Palais d'Amour" in Hamburg. First, a word on the entire Reeperbahn, or St. Pauli, area, which is the sex district in Hamburg, the most liberal city in Germany. There are many, many sex shops, nightclub sex shows (where the women make love on stage, sometimes to German Shepherds, among many other strange practices), and huge, factory-like whorehouses. The Germans do go to excess in some of these matters. Of course, there are also a lot of fine restaurants, where the Germans enjoy gustatory pleasures before or after their sexual adventures. It's also interesting that the Germans are very proud of their Reeperbahn sex district, and bring their children to see it. The Germans (some of them, anyway) see nothing wrong with this, and believe that sex is an important and pleasurable part of life, and the kids should at least begin to get acquainted with it early on.

My sexual experiences on the Reeperbahn took place on several occasions at the aforementioned Palais d'Amour. This is a huge, bunker-like building with hundreds of small rooms without windows, basically equipped with a double bed, a table for drinks, and little else. A sex factory, as I said.

The "presentation" or "lineup" at Palais d'Amour is in a large room, where the girls and the visitors circulate, rather like at a big cocktail party. On my first trip, I picked a modest, sensitive brunette who was upfront with me about the prices, which I appreciated. The prices, incidentally, were 50 marks (a mark was worth about half a dollar, at the time) for vaginal sex, 50 marks for fellatio, and there was another option, which I cannot recall. Anyway, we went upstairs and I had a very pleasurable time. I wish that girl well.

On my second trip, as late as 1992, I was not so fortunate. I picked a garishly dyed blonde who looked good in the dim light of the presentation, but not so good, close up, in the better light upstairs. She was trying to be a tough little tart, and lied to me downstairs about the prices. Anyway, this was in about 1992, and the AIDS epidemic was rampant. And the girl's noxious manners did not help any. On this occasion, I could not perform. So I paid and went out and enjoyed a nightclub sex show, German Shepherds and all, and also had a good dinner.

That about covers my overseas experiences. Oh yes, in the Rappongi sex and entertainment district of Tokyo, I danced in a nightclub with a pretty nightclub dancer clad only in a G-string. I don't know if I could have made an assignation with her or not, but I was on a trip hosted by the Japanese Government, so I thought I'd better be discreet.

I hope all of the above tells you a little more about me, and that it may help someone else. I'll add that I am comfortable (usually) with prostitutes, and that I like my sex to be objectified. Yes, women (some of them) are beautiful sexual creatures. But I eschew the subjective in this and other matters as much as I can, because, as I have described previously in the Psychology Section and other Sections of this Memoir, the subjective has led me in the past into miasmic chaos, in which everything is possible, and consequently nothing is possible or means anything, and there's no sense or point to anything, in this world, anyway, and that's the only world I care about. I try to avoid those "subjective" states of mind and have been reasonably successful in doing so.

I have ended my "Memoir" with a discussion of some of my whoring experiences, just as I began it. These experiences have been very important to me. I don't know if these events were THE most important thing in my life, but they counted for a lot. Sex is, after all, one of the main reasons I went to the psychiatrists in the first place. If I'd been smart, I would have skipped the psychiatrists altogether and concentrated on the whoring. I spent about an equal amount of money (perhaps $50,000 for each) on the one as on the other. I consider that the whoring money was much better spent. Anyway, perhaps, dear reader, you consider whoring a low occupation, and maybe it is, but it's better than killing people you don't know, at the command of somebody else, as all our young heroes must do in the military. And whoring is a vivid part of Life, and for me at least, as somebody who has lived on the fringes of Society, it affirms Life, and that's important to me. I hope my tale, in this respect and others, has been helpful to at least some of you.